DECODING INTOLERANCE

OTHER LOTUS TITLES

Ajit Bhattacharjea	*Sheikh Mohammad Abdullah: Tragic Hero of Kashmir*
Anil Dharker	*Icons: Men & Women Who Shaped Today's India*
Aitzaz Ahsan	*The Indus Saga: The Making of Pakistan*
Alam Srinivas & TR Vivek	*IPL: The Inside Story*
Amir Mir	*The True Face of Jehadis: Inside Pakistan's Terror Networks*
Ashok Mitra	*The Starkness of It*
Dr Humanyun Khan & G. Parthasarthy	*Diplomatic Divide*
Gyanendra Pandey & Yunus Samad	*Faultlines of Nationhood*
H.L.O. Garrett	*The Trial of Bahadur Shah Zafar*
M.J. Akbar	*India: The Siege Within*
M.J. Akbar	*Kashmir: Behind the Vale*
M.J. Akbar	*The Shade of Swords*
M.J. Akbar	*Byline*
M.J. Akbar	*Blood Brothers: A Family Saga*
Maj. Gen. Ian Cardozo	*Param Vir: Our Heroes in Battle*
Maj. Gen. Ian Cardozo	*The Sinking of INS Khukri: What Happened in 1971*
Madhu Trehan	*Tehelka as Metaphor*
Mushirul Hasan	*India Partitioned. 2 Vols*
Mushirul Hasan	*John Company to the Republic*
Mushirul Hasan	*Knowledge, Power and Politics*
Nayantara Sahgal (ed.)	*Before Freedom: Nehru's Letters to His Sister*
Nilima Lambah	*A Life Across Three Continents: Recollections of a Diplomat's Wife*
Sharmishta Gooptu and Boria Majumdar (eds)	*Revisiting 1857: Myth, Memory, History*
Shashi Joshi	*The Last Durbar*
Shashi Tharoor & Shaharyar M. Khan	*Shadows Across the Playing Field*
Shrabani Basu	*Spy Princess: The Life of Noor Inayat Khan*
Shyam Bhatia	*Goodbye Shahzadi: A Political Biography*

FORTHCOMING TITLES

M.B. Naqvi	*Pakistan on Knife's Edge*
M.J. Akbar	*Have Pen, Will Travel*
Robert Hutchison	*The Raja of Harsil*
Sunil Gupta	*Living on the 'Adge' in Jhande Walan Thompson*

DECODING INTOLERANCE

RIOTS AND THE EMERGENCE OF TERRORISM IN INDIA

Prateep K. Lahiri

LOTUS COLLECTION
ROLI BOOKS

This book is dedicated to my father

Shri B.N. Lahiri (IP), a true karmayogi:

the first Indian Inspector General of Police, Uttar Pradesh.

Lotus Collection 2009

First published in 2009
The Lotus Collection
An imprint of Roli Books Pvt. Ltd.
M-75, G.K. II Market, New Delhi 110 048
Phones: ++91 (011) 2921 2271, 40682000. Fax: ++91 (011) 2921 7185
E-mail: info@rolibooks.com; Website: rolibooks.com
Also at Bangalore, Chennai, Jaipur, Kolkata, Mumbai, Varanasi

Cover Design: Nitisha Mehta Sharma

ISBN: 978-81-7436-743-3

Printed in India at Saurabh Printers, New Delhi

Contents

IN RETROSPECT: A FEW CASE STUDIES

Foreword

Bashir returns home after the first day at school and asks his mother why the boy who shares his desk calls himself Ram. Why is his name different from his or his cousin's, Imtiaz? The mother explains that we are Muslims and they are Hindu. Ram is theirs. Bashir keeps quiet but remains unconvinced about why the different names should make them separate communities.

Do such perceptions take birth in schools? Or is it the home where the differences are articulated? True, the two religions, Hinduism and Islam, are poles apart. But how similar do their followers look when they bow at the prayers? It is not the faith that divides them. It is the assertion that one is superior to the other that injects the bias. Both Bashir and Ram, or for that matter, Muslims and Hindus, harbour the belief that their religion alone teaches what is right, what is god-ordained.

In India where both communities share the same history and the same culture, their nationality is the same. Some are Muslims and some Hindus but both are Indians. Differences are deliberately cultivated and then exaggerated by vested interests or religious leaders so as to keep the two communities distant for electoral and other reasons. This separation feeds prejudice and fanaticism.

If one were to analyze the causes of any riot, whether at Jamshedpur, Bhagalpur or Mumbai, one would not but come to the same conclusion: bigotry takes over when the voice of reason weakens. Both communities kill in the name of religion which teaches them amity and accord. Worse, the police force too has become partisan. Many riots begin with a clash between Hindus and Muslims and end up with the confrontation between Muslims and the police. Many inquiry reports have pointed out how the police force has got contaminated and how it often sides with the majority community.

Whether it was a tug of conscience or sheer sensitivity, some senior police officers have been meeting Prime Minister Manmohan Singh to argue that 'any communal disturbance' can be 'effectively contained within a few hours'. Their experience tells them that wherever riots prolong, there is the partisanship of police to contend with.

More than a decade ago, a senior police officer from UP studied ten major riots for a research project on police neutrality during communal riots. He came to the conclusion that in all the riots he had analyzed, the police 'did not act as a neutral law enforcement agency'. He also found a 'perceptible discrimination' in the use of the force, preventive arrests made, reporting of the facts, investigation, prosecution, etc. His study showed that no communal riot could last beyond twenty-four hours 'without the connivance of the authorities'.

Every commission of inquiry – some thirty of them since independence – has brought out 'how utterly negligent and callous the local police were'. The mandatory supervision by senior officers even in heinous offences has been absent. For example, the various probes which went into the 1984 riots came to infer that in a large number of cases, complaints made to the police were simply mentioned in the case diaries of FIRs and considered as good as disposed of. No attempt was made to record evidence of witnesses. Nor was there any identification of the accused.

Strange, the authorities have learnt no lesson. The Gujarat riots were worse. In fact, they were not riots. It was a pogrom. The cadre of a political party imbued by communal considerations, indulged in killing, looting, arson, etc., with impunity. It was a major failure of governance. Till today the government remains prejudiced and the citizen indifferent.

Two recommendations made by many inquiry committees are pertinent. One, the administration and its officers should be held accountable. Two, the victims of mob violence should be fully compensated as if they were insured and their homes and sources of livelihood fully restored. The hitch comes when the state is itself involved as is the case in Gujarat. Such instances erode the confidence of Muslims and other minorities in the 'commitment' of India to protect their life and property.

In fact, it is said that whichever the ruling party, in a state or at the centre, it tends to condition the attitude of the police and, therefore, politicize the force. This happened also during the

Emergency (1975-77) when the police became a willing tool of tyranny. Blank warrants of arrest were issued. The authorities also settled their personal scores.

The Justice Shah Commission which went into the excesses of the Emergency says: 'The government must seriously consider the feasibility and the desirability of insulating the police from the politics of the country and employing it scrupulously on duties for which alone it is by law intended. The policemen must also be made to realize that politicking by them is outside the sphere of their domain and the government would take a very serious view of it.' Yet the centre has done nothing and the police force has not improved even after the commission's advice. In fact, the recommendations by the National Police Commission have not been implemented because Prime Minister Indira Gandhi did not accept any probe conducted during the Emergency. The police are still governed by a British law which is more than 100 years old.

The failure of the police and the steps to politicize the force are interlinked. I am not going into them. Even the best of my effort will look puny before the tremendous work which P.K. Lahiri, a distinguished civil servant, has done. He saw several Hindu-Muslim riots from close quarters and has done an excellent job in analyzing the cause and effect. I have been fascinated by the account he has given about riots, even the minutest detail.

I agree with Mr Lahiri that Hindu-Muslim riots cannot be compared to the clash of civilizations. Nor do they relate to the question of ethnicity. It has more to do with identity, the fear that the majority will blot out the numerically few. The rest is prejudice and bias. Fanatics and religiously inclined political parties are responsible for it. Lahiri's book has added to my knowledge. This will happen to you too – the readers. You will go through the same experience. This scholarly work done by Lahiri deserves a doctorate. I hope some university will confer on him this honour.

Kuldip Nayar
New Delhi

Acknowledgements

Although I have always taken keen interest in the subject of interreligious conflict in India, certain people and events of importance that happened on my watch have enabled me to attempt a book on Hindu-Muslim riots. Herein I acknowledge the presence and assistance of those people, without whom this book may not have been written.

My father, late Shri B.N. Lahiri, to whom the book is dedicated, was my first administrative guru. I was fortunate that his guidance was available to me not only in my formative years but right through my career in the civil service. My mother, Susmita Devi was instrumental in fostering my interest in reading about all manner of subjects. My elder brother, Pradosh and his spouse, Nandita have encouraged me in this project.

My wife, Ratna has always been a great source of strength for me and acted as a sounding board. Many of the ideas and views that find place in the book have been shaped and honed through our discussions.

The 'gen-next' of our family, Ruchira, Arjun, Radhika, Shantanu, Kexin and grandson Krishna, all live abroad; even so they have all shown a lively interest in the writing of this book.

It is appropriate to acknowledge the debt I owe to my mentors. I was fortunate to have served under the stalwarts, Shri M.S. Chaudhary and Shri M.P. Sriwastava in the earlier years, when I worked mainly in the field, and later under Shri S.B. Lal. All of them have been my guiding lights.

I must express my gratitude to Dr Manmohan Singh, then finance minister, for the guidance, encouragement and support he gave me in the concluding phase of my career in the civil service, when I was reporting to him, first as revenue secretary in the central government and then as executive director, Asian Development Bank, Manila.

My friend from college days, P. Goswami went over the entire manuscript and gave valuable inputs, as did my colleague, Najeeb Jung, who has encouraged me at every step.

Dr Partha De has been extremely helpful in accessing and researching the materials and sources, which have been used during the writing of this book.

I have benefited from discussions on the subject with Naresh Narad, Murad Baig, Ashraf Rizvi, K.K. Baksi and some of their ideas find place in the book.

Prof T. Kumar, Col P.S. Sandhu and many others of the ISM University, an institution I have been closely associated with for a decade, have extended a helping hand at every stage.

I must also gratefully acknowledge the secretarial assistance rendered to me by S.D. Balooni, Tapas Dasgoswami, Tapan Chatterjee and Goutam Banerjee in drawing up the manuscript.

I am indeed grateful to eminent journalist, author and former diplomat Shri Kuldip Nayar for writing the Foreword to this book.

Above all, I must thank my publisher Pramod Kapoor for accepting this book of a first-time author, Nandita Bhardwaj for overseeing its publication at every step, and Richa Burman for the meticulousness with which she carried out her editorial responsibilities.

Introduction

Friends and well-wishers have often suggested that I write my memoirs. I have hesitated to do so because, barring one or two exceptions, the memoirs of civil servants I have come across, abound in descriptions of their perceptive and brilliant interventions in resolving knotty problems that have resulted in favourable outcomes. Besides, the readers are told of the innumerable occasions on which they stood up to interfering politicians and bosses and prevented them from materializing their nefarious designs. Avoiding the route of any such ego trip, I decided to write about a specific subject, that is, Hindu-Muslim riots. The account is experiential only to a limited extent.

The subject of communal disturbances, specifically of Hindu-Muslim riots, has been an area of interest for me virtually from the beginning of my career in the civil service. After completing my induction training in the National Academy of Administration (NAA) I was allotted the Madhya Pradesh cadre and posted at Jabalpur for district training, which included working as a judicial as well as an executive magistrate. During this period, in February 1961, a Hindu-Muslim riot broke out in Jabalpur. I was assigned certain magisterial duties and thus gained some first-hand experience of dealing with a communal riot. The events of this riot have been described in the book.

This riot has special significance in the chronology of Hindu-Muslim conflict in India. Once Pakistan was made a separate entity and the Partition riots subsided, Hindu-Muslim discord was relegated to the background of public debate. In the decade since 1950 no major communal riot took place in the country. It was widely believed that communal disturbances would soon become a thing of the past. The 1961 riot of Jabalpur therefore signalled a return of the earlier era of episodic conflicts between Hindus and Muslims.

Some years later I was posted as district magistrate (DM) at Indore, when I had to deal with another Hindu-Muslim riot, which has also been described in this book. Apart from these two riots, during the early part of my career, when I was continuously posted in the field first as sub-divisional magistrate (SDM) and then collector and DM, successively in three districts, there were several occasions when I had to deal with law and order problems, quite a few of them involving confrontation between the Hindu and Muslim communities. Fortunately, in most of these cases, through appropriate interventions we were able to prevent rioting and violence. Nevertheless, the first-hand experience of dealing with the question of communal conflicts has kept me interested in the subject.

In time I decided to explore the enduring phenomenon of Hindu-Muslim riots in some depth and the idea of writing this book was born. I realized that the issue of conflict between Hindus and Muslims in India had wide ramifications and justice could not be done to it based merely on my experience of dealing with two Hindu-Muslim riots, which too had occurred some four decades ago.

Before proceeding further I must explain the sense in which the words 'communal' and 'communalism' have been used in the book to describe the conflict between Hindus and Muslims. Some writers describe conflicts between the two communities as 'ethnic' rather than 'communal'. The latter term then is used for describing intra-religious conflicts, that is, between castes or different groups following the same religion. However, many of us construe the term more narrowly to refer only to racial or linguistic distinctions. This definitional issue has been discussed by Ashutosh Varshney who has used the broader definition of the term 'ethnic'. Therefore, for him Hindu-Muslim conflicts can be classified as being ethnic ones.[1] I, however, subscribe to the terminology commonly used in the media and official documents that refer to Hindu-Muslim clashes as 'communal' rather than 'ethnic' conflicts. In this respect I have adopted the definition of 'communalism' given by Bipan Chandra that has been quoted verbatim in the chapter, 'Origins and Dimensions of the Problem', in this book.

To reiterate, this book is confined to Hindu-Muslim riots and issues related thereto. When referring to communal clashes I have confined myself to the conflicts between Hindus and Muslims and not the followers of other religions. Clashes between Hindus and Sikhs or Hindus and Christians are outside the scope of this book.

PLAN OF THE BOOK

The first section of the book examines the phenomenon of Hindu-Muslim riots in India through discussion of the major issues arising out of these incidents. In the first chapter of this section, a brief overview of the history of Hindu-Muslim riots in India has been given, followed by an assessment of the actual nature and extent of the problem. It would be seen that though the phenomenon of Hindu-Muslim riots has been a long-standing and persisting one, it is not as widespread in the country as is generally believed. Though endemic in nature it is largely confined to certain urban centres. To mention just a few, these are Aligarh in Uttar Pradesh, Bhagalpur in Bihar, Ahmedabad in Gujarat and Hyderabad in Andhra Pradesh. Most of rural India remains unaffected to this day by the malaise.

The second chapter critically examines the reasons why these riots occur and continually bring interreligious relations to a crisis. This subject has been studied by a number of social and political scientists. Prominent among them are Paul Brass, Ashutosh Varshney and Steven I. Wilkinson, who have researched the subject thoroughly and offered their perspectives on the question, which I have discussed in detail. While the social scientists have based their conclusions on the data collected and research done in the field by them, I have attempted to synthesize the differing perceptions and present a holistic view of the causal factors and dynamics of these riots.

The next chapter provides statistics of the losses suffered by Hindus and Muslims in communal riots and the role of the state and the police in handling the riots has been examined from the point of view of their neutrality in dealing with the two communities. It may be mentioned that a senior serving officer of the Uttar Pradesh police, V.N. Rai, has made a detailed study of the issue of police neutrality and his findings have been cited extensively in the chapter.

In the fourth chapter I have tried to put together, for the benefit of administrators and policemen, the legal provisions to be invoked in dealing with and controlling riots, and have suggested how best they can tackle situations that can be diffused if handled deftly. These are practical tips, culled from hands-on experience, for dealing effectively with crisis situations in the field.

In the second section I have taken up certain issues that affect Muslims in India. This has a significant bearing on the question of communal riots because after a riot is over, it is generally the Muslims who are blamed as the perpetrators, for their presumed conservatism and for orthodox beliefs and practices. These issues are focused upon by those who wish to brand them as anti-secular, anti-national or disloyal to the country.

The first chapter relates to the oft-repeated claim that Muslims are averse to adopting the small-family norm and that their population is multiplying exponentially – to such an extent that eventually they could outnumber the other communities in the country. The second chapter relates to the allegation that Muslims are opposed to adopting the Uniform Civil Code and that this has come in the way of implementation of one of the directive principles of state policy enshrined in our Constitution. I have examined these two issues as objectively and dispassionately as possible so that the reader can get a balanced picture.

The third chapter in this section examines the question of the alleged deprivation of Muslims in areas such as education, employment and representation in elected bodies and also deals with the question whether affirmative action to protect interest of the Muslims ought to be considered as a matter of state policy. Deprivation of Muslims is also cited by a few as the cause for some members of the community turning seditious.

A study of these issues facilitates a seamless transition to the third section of the book, which deals with topics that have wider ramifications and, in some instances, need to be looked at in a global perspective. I have dealt with certain overarching issues which affect many countries in the world, including India, since the same have, at times, a causal relationship with the micro-level phenomenon of communal riots in this country. However, these chapters can also be read as independent essays on the concerned topics.

The struggle between 'fundamentalism' and 'liberalism' in Islam, for one, transcends our borders and has been encapsulated in the first chapter. The chapter on terrorism, after drawing on a history of the phenomenon deals with the specific problem India is facing today. The chapter on secularism brings together the varying perspectives on the issue and makes a distinction between the Western and Indian versions of secularism. In this chapter I have also highlighted how important the Gandhi-Nehru construct of secularism is for the healthy development of our polity.

In the two chapters on religious nationalism, one dealing with the Muslim aspect of the issue and the other dealing with the Hindu one, the historical developments have been traced and it has been shown how the opposing attitudes have hardened over time.

....

The chapter on 'clash of civilizations' takes up Samuel P. Huntington's thesis[2] that civilizational (religious) conflicts would be the order of the day in the post Cold War era and posits against it the counterarguments demolishing the thesis. In this context the issue of politics of 'identity', which is at the root of the Hindu-Muslim divide in India, is also discussed.

In the fourth and last section of the book I have dealt with five episodes of Hindu-Muslim riots to give the reader an understanding of how riots erupt and play out on the ground. The first two chapters deal with the 1961 Jabalpur riots and the 1969 Indore riots. Thereafter, I have taken up for description and analysis three major riots that occurred at Bhagalpur, Bihar (1989), Bombay (December 1992 to January 1993) and in Gujarat in 2002. The first two have been covered because of my direct exposure to the events as they unfolded. At Jabalpur in 1961 and at Indore in 1969 I was not merely a witness to the incidents but had a definitive role in tackling the volatile situations as part of the state machinery.

I have taken up the other three riots mainly for two reasons: firstly because in scale and magnitude, loss of lives and destruction of properties, these were perhaps the most violent riots to have occurred in independent India; secondly, they have a representative character inasmuch as all the three riots are a fallout, in one way or another, of the concerted political mobilization carried out by the Sangh Parivar around the movement to build a Ram temple at Ayodhya. The genesis of and the developments relating to this movement have been traced in the earlier chapters, 'Origins and Dimensions of the Problem' and 'Religious Nationalism and Hindutva'.

The history of post-Independence India is literally littered with hundreds of Hindu-Muslim riots. In his book,[3] Asghar Ali Engineer has attempted to give an account of all the riots that have taken place from 1950 to 2002. Even this account is perhaps not comprehensive since he has not mentioned a few cases, like the 1969 Indore riots. My intention to present these five riots as case studies is to pinpoint the common strands that run through most such riots. Inter alia, these are: the failure to counter false rumours spread by elements interested in fomenting trouble; playing up of a minor incident by interested parties or the media so that it becomes the 'precipitating incident' which causes a riot; the failure of intelligence; ineffective enforcement of prohibitory orders including curfew; and the failure to call in the army in time to quell escalating violence.

These five communal riots may thus be considered archetypal of the episodes of Hindu-Muslim violence and if the inherent problems listed above are addressed, the recurrence of such riots can be obviated or at least mitigated. These incidents also serve as an illustration of the causal factors and the different analyses presented in the first section of the book. The backdrop is provided in the description of the five riots which the reader may refer to while going through the analyses.

In the epilogue, 'A Non-astrological Peep into the Future', I have attempted to foresee as to how the relations between Hindus and Muslims will play out in the future. Although Hindu-Muslim riots have been an enduring phenomenon for nearly a century, I do see certain portents that signal a cessation of this cycle of episodic violence in the proximate future. The elections of 2009 have dealt a body blow to the reactionary forces which have a vested interest in keeping the embers of communal discord alive. Besides, fast-paced economic and social development, if it is really inclusive, will surely lead to diminution of tensions between communities which at times have a fallout in terms of overt violence.

NOTES

1 Ashutosh Varshney, *Ethnic Conflinct and Civic Life – Hindus and Muslims in India* (New Delhi: Oxford, 2005), pp. 4-5.

2 Samuel P. Huntington, *The Clash of Civilizations and the Remaking of World Order* (New York: Simon & Schuster, 1996).

3 Asghar Ali Engineer, *Communal Riots After Independence: A Comprehensive Account* (Delhi: Shipra, 2004).

List of Abbreviations

ACP	Assistant Commissioner of Police
AIMPLB	All-India Muslim Personal Law Board
AIR	All India Reporter
AMU	Aligarh Muslim University
BJP	Bharatiya Janata Party
CID	Criminal Investigation Department
CrPC	Code of Criminal Procedure
CSP	City Superintendent of Police
DM	District Magistrate
HUJI	Harkat-ul-Jihad-al-Islami
IB	Intelligence Bureau
INC	Indian National Congress (or just Congress)
IPC	Indian Penal Code
ISI	Inter-Services Intelligence
J&K	Jammu & Kashmir
JeM	Jaish-e-Mohammad
LeT	Lashkar-e-Toiba
NDA	National Democratic Alliance
NHRC	National Human Rights Commission
PAC	Provincial Armed Constabulary
POTA	Prevention of Terrorism Act
RAW	Research and Analysis Wing
SHO	Station House Officer
SIMI	Students Islamic Movement of India
SP	Superintendent of Police
SSP	Senior Superintendent of Police
ULFA	United Liberation Front of Assam
UPA	United Progressive Alliance

HINDU-MUSLIM RIOTS: A RECKONING

Origins and Dimensions of the Problem

Communalism in India is responsible for the Hindu Muslim divide, which, in turn, is at the root of the outbreak of riots involving the two communities. Whenever a major communal riot occurs, we tend to look at the immense suffering of the affected people and despair at the brutality and uselessness of it all and lay the blame at the door of either the religious fanatics of one community or the machinations of a few political opportunists. Both groups may well be faulted but it would be interesting to trace the beginning of communalism and its recurrent fatal and violent impact on the lives of the two major Indian communities. As has been succinctly explained by the noted historian Bipan Chandra:

> Communalism is the belief that because a group of people follow a particular religion they have, as a result, common social, political and economic interests. It is the belief that in India Hindus, Muslims, Christians and Sikhs form different and distinct communities which are independently and separately structured or consolidated: that all the followers of a religion share not only a community of religious interests but also common secular interests, that is, common economic, political, social and cultural interests; that Indians inevitably perceive such interests through the spectacles of the religious grouping and are bound to possess a sense of identity based on religion, i.e. religion has to become the basis of their basic social identity and the determinant of their basic social relationships ...[1]

Communalism will remain in the forefront of public discourse so long as all other identities of persons are subjugated or even subsumed under their religious identity. Bipan Chandra goes on to observe that communal riots are not the main form or content of communalism:

> They were, in the main, its reflection, its active episodic expression, its bitter and virulent manifestation and consequence, and one of the instruments and agencies for its spread. The communal riot was sudden and spasmodic, was an aspect of social pathology, and its causation lay either in the prevalence of a communal atmosphere generated by communal politics and communal ideology or in conjunctural causes, involving religious feelings along or in combination with some particular local interests ...[2]

Prior to British rule communalism had not taken on an ideological dimension. It was the British period that saw Muslim and Hindu communalism develop into competing ideologies. The Muslim communalist ended up believing that in medieval India, Muslims constituted the ruling class and Hindus were the ruled. This view is well encapsulated in the words of Mohammad Ali Jinnah.

> 'Our demand is not from Hindus because the Hindus never took the whole of India. It was the Muslims who took India and ruled for 700 years. It was the British who took India from the Musalmans.' In 1942, he asserted that if the British handed over the government of India to the Muslim League, they 'will be making full amends to the Muslims by restoring the government of India to them from whom they had taken it ...'[3]

The Muslim communalist portrayed the medieval period of Indian history, when the Mughals were in power, as a glorious one, whereas the Hindu communalist adopted and propagated the imperialist view that the medieval period represented Muslim tyranny. Although Muslims came to India a thousand years ago and majority of them were descendants of converts to Islam, many Hindus nevertheless viewed them as foreigners who had forcibly planted themselves in the land that ought to be their (Hindus') exclusive heritage. In the Hindu communal view, thus, the medieval period was considered to be full of conflict, persecution, subjugation, etc., by the Muslims, whereas ancient Indian society was declared free of social and religious tensions and conflict.

THE POLICY OF DIVIDE AND RULE

Communalism, as it is understood today, came into existence in the

British period. Consequently, communal riots that are 'episodic manifestations' of communalism, were not known to have occurred prior to the nineteenth century. During the nationalist movement against British rule, in the phases in which Hindus and Muslims cooperated in the struggle, the incidence of communal riots showed a marked decline. As Bipan Chandra has rightly pointed out:

> [T]he British Indian administration did not support a particular 'community' or communalism for the love of that 'community' or communalism. The aim of the British policy of divide and rule was to check the politicization of the Indian people, to curb their consolidation and unification and to disrupt the process of the Indian nation-in-the-making. Once the anti-imperialist nationalist movement arose, the policy was also directed towards checking its growth, dividing its actual or potential supporters and preventing Muslims (as also landlords, capitalists, Panjabis, etc.) from joining it ...[4]

It is interesting to note Winston Churchill's views, as expressed in the cabinet meeting on 2 February 1940, which are recorded as follows in the cabinet papers:

> ... he did not share the anxiety to encourage and promote unity between the Hindu and Muslim communities. Such unity was, in fact, almost out of the realm of practical politics, while, if it were to be brought about, the immediate result would be that the united communities would join in showing us the door. He regarded the Hindu-Muslim feud as the bulwark of British rule in India.[5]

The British did face a dilemma in that they tried, in general, to douse communal passions when they rose too high. But they preferred to face administrative problems created by communalism rather than let the unification of the Indian people in an anti-imperialist movement proceed unhindered. As Hamilton, the secretary of state wrote to Elgin, the viceroy in 1897: 'One hardly knows what to wish for. Unity of ideas and action (among Indians) would be very dangerous politically, divergence of ideas and collision are administratively troublesome. Of the two the latter is the least risky, though it throws anxiety and responsibility upon those on the spot where the friction exists.'[6]

....

The British preferred to extend support to Muslim communalism instead of Hindu communalism, because Hindus being in a majority, if united, could prove to be more dangerous to colonial rule. Since Hindus were splintered by caste divisions, encouragement to Hindu communalism would integrate them into a single 'community' and would, therefore, serve a contrary purpose. However, the British did not, as a matter of policy, engender communal clashes between Hindus and Muslims – these were a fallout of their 'divide and rule' policy.

Before the 1857 revolt, a few communal riots in the modern sense had taken place. 'Banaras (1809), Kiol (1820), Moradabad, Sambhal, Kashipur (1833), Shahjahanpur (1837), Bareilly, Kanpur, Allahabad (1837-1852) had witnessed clashes between Hindus and Muslims that can be termed as communal riots ...'[7] But in the struggle during 1857-58, Hindus and Muslims were completely united; it is noteworthy that in those two years there were no communal riots.

From 1858 to 1919, however, there were several Hindu-Muslim riots, including the ones 'in Bareilly (1871), Mau (1893), Mumbai (1893), Nasik (1894), East Bengal (1907), Peshawar (1910), Ayodhya (1912), Agra (1913), Shahabad (1917) and Katarpur (1918) are noteworthy ...'[8]

Under the leadership of Mahatma Gandhi, the Hindus made common cause with the Muslims in the Khilafat and Non-Cooperation movements against the Rowlatt Act, the Jallianwala Bagh massacre and for the restoration of the Turkish Khalifa. Not surprisingly, the years 1919-20 did not witness any significant communal riots.

While the Hindu-Muslim alliance was in the process of consolidation, two events dealt crippling blows to it. The first of these was the Moplah rebellion in 1921. The Moplahs are a Muslim community settled on the Malabar Coast of South India. These people, comprising mostly poor peasants and fishermen, were a fanatical and unruly lot who had clashed with British authorities and the more prosperous Hindu landlords and moneylenders even in the past. One of the leaders of the revolt proclaimed:

> 'We have extorted Swaraj from the white man and what we have secured we are not going to give up so easily ... We shall give Hindus the option of death or Islam ... The Jews and Christians, as believers in a revealed book, may be tolerated but the idolatrous Hindus can only be allowed to

> live in a Muslim state on sufferance.' The rebels murdered four Europeans but their real victims were the Hindus. They ruthlessly murdered, converted people forcibly to Islam, raped women, desecrated temples, and pillaged and destroyed property. It was only strong and sustained military action that brought the situation under control at the end of the year ...[9]

The second setback to Hindu-Muslim unity was the withdrawal of the Non-Cooperation movement by Mahatma Gandhi consequent to the Chouri-Choura incident, when Gandhiji called off the movement for the reason that it had turned violent. This led to the collapse of the Hindu-Muslim unity forged during the Non-Cooperation movement against British rule. The British could once again continue to 'divide and rule'.

GENESIS OF THE AYODHYA TEMPLE DISPUTE

The developments since 1949 to the present day – pertaining to the movement to build a temple for Lord Ram at the site where the Babri Masjid had come up during the reign of Emperor Babar – have been described in some detail in the chapter on Hindutva. It is, however, interesting to note that the genesis of the dispute can be traced back to much earlier times, when the British contributed to keeping it alive to serve their divisive policies.

In 1853, Maulavi Amir Ali got the information that the Babri Masjid in Ayodhya had been destroyed by members of the Bairagi sect. He then gave a call for the jihad. Nawab Wajid Ali Shah sought the intervention of the East India Company to restrain the Muslims, but the British Resident deliberately declined to do so. Wajid Ali Shah then sent his troops and in the ensuing fight Maulavi Amir Ali was killed.

The rumour of the destruction of Babri Masjid was of course false. It was to be actually destroyed over a hundred years later. At the time in 1855, the elders of the Hindu and Muslim communities got together and the problem was temporarily resolved.

It is noteworthy, as contemporary historical records show, that the British kept alive the Ayodhya dispute as part of their strategy to keep the two communities at loggerheads. The consequences of the British action (or inaction) to settle the dispute reverberate till today.[10]

....

RUPTURES IN THE NATIONALIST MOVEMENT

A stratagem of the British to keep Hindus and Muslims divided was to introduce communal or separate electorates. This was done through successive stages of constitutional reforms till 1935. The introduction of separate electorates served to strengthen the communal divide. It was designed to favour Muslims who were guaranteed seats in proportion to their population in elected bodies. This was resented by the Hindus who felt deprived because they would otherwise win a vast majority of the seats on the basis of their numerical strength.

Yet, in the 1937 elections, the Indian National Congress came out victorious in large parts of the country. Alarmed at the consolidation of nationalist forces under the Congress, the British played the communal card to the hilt and extended open support to the Muslim League. When the Second World War broke out in 1939, Congress agreed to extend cooperation to the British on the condition that a declaration be made that India would attain independence after the war. Not willing to concede this demand outright, the British relied on and backed the Muslim League as a counterpoise to the Congress.[11]

The British also extended the system of reservations for minorities in education and employment. With the introduction of separate electorates and reservations for the minority community, the state became more 'consociational'.[12] Contrary, however, to Arend Lijphart's hypothesis that increased 'consociationalism' leads to reduction in communal violence, reservations actually exacerbated the communal divide in India; its fallout was seen in terms of subsequent riots, such as the one in Calcutta in 1946. The issue of consociationalism and communal violence has been discussed separately in the chapter on causal factors.

Vibhuti Narain Rai, a senior officer of the UP police, has described how the British mishandled the Kanpur riot of 1931 resulting in huge loss of lives and property, which a proactive administration could have prevented or minimized. Two enquiry commissions corroborated the conclusion that the attitude of the official machinery went beyond mere inactivity and actually encouraged the rioters.[13]

Bipan Chandra has noted that 'a large number of contemporary public persons and the Press expressed the opinion that the British authorities deliberately instigated and engineered or at least connived at communal riots, especially when faced with nationalist or class upsurge, through agent provocateurs, aid to the instigators and organizers of the riots and such other methods ...'[14] He has also mentioned that the policy of inactivity of the administration cost thousands of lives during the communal killings of 1946-47. This happened both in Bengal and Punjab where the administrative machinery remained passive and inactive when mass killings and one-sided pogroms happened.

After the post-Partition riots were brought under control, the incidents of communal violence came down sharply. The liberals believed that secular ideology had finally taken hold of the national imagination and the communal divide between two major communities was getting bridged. The 1961 communal riots in Jabalpur thus mark a watershed since they shattered this illusion.[15]

DIMENSIONS OF THE PROBLEM

Hindus and Muslims together constitute about 95 per cent of the total population of the country. Among all countries in the world, India has the second-largest Muslim population. It is for this reason that the persistence of communal discord between the two major communities, resulting in violent clashes from time to time at different focal points in the country, is a matter of grave concern.

Although the communal divide between Hindus and Muslims has persisted over time and there have been many incidents of violence involving the two communities, we should not overstate the magnitude of this problem. Approximately 10,000 deaths and 30,000 injuries have occurred in the reported Hindu-Muslim riots since 1950.

This is only a fraction of the 60,000 people who die each year in road accidents in India and is also much lower than the number of women murdered in 'dowry deaths' (3,000 to 4,000) each year.[16] In 1989, for example, when the Ayodhya agitation was nearing its peak, 521 people died in communal riots compared to 3,894 women killed over dowry.

In per capita terms too, the death rate from Hindu-Muslim riots is low compared to certain other parts of the world where ethnic conflicts have been a persistent phenomenon. For instance, the death rates in Northern Ireland arising out of ethnic clashes since 1969 are 50 times the per capita death rate in India which arises out of the Hindu-Muslim discord.[17]

The pattern in which Hindu-Muslim riots have occurred between 1950 and 1955, and the number of the resulting deaths, is clearly brought out in the graph given here:

Hindu-Muslim Riots since Independence
(Data from Varshney and Wilkinson)

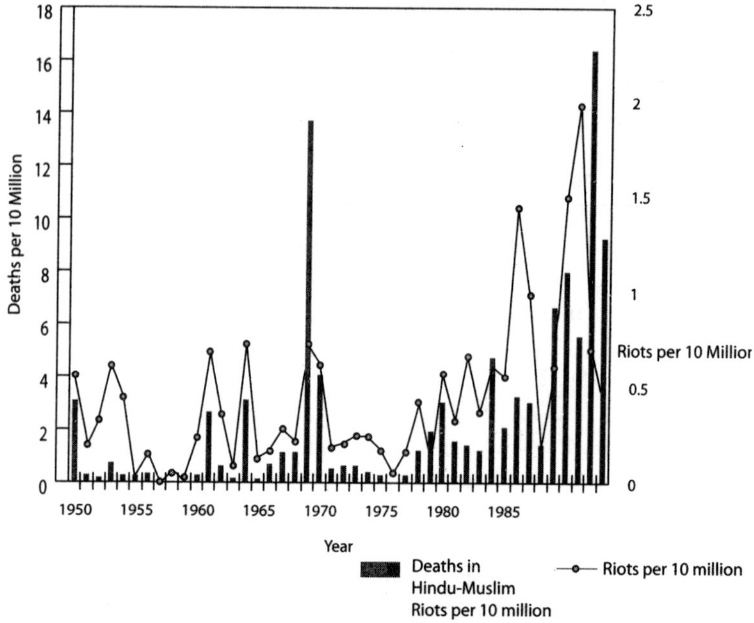

Source: Votes and Violence, *Steven I. Wilkinson, p. 12.*

Hindu-Muslim riots are not as widespread in the country as is generally believed. By and large the rural areas, where approximately 60 per cent of our population lives, are hardly affected by riots. Even when there are incidents of communal clashes in rural areas, the origins usually lie in an urban centre from where the virus spreads to the adjacent rural hinterland. This is what happened, for instance, in the case of the riots in Jabalpur in 1961.

Varshney's view is that rural areas remain relatively immune from communal clashes because the quotidian or everyday engagements between members of the two communities are more intense in the villages than in towns or cities. The bond forged through such engagements prevents minor disputations between individual Hindus and Muslims from degenerating into riots.

Varshney's hypothesis is perhaps correct but the reasons are also embedded in our history. The majority of Muslims in India are actually converts; their conversion to the Muslim faith started from the eleventh century, during the many invasions of the Muslims from the north. The conversions were mostly done at the point of a sword but many of those oppressed by discrimination in the Hindu caste system also willingly embraced Islam.

For several centuries since then, the Muslim converts and the Hindus lived and died side by side in the villages and cities of medieval and modern India. An easy bond, based on past kinship and present advantages of coexistence, kept them together. Due to the machinations of the British, India missed out on the industrial revolution and remained rooted to its past. Minimal or no changes occurred in the socio-economic sphere in India; while the urban areas received the benefits of the railways and of modern institutions like education and judiciary, the effect on rural India was negligible. Villages continued to remain literally in the umbra of modern society and received no blessings of the 'march of civilization' in either the material or the intellectual fronts. A salubrious period of peaceful coexistence continued in the villages, where the Muslims and the Hindus doggedly continued to follow their beliefs without getting into violent communal situations.

This did not remain the case for the people in the urban areas. The British found a very effective weapon against Indian nationalistic aspirations in the form of a 'divide and rule' policy. It enabled them to rule the country more easily and for longer but it sundered the two communities in a lasting manner.

That Hindu-Muslim riots are essentially an urban phenomenon is well illustrated in the graph below:

Rural-Urban Breakdown of Riots by Year, 1950-95

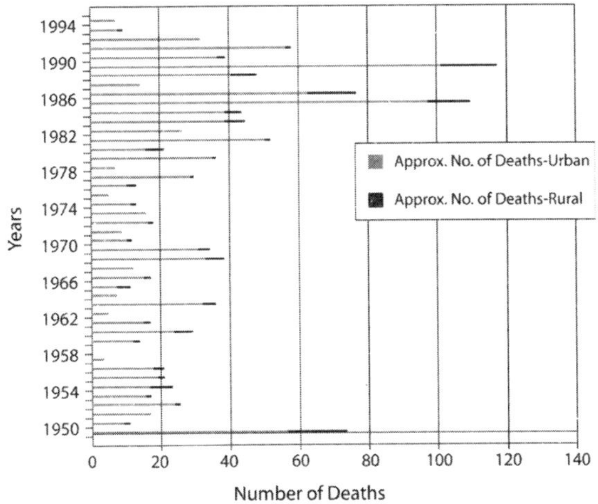

Source: Ethnic Conflict and Civic Life, *Ashutosh Varshney, p. 96.*

But even with respect to urban India, riots have been a recurring phenomenon only in specific locations. On the basis of detailed analysis of data, Varshney has identified certain urban centres as 'riot prone'. The riot-prone cities and towns have, in turn, been classified – on the bases of the number of communal riots that have occurred at these places, their periodicity, and the number of deaths in such riots – into four categories. These categories are RP_1, RP_2, RP_3, and RP_4 in ascending order of 'riot proneness'. The total number of cities and towns that are deemed to be riot-prone are twenty-eight (RP_1); of these only eight qualify to be RP_4 where a minimum of fifty deaths have occurred in at least ten riots over five-year periods. These cities are Ahmedabad and Baroda (Gujarat), Meerut and Aligarh (Uttar Pradesh), Mumbai (Maharashtra), Delhi, Hyderabad (Andhra Pradesh) and Kolkata (West Bengal).

Varshney has pointed out that these eight most riot-prone cities (RP_4) account for 45.5 per cent of total deaths in urban India and 49 per cent of all deaths in the entire country due to riots. However, these eight cities hold only 18 per cent of the urban population of the country. If the rural population is also taken into account it becomes evident that 'riot proneness' in the true sense is confined to only 5 per cent of India's population.[18]

In an all-India perspective it is evident that there are four states, viz. Gujarat, Maharashtra, Uttar Pradesh and Bihar, which have suffered the most deaths from rioting. This is illustrated in the following graph:

Incidents of Riots with One or More Deaths

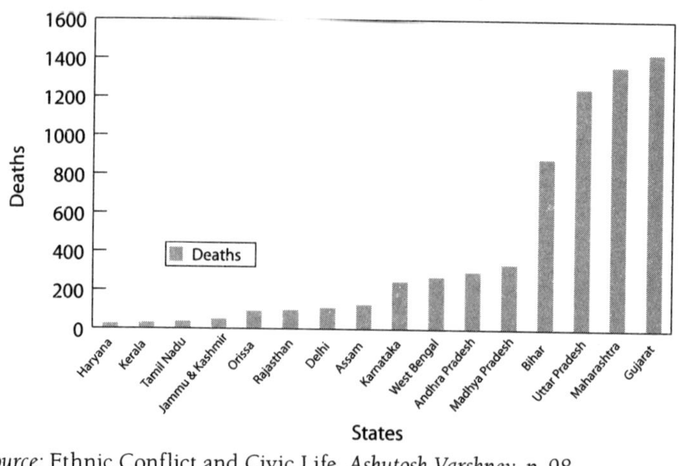

Source: Ethnic Conflict and Civic Life, *Ashutosh Varshney, p. 98.*

Thus, the malaise of recurring Hindu-Muslim riots, instead of being uniformly spread across the country, is actually a localized one. It is often said that the problem of Hindu-Muslim riots in India is endemic in nature. It is endemic only insofar as four of our states are concerned and eight cities, five of which lie within these states. In Bihar, no one or two cities can be identified to be the most riot-prone as the problem is spread all over the state.

The picture which emerges is that the matter for concern regarding Hindu-Muslim riots is one of their persistence rather than their spread across the country. With the problem areas and locations being clearly identified, state policy should be directed toward dealing with the problem in these specific places, so it can be tackled in a focused way and be overcome sooner rather than later.

NOTES

1 Bipan Chandra, *Communalism in Modern India* (New Delhi: Vikas Publishing House Pvt Ltd, 1984), p. 1.
2 Ibid., p. 5.
3 Ibid., pp. 219-220.
4 Ibid., pp. 245-246.
5 Ibid., p. 245, footnote.
6 Ibid., p. 248.
7 V.N. Rai, *Combating Communal Conflict: Perception of Police Neutrality During Hindu-Muslim Riots in India* (New Delhi: Manas Publications, 2008), p. 19.
8 Ibid., p. 21.
9 S.M. Burke and Salim Al-Din Quraishi, *The British Raj in India: An Historical Review* (Chennai: Oxford, 2004), pp. 232-233.
10 Rai, *Combating Communal Conflict*, pp. 21-22 and 37-38.
11 For how the creation and support of the Muslim League led to the consolidation of communalism in the subcontinent, refer to the chapter 'Religious Nationalism: The Muslim Version'.
12 This theory, propagated by Arend Lijphart in the '60s, contends that a stable democracy can be attained by consensual power-sharing in proportion of the population of different groups.
13 Rai, *Combating Communal Conflict*, pp. 38-42.
14 Chandra, *Communalism in Modern India*, p. 285.
15 *See* chapter 'Jabalpur, Madhya Pradesh, 1961' for details of the incident.
16 Steven I. Wilkinson, *Votes and Violence: Electoral Competition and Communal Riots in India* (Cambridge, UK: Cambridge, 2005), pp. 12-13.
17 Ibid., p. 13.
18 Ashutosh Varshney, *Ethnic Conflict and Civic Life – Hindus and Muslims in India* (New Delhi: Oxford, 2005), pp. 100-103.

Causal Factors and Dynamics of Communal Riots

Hindu-Muslim riots have been an enduring phenomenon across several states, even though in terms of endemicity they are confined to certain known locations. Often, when a riot occurs, a 'precipitating incident' is identified as the cause which triggered the riot. But the underlying factors are many and diverse. It can be self-defeating to pinpoint a single incident as the reason for a particular riot breaking out. It may be that tensions have been simmering for a long time between the communities at a given location and a particular incident is seized upon by members of one community to attack those of the other community to settle old scores. The incident could even be an engineered one. Paul Brass[1] has rightly pointed out that riots are generally erroneously perceived as spontaneous occurrences arising out of petty quarrels; and that the latter turn into mass frenzies through the spread of rumours exaggerating the precipitating incidents.

Wherever Hindus and Muslims live side by side it is natural that minor frictions will occur from time to time. Normally such incidents should not result in sparking off large-scale violence. But when there is underlying tension prevailing between the two communities and a history of antagonism, any minor incident can be seized upon by elements who have a vested interest in fomenting trouble, and be blown out of proportion to create a riotous situation.

The 1961 riots in Jabalpur were triggered precisely by such an incident. The veracity of the incident was in doubt but it was highlighted and splashed in a local newspaper with the intent of rousing passions within one community against the other (see the chapter on the Jabalpur riots for further details).

While most of the social scientists who have researched the subject are agreed that it is simplistic to overplay the importance of the precipitating incidents, they have divergent views regarding the underlying causal factors and dynamics of such riots. These views have been discussed below.

I – CIVIC ENGAGEMENTS BETWEEN HINDUS AND MUSLIMS

Ashutosh Varshney has argued quite persuasively that the non-existence of civic ties between Hindus and Muslims, at the town level, is the primary cause of conflict between the two communities.[2] On the basis of certain criteria pertaining to the incidence of riots, he has identified particular cities and towns as being riot-prone. Varshney emphasizes city-level variations in the incidence of riots to make the point that the occurrence of riots has little to do with the actions and policies of the central government, state governments or the police. In the state of Uttar Pradesh, riots have frequently occurred in Aligarh but not in Lucknow. Similarly in Gujarat, Ahmedabad has witnessed many communal riots whereas Surat has generally remained peaceful. It is not logical to suggest that the state government or the police would actively promote or foment riots at one location, say in Ahmedabad, and at the same time act firmly to prevent such occurrences in another city in the same state, like in Surat.

While thus downplaying the role of the state and police, Varshney homes in on the levels of prevailing civic engagement as the main determining factor which influences riot-proneness in the concerned city or town. Varshney's hypothesis, wherein he seeks to establish an integral link between the structure of civil society and communal violence, is interesting and worth exploring. His emphasis is on inter-communal, not intra-communal networks of civic life, which bring different communities together. These networks are of two types: the 'associational' forms and the 'quotidian', or the everyday forms of civic engagement.

Examples of associational forms are business and professional organizations, different social clubs, festival associations, and trade unions and cadre-based political parties. Everyday forms of engagement consist of routine interactions in daily life among Hindu and Muslim families, such as visiting each other, eating together, jointly participating in festivals, their children playing together, etc. Both forms of engagement, if robust, promote peace. Their absence or weakness opens up the space for communal violence.

Paired Comparison of Cities

Having statistically established that communal violence is city-centric, and among cities too only some are really riot-prone, Varshney has selected six cities for the purpose of paired comparison: three from the list of eight riot-prone cities and three peaceful ones.

It was ensured that the two cities in each pair had roughly similar Hindu-Muslim percentages in the city population.

The first pair, Aligarh and Calicut, was based on comparable percentages of population alone. The second pair of Hyderabad and Lucknow added two more criteria: previous Muslim rule and reasonable cultural similarities. The third pair of Ahmedabad and Surat also shares history, language and culture. All the cities have a population in excess of 5,00,000.

The central finding of Varshney's project is that where strong local networks of civic engagement between the two communities exist, division and confrontations are mainly contained; where they are missing, communal identities lead to endemic and ghastly violence. Both associational and everyday forms of engagement promote peace, but the capacity of associational forms to withstand national-level exogenous shocks, such as India's partition in 1947 or the demolition of Babri Masjid in 1992, is substantially higher.

However, Varshney recognizes the paradox wherein rural India, which has everyday forms of engagement but hardly any associational forms, is relatively free from communal violence, whereas cities, with more associational forms, are centres where communal riots largely occur. His answer to the paradox is that informal engagements may help in keeping peace in villages but not in cities which tend to be less interconnected and more anonymous.

In the development of associational structures in the country, Varshney highlights Mahatma Gandhi's contribution which was responsible for transforming the freedom struggle into a national movement that involved Indians from all walks of life. For Gandhi, the objective of the freedom movement included a social transformation of the country – he stressed upon Hindu-Muslim unity, abolition of untouchability and the upliftment of other depressed classes. Thus, the foundations of India's associational civic order were laid by the Gandhian shift in the national movement.

In the process of national integration, a whole host of organizations came into being between 1920 and the 1940s. The biggest among these was the Congress party which led the movement politically and developed cadres all over India. In Varshney's words,[3]

> The movement had greater success in forging Hindu-Muslim unity in the South where a Hindu-Muslim cleavage had not already emerged in local politics. ... If local politics

emphasized some other cleavage for example caste cleavage among Hindus, or Shia-Sunni divisions among the Muslims, then the Congress party and the Gandhian social workers found it easier to bring Hindus and Muslims together in local civic life.

Comparison of Lucknow and Hyderabad[4]

Both Hyderabad and Lucknow have been viewed as centres of syncretic Hindu-Muslim culture. They had Muslim rulers: Nizams in Hyderabad and nawabs in Lucknow. The Hindu-Muslim population percentages in both the cities have been in the same range. Moreover, Muslims constitute a significant voting block in terms of electoral competition in both the cities.

Despite these commonalities, the two cities have sharply constrasting records vis-à-vis communal violence. Lucknow's only major Hindu-Muslim riot in the twentieth century took place in 1924. The city remained virtually free from communal violence during the Partition phase; in the midst of widespread communal clashes when the Ayodhya movement was at its peak; and also after the demolition of the Babri Masjid. Since 1938, when communal peace was first broken, Hyderabad, however, has turned into one of the most riot-prone cities in India. After the 1960s, it has witnessed numerous communal riots.

Searching for the causes of the stark contrast these two cities present in terms of their record of communal violence, Varshney has argued that historically, the dominant cleavage in Lucknow has been an intra-religious one between the Shia and the Sunni sect of Muslims, not an interreligious one. In Hyderabad, on the other hand, the mass politics that emerged in the 1930s was superimposed on Hindu-Muslim and not Shia-Sunni differences.

The turning point was the refusal of the seventh Nizam of Hyderabad to concede popular rule in the state, where Hindus were in a majority but Muslims dominated the power structure. The Nizam used his autocratic powers to block the emergence of mass-level organizations that could have promoted civic integration of Hindus and Muslims. In Hyderabad, thus, the associational space for inter-communal engagement steadily shrank.

In the backdrop of these historical developments, most Hyderabad politicians have used Hindu-Muslim polarization and violence as a strategic political tool, whereas Lucknow politicians have usually sought to build bridges in times of communal tension.

....

In Lucknow, the biggest source of mass-level civic engagement is economic activity. The embroidered-textile industry comprising Chikan and Zardozi is at the heart of Lucknow's economy. Almost the entire workforce in this industry is Muslim and it is estimated that 2,00,000 to 3,00,000 persons are dependent on the industry, or almost 30 to 50 per cent of the entire Muslim population. While the workers are overwhelmingly Sunni Muslims, the traders and entrepreneurs are Hindus.

Hindus have historically enjoyed a cordial relationship with the Shia community and with the Chikan and Zardozi industry taking root in Lucknow, a large number of Hindus and Sunni Muslims too have come together 'in a mutually dependent relationship'. It is important to note that the industry does not function through wage contracts or any other kind of legally binding arrangements. The system works on trust.

Both communities recognize that any discord would hurt the poor Muslims who provide the workforce as well as the rich Hindus whose investments ride on the industry. Thus, if any communal violence were to occur, Lucknow's economy would collapse and this factor alone works in the favour of maintaining communal harmony.

There is nothing comparable to this situation in Hyderabad. Though it has a number of different industries, there is no large-scale employment of workers from one community in a single industry, unlike in Lucknow. Consequently, there is no economic symbiosis. Muslims in Hyderabad were largely poor but the community received an economic boost from migration to the Middle East since the mid-1970s. In Hyderabad, they are mostly engaged in the trade of fruits and vegetables, shoes, metal scraps, auto mechanics, etc., but none of these activities leads to any significant trader-customer linkages between Hindus and Muslims. Here, the two communities are not locked into solid economic and associational links.

The second hypothesis concerns political organizations and trade unions which are considered instrumental in bringing people and communities together. Such organizations in Hyderabad link individuals intra-communally whereas in Lucknow the links are inter-communal. In most parts of India, after Independence Muslims embraced the Congress party which, barring periods of aberration, has remained committed to secularism. In Hyderabad, however, deviating from the all-India pattern, 'Muslims overwhelmingly supported a Muslim party called Majlis-e-Ittehadul Muslimeen

(MIM)'.[5] Thus, secular political organizations in Hyderabad were unable to play the role of bridge-building between the two major communities. Contrarily, the MIM strength in the city has created fertile ground for Hindu nationalist organizations to polarize Hindus; and the fault lines between the two communities have been exacerbated.

The religious campaigns initiated by MIM and the Hindu organization, Arya Samaj, a decade earlier, culminated in 'competitive proselytization'. The MIM converted Hindus to Islam and the Arya Samaj engaged in re-conversion (*shuddhikaran*). Religious conversions and re-conversions added to the bitterness between the two communities. The riots that broke out in Hyderabad in 1938 were by-products of this competitive proselytization.

Due to the economic symbiosis between Hindus and Muslims in Lucknow, political leaders and local, organic peace committees come together to contain tensions and rumours. Unlike in Lucknow, there is a good deal of civic interaction between Hindus and Muslims in Hyderabad at the elite level. It takes place through the many clubs in the city, modern NGOs and other organizations that have sprung up in recent times. In Hyderabad, however, peace committees do not emerge from below but are put in place by the local administration from above. These committees therefore prove to be ineffective.

Civic engagements among different communities also take place through festivals. In Hyderabad, however, processions taken out by Hindus to celebrate Ganesh Chaturthi have excluded Muslims and, in fact, the intent has been 'to demonstrate to Muslims how united the Hindus could be'.[6] In response, the MIM engineered a new collective rite for Muslims called the Pankha Procession. Varshney recalls that in 1984, the Pankha and Ganesh processions followed in quick succession leading to the worst violence of the decade. Thus, the popular civic arena of festivals too has been polarized in this city.

Lucknow has also been a centre of 'festival politics' involving a large number of people, but the dispute there is among the two major Muslims sects. The festival of Muharram creates a problem each time as it is essentially celebrated by Shias. Since Lucknow was ruled by Shia princes, this festival is traditionally celebrated with much fanfare and pageantry. The celebrations have led to Shia-Sunni clashes in the past but not Hindu-Muslim clashes.

Varshney has similarly compared Surat with Ahmedabad and Aligarh with Calicut, reaching practically the same conclusions.

Briefly stated, the conclusion is that cities with strong associational civic engagements remain largely free of communal tension. It can be said that in these cities an 'institutionalized peace system' exists, where organizations are communally integrated. These civic organizations assist the local administration in maintaining peace and order. And the opposite is true of the cities where communal tension and violence is a regular feature.

When the civic edifice is inter-ethnic and associational, it can take on 'ethnic earthquakes' such as the Partition and the desecration of a holy place. But if the form of civic engagement is essentially intra-ethnic, 'earthquakes' of much smaller intensity can bring the edifice down.

II – ELECTORAL COMPULSIONS AND COMPETITION

Socio-political analyst Steven I. Wilkinson in his book, *Votes and Violence: Electoral Competition and Communal Riots in India*, identifies electoral politics and competition as the principal causative factor for the occurrence of communal riots in India.

Wilkinson and Varshney have collaborated in their research of communal riots and even shared some of the data sets. But when it comes to identifying the causative factors, they have trodden divergent paths. Wilkinson's central argument is that town-level electoral incentives account for the outbreak of Hindu-Muslim violence and state-level electoral incentives account for state governments using their police force to prevent such an outbreak.

Based on his analysis of empirical data, Wilkinson posits that 'democratic states protect minorities when it is in their government's electoral interest to do so'. When the number of minority votes in a state is considerable and there is a high level of party competition, the state government and the politicians provide security to minority communities.[7]

In his analysis, the states in India are placed in three broad categories. Taking the Gujarat riots of 2002 as a reference point, the states of Kerala, Bihar and Orissa are put in the first category, where there were three or more parties and a high level of party competition existed in the state. In the second category are placed the states of Andhra Pradesh, Madhya Pradesh and Rajasthan that primarily had only two competing parties, or 'bipolar competition', but the government relied heavily on minority votes. The state of Gujarat alone is placed in the third category, where, despite bipolar competition, there was no reliance on minority votes.

Logically, the state governments under the first two categories worked proactively in preventing riots in 2002, after the Godhra incident. The situation in Gujarat has been depicted as the worst-case scenario, wherein the BJP government in power did not have an electoral support base in the minority community nor did the other parties in the state offer enough competition for them. Thus, it had no incentive to protect the Gujarati Muslims.[8]

It is important to summarize Wilkinson's hypothesis about the way electoral competition creates and sustains the communal divide between Hindus and Muslims, which is at the root of occurrence of riots.

Use of Ethnic Wedge Issues

'Politicians in India choose an ethnic or non-ethnic identity which, in their judgment, voters will identify themselves with. Thereafter, they face the challenge of how to make this identity the most politically salient among their target voters.' In such a situation, the main rival political parties use ethnic wedge issues most likely to favour their party. In order to mobilize and consolidate Hindu votes, in areas where Muslims are a sizeable part of the population, 'upper-caste dominated parties may highlight anti-Muslim wedge issues: bringing up Muslim's alleged slaughter of cows; taking a Hindu procession through a Muslim neighbourhood; laying "Hindu" claim on a plot of land occupied by Muslims, etc.'[9]

When this happens, defensive counter-mobilization by minorities takes place and increases the probability of ethnic violence. The minority counter-mobilization or ethnic violence that results from such electoral mobilization does not make all Hindu swing voters support the pro-Hindu party. But to win an election, the party attempts to influence the pivotal swing voters. Elections can be won or lost depending on the success in influencing such voters.[10]

Many politicians are 'quite open about the relationship between communal violence and an improvement in their electoral prospects. For instance, in January 1986, riots broke out in Aurangabad, Maharashtra, following processions and protests organized by the Shiv Sena, a Maharashtra-based Hindu right-wing organization. The riots helped the Sena defeat the Congress in the subsequent elections, and the Shiv Sena chief in the city, Chandrakant Khaire claimed that the riots were critical in building support for the Sena and that "ever since the first stir our party has received tremendous sympathy from the Hindus"'.[11]

....

Making a study of communal riots in Uttar Pradesh, Wilkinson finds that 'polarizing the electorates through communal processions and other events, likely to divide people and increase the salience of religious identity, have proved to be a highly effective electoral strategy. Between the 1989 state elections and 1991 state elections in Uttar Pradesh, thirty-three riots took place in which 295 persons died. The precipitating event for violence in each case was an organized Hindu nationalist attempt to disrupt a Muslim procession, to hold an anti-Muslim public meeting, or to raise the fear that Muslims were about to turn upon Hindus'. The riots in Agra and in Aligarh in December 1990 have been cited as examples.[12]

The electoral impact was that in the towns affected by the riots, the vote share of the BJP went up by an average of 24 per cent, while in the unaffected town the BJP vote share went up by only 7 per cent. In the final electoral results, the BJP defeated candidates from the Muslim-supported Janata Dal in all but two of the riot-affected towns, and in eight towns its share of votes rose to around 50 per cent.[13]

Christophe Jaffrelot's research on riots in state elections in Madhya Pradesh also shows similar favourable impact on the electoral fortunes of the BJP in that state.[14] In the 1993 election, in a complete turnaround for the first time in the state's history, not a single Muslim was elected from Bhopal. The impact of such communal polarization was observed in other urban constituencies too, such as in Burhanpur, a town with a 22 per cent Muslim population, where the winning candidate was a VHP sadhu.

It is worth recounting briefly, two more examples of how electoral competition affects riot prevention and how party fractionalization actually helps in maintaining peace. In Uttar Pradesh, when the BJP was in power in 1991, its ally the VHP was allowed to conduct a religious procession and ceremony with a minimal police escort in the sensitive city of Varanasi.[15] The procession went through a heavily Muslim-populated area in the old city. The processionists chanted provocative slogans and set off fireworks, which injured a Muslim. This resulted in a fracas and the situation soon escalated into large-scale riots. As is usual in such cases, false rumours about possible Muslim attacks on Hindus were spread, which resulted in worsening the situation. In the four days of rioting, seventeen people were killed and in certain localities, properties of Muslims were looted and destroyed.

The local DM was opposed to the procession but was prevailed over by the state government to allow it. The key reason for the procession being taken out was that by-elections to fourteen state assembly districts were due in two weeks. The BJP recognized the Hindu voters sympathetic to Hindutva, who were also fearful of the alleged 'Muslim threat', as the main constituency it needed to influence. This led the party in power to virtually engineer the riots in Varanasi.

The second interesting incident, where electoral compulsions prompted the administration to act differently, resulting in a happier denouement pertains to Mathura, also in Uttar Pradesh.[16] In August 1995, BJP and its allied organization, the VHP announced their intention to carry out a Vishnu *mahayagna* (grand fire ritual) and a *parikrama* (circumambulation) around the disputed complex that houses both the Keshav Das Temple and the Muslim Shahi Masjid Idgah. The temple-*idgah* complex is one of the many disputed mosque-temple sites in the country, and therefore, 'a natural choice for anti-Muslim mobilization'. The temple is associated with Lord Krishna, an important icon for Yadavs, a backward community; the campaign intended to win over a large number of backward class votes for the upper-caste dominated BJP.

At this time, Mayawati of the BSP was the chief minister, leading a coalition with the BJP in the state. She, however, realized that the Mathura *mahayagna* would pose a serious threat to her ethnic political base. Fearing the loss of Muslim votes, she took a firm public stance against the ritual. Both the VHP and the BJP, her coalition partners, put pressure on her to allow both the rituals to be carried out as planned but Mayawati did not relent and even threatened to resign.

The BJP had no choice but to settle for a compromise. The VHP was allowed to hold the *mahayagna*, not the circumambulation around the complex, and that too well outside the three-kilometre security cordon around it. This plan worked and no Hindu-Muslim riot broke out.

III – DYNAMICS OF HINDU-MUSLIM RIOTS AND INSTITUTIONALIZED RIOT SYSTEMS (IRS)

Paul Brass, a professor in the University of Washington, has researched the subject of Hindu-Muslim riots in depth, with particular focus on Aligarh in UP, where such riots have been endemic over time.[17] Brass has brought in a perspective quite different from that of most other social scientists in that he shifts the focus from a search for causes to a historical evolutionary process and the dynamics of the relations between Hindus and Muslims.

According to him, these riots have occurred in 'waves' or 'chains' historically. Before Independence, such periods were 1923-27, after the collapse of the Khilafat movement against British rule, and 1946-48, before and after the Partition.[18] The third such period began in the late 1980s and early 1990s, when the Ayodhya movement was reaching its peak, and continued till 1993. In order to find a satisfactory explanation for the occurrence of riots in India over such broad periods and in the disparate sites, it was necessary to examine them beyond the formulation of 'chains' or 'waves'.

Brass analyzes conditions and causes in Aligarh and takes the site as an archetype for most other places in India, where Hindus and Muslims cohabit and where riots have been endemic. He argues that a larger 'discursive framework of communalism' operates in all these places, like in Aligarh, though derivatively.[19] For Brass, Aligarh is an apt choice of 'riot persistence' especially because of the Aligarh Muslim University (AMU). Since the Pakistan movement was virtually born out of AMU, for many Hindus the university stands for the Indian Muslim, the creation of Pakistan and the problems that arose in Indian society thereafter.

Among the different forms of collective protest that took root in the nineteenth century, like nonviolent civil disobedience movements, riots too became established as a form of collective, albeit communal, action. Paul Brass has tried to establish that the entire political order in post-Independent North India has become embedded in Hindu-Muslim riots. These riots offer distinct political benefits for certain organizations as well as larger political uses. He avers that the Hindu-Muslim conflict is the main justificatory cause for the existence of Hindu nationalist organizations, at whose core is the RSS. This set of organizations, whose task is to mobilize Hindus, is collectively known as the Sangh Parivar. The Parivar has greatly profited from the perpetuation of this conflict by consolidating the political support of Hindus, as elaborated later in the chapter on Hindutva.

Hindu-Muslim riots take place in the backdrop of the communal discourse which has been set in a historical perspective. Brass is in agreement with leftist historians, according to whom the representations of a collective 'Hindu' past are key in contributing to the persistence of communal violence in India. Evidence exists to show that this memorialization leads to demonization of the 'Other', who in the case of India, are the Muslims.[20]

Thus, the political benefits of kindling communal fires and keeping them alive brings us to the theory of 'institutionalized riots systems (IRS)' that exist at places where riots are endemic. These systems are aimed at distorting events and information so that communal violence can occur or be aggravated.

IRS has been conceived akin to 'dramatic production' in a theatre. The dramatis personae include 'conversion specialists' and 'fire tenders'. The former category plays up a trivial everyday incident that can result in communal violence. The role of the fire tenders, on the other hand, is to keep the fires of communalism smouldering, so that when the opportunity arises, the fire may be stoked into a flame – into one of those deceptively spontaneous conflagrations that are then seen as an inevitable outcome of the 'precipitating incident'.

Another set of people involved in riot production are the 'communalist mobilizers', who capitalize on the latent hostilities and create incidents for those hostilities to be acted upon. In this category are politicians, professionals and activists, mostly associated with the Sangh Parivar, and others leaning towards the Hindu right. Particularly in Aligarh, this category includes rabble-rousing students of the Hindu-majority colleges as well as those of the AMU. Brass explains:

> The institutionalized riot systems or networks that exist in riot-prone cities and towns comprise a multiplicity of roles ... they include informants who carry messages to political group leaders of the occurrence of incidents that may affect the relations between Hindus and Muslims; propagandists who create messages to be conveyed to particular segments of society, to the press, to the general public; vernacular journalists who publish these messages in the form of 'news,' poster plasterers who place them on walls, rumormongers who transmit them by word of mouth; recruiters who collect crowds from colleges and universities and *goondas* (thugs) to kill, loot, and burn when the time is ripe.[21]

Since Aligarh has witnessed numerous Hindu-Muslim riots over time, it qualifies as a centre where IRS exists. Brass gives the example of one such riot that occured in 1990.[22] On 8 December 1990, a mob of Hindus attacked the Gomti Express and butchered a number of Muslim passengers. Two days later, on 10 December, false news reports appeared in leading Hindi newspapers, *Aaj*, *Dainik Jagaran* and *Amar Ujala*, that many Hindu patients had been murdered at the AMU Medical College Hospital. This fabricated story was published and widely circulated in the Hindi belt of North India. The rumour served the purpose of diverting attention from the massacre of the Muslim passengers in the train and setting off another round of anti-Muslim agitation in the form of riots. Brass contends that the three newspapers, their journalists and editors fed into the IRS that exists in Aligarh, and in North India, and that they have to bear responsibility for the rioting and deaths that occurred.

IV – OTHER EXPLANATIONS

I have covered, in some detail, the interpretations regarding causal factors and dynamics of Hindu-Muslim riots given by the three social scientists, Ashutosh Varshney, Steven I. Wilkinson and Paul Brass. Each of them has studied the subject in-depth but reached differing conclusions about the reasons for the origin and persistence of this enduring phenomenon. It is to be noted that unlike numerous scholars, who while writing on the subject of Hindu-Muslim riots, base their theories on intellectual – at times rather esoteric – arguments, this trio of social scientists has drawn the conclusions from research done in the field. Their views thus are more grounded in reality than many others who would like to convert the subject into a merely conceptual debate.

Herein, I summarize the other explanations that emerge from different studies to assess whether they are tenable and also if they can be considered along with the other broader explanations. These explanations have been considered by Wilkinson[23] and I offer my own interpretations here.

Economic Explanation

There are two main economic explanations applied to these kinds of riots. The first – 'identified with the 1992-93 riots in Bombay and Calcutta and the 2002 riots in Ahmedabad – sees communal violence as strategy used by slum lords and real estate developers to displace people from valuable land which can be sold for a high price'.[24]

The second theory sees riots as the result of growing competition in 'ethnically divided labour markets'. For a long time, the labour force in industries, especially small-scale ones, has been predominantly Muslim, while the owners and merchants have been Hindu. Increasingly, as Muslims have begun to move into these trades as entrepreneurs, the existing Hindu merchants are getting uncomfortable. Thus, according to this formulation, riots occur or are engineered because of the emerging competition from members of the Muslim community who had hitherto been restricted to the role of artisans and labourers.

Among the examples given by scholars are the 1984 riots in Bhiwandi (Maharashtra), which was an organized attempt by Hindu cloth merchants to damage the properties of the new Muslim competitors in the region. In Meerut (UP), the Hindu business castes, which controlled the wholesale cloth trade, sparked off riots to destroy the Muslim loom-owners who wanted to come into this business. Other examples of riots in Jabalpur (MP), Kanpur and Moradabad (UP) have also been proved as organized attempts to drive out new Muslim competitors in the *beedi* and brassware industries respectively.[25]

Two arguments are urged in favour of this theory. The first is that Hindu-Muslim riots in India mostly take place in towns where small-scale industries thrive along with intense economic competition among the two communities. The other evidence used to support this formulation is related to the proportion of Muslim casualties and property losses – which is much higher than that of Hindus – due to such violence. V.N. Rai's substantive findings have been given in the chapter on the neutrality of the state and the police. Therefore, the change in ethnically divided labour markets in favour of Muslims and the consequent losses they have to suffer indicate that riots are economically motivated against rising Muslim competition.

Paul Brass, however, is of the view that there is little evidence of economic competition between Hindus and Muslims being the cause of riots. 'Rather, there is more evidence that, in particular localities, competition between Hindus and Muslims in the same traditional trades – such as butchering – has been a factor providing recruits from particular castes and *baradaris* for riotous activity against each other.'[26]

Brass has further contended that when communal riots have occured (due to other reasons) Hindu businessmen have taken advantage of the situation to target poor Muslim artisans to gain economic advantage. According to him, riots 'occur in a communal discursive context and are almost always associated with political activities'. In short, Brass tends to see the economic correlation with riots as an effect rather than a cause.

In my view it would rarely be the case that business rivalry or economic competition would cause a riot. It is more likely that once a riot breaks out, economically motivated violence against a particular community takes place. It so happens that in most instances, where members of both communities are involved in a business – even in different capacities – both communities suffer. It is in the interest of neither to have their business or industry disrupted. Hence, it is reasonable to assume that neither the Hindus nor Muslims would like to engineer a riot that would prove counterproductive for both. But once this does happen independently of their volition, members of the either community may try to take advantage of the situation to cause harm to the other community.

Wilkinson has cited the contention of some scholars that 'ethnically divided markets might actually promote economic interdependence and peace between Hindus and Muslims rather than economic competition'. For instance, in Varanasi, a major riot was prevented by the local Hindu traders' association, the Kashi Vyapar Mandal, who were staunch supporters of the Ayodhya movement. However, protecting their shared economic interest took precedence over their personal religious agenda.[27] Varshney's example of the Chikan and Zardozi industries in Lucknow also shows how economic symbiosis among Hindus and Muslims may act as a deterrent against the outbreak of communal violence.

Ethnic Balance Explanation

It has also been theorized that there is a relationship between a town's Muslim population and its levels and recurrence of Hindu-Muslim violence. Social scientists do not appear to agree on how the balance in the population of Hindus and Muslims, at a particular location, makes it prone to conflicts between the two communities. This is evident from the following excerpt:

> In 1951 Richard Lambert, in one of the first serious social-scientific studies of Hindu-Muslim violence, noted that 'Urban riots occurred generally in localities where the communities were more balanced in numbers.' More recently, Moin Shakir has argued that Hindu-Muslim riots occur where Muslims are 'numerous enough to be reckoned with, yet not sufficient to be overwhelming,' while P.R. Rajgopal claims that 'As a general proposition, communal riots occur in places where neither of the communities has a preponderance in number.'[28]

It is true that riots rarely occur in towns, cities or even states where Muslims constitute an insignificant minority. The states of Himachal

Pradesh, Haryana and Rajasthan are cases in point, where communal riots are virtually unknown. But it does not necessarily follow that riots would frequently occur where the percentage of Muslims in the population is substantial. West Bengal and Kerala, for instance, are the exceptions where riots have occurred very rarely despite the fact that Muslims live in substantial numbers almost in every part of these two states. Thus, the argument about 'ethnic balance' cannot be generalized and is unviable.

Embittered Refugee Hypothesis

It has been argued with some logic that those who have been displaced and forced to flee from their homes due to persecution are wont to seek revenge on members of the group or community they identify with their erstwhile persecutors. In India, this applies to the displaced persons or refugees who had to flee from their homes in Pakistan and migrate to India. Between 1947 and 1950 there were several riots involving attacks by Hindu and Sikh refugees on local Muslims on whom the refugees vented their wrath. Similarly, some scholars have noted that a large number of communal riots have taken place in certain towns in UP and Gujarat where the refugees had settled down. There is evidence that these places tend to be communally sensitive. It is also true that many of the refugees and their descendents actively support the Hindu right and are to be found in substantial numbers in the cadres of the RSS.[29]

Consociational Explanation

'The consociational model was first developed in the late 1960s by Arend Lijphart to explain the puzzle why Belgium, Netherlands and Switzerland are stable and democratic, when their religious and ethnic diversity ought to have led to democratic instability and violence.'[30] Applying this model to India, Lijphart argues that in the years following Independence till mid-1960s, Hindu-Muslim violence was largely contained because India had been a 'de facto consociational state'. This was because it was ruled by an ethnically inclusive 'grand coalition', that is, the Congress, which 'granted cultural autonomy to religious and linguistic minorities, ensured minority "proportionality" in politics, education and government employment and gave minorities a veto over important social and religious legislation'.[31] Hindu-Muslim violence increased since the 1960s because India became '"less firmly consociational" with the multi-ethnic Congress party losing power in many states'.[32]

....

Wilkinson has questioned the application of the consociational model to India by Lijphart. Tracing the history of consociationalism in India, Wilkinson finds that India was a consociational state from 1919 to 1947. In this period, Muslims were guaranteed political representation through the creation of constituencies in which only they could vote. Muslims were also guaranteed a minimum percentage of representation in provincial assemblies in provinces where they were in a minority. Moreover, Muslims, Sikhs, Christians and Anglo-Indians had their share of government jobs guaranteed through reservations in proportion to their population.

'Muslims, Hindus and Sikhs also administered their own personal laws and the state guaranteed minority cultural rights, like Muslims' right to slaughter cows for food.' Urdu also 'enjoyed equal status with Hindi as an official language'.[33]

After Independence, India became much less consociational. Separate electorates were abolished wherever they had been introduced earlier. In the central government, job reservations for Muslims, Sikhs and Christians were abolished in 1949. Thus, contrary to Lijphart's assertions, consociationalism was virtually done away with in the post-Independence period.

Wilkinson further argues that since the mid-1960s, India has become increasingly consociational. Job reservations have been extended to the schedule castes, schedule tribes and other backward classes among Hindus, as well as other minorities, in different states. Empowerment of the depressed classes has resulted in their gaining political power and leverage across many states.

Contrary to Lijphart's contention, Wilkinson concludes that 'once we recode India's consociational character and realize that India was consociational from 1919 to 1947, nonconsociational from 1947 to 1966, and increasingly consociational since the 1960s, we can see that consociationalism seems, if anything, to have been accompanied by higher national levels of Hindu-Muslim violence'.[34]

OVERALL ASSESSMENT

From the foregoing discussion it will be evident that many theories and hypotheses have been propounded by scholars who have studied the phenomenon in India about the causal factors and dynamics of these riots. It is clear that there are no generic explanations that can satisfactorily cover the varying situations which lead to these incidents. Even the scholars whose arguments I have cited – Ashutosh Varshney, Steven I. Wilkinson and Paul R. Brass – have differing takes on this issue.

Varshney has emphasized the importance of civic engagement, but in doing so he perhaps ignores or underplays the importance of political mobilization and party competition in the production of riots.

Paul Brass's comparison of riots to a dramatic production is quite original and appears to be conceptually attractive but the existence of the IRS cannot be empirically tested. Brass's belief that his findings, based on detailed micro-level study of riots in Aligarh, can be generalized and extrapolated to other parts of India does not seem very feasible. The dynamics of the relations between the two communities differ at different locations and the same circumstances would not always prevail. Brass, while rightly dismissing the theories of complete 'spontaneity' in causing riots, swings to the other extreme of treating them wholly as a product of rational planning and preparation. Treating riots as dramatic productions is an oversimplification since everyone concerned participates in dramatic productions of their own free will, whereas in riots, large number of people get involved in the situation against their will or inclination. Moreover, every development that takes place in a play as it unfolds is planned and choreographed in advance. There is hardly any element of losing one's reason that seems to inform many of the actions of rioters in a real life situation.

Wilkinson focuses mainly on the relationship between electoral competition and communal violence. Elections are almost a perpetual feature in a democratic polity such as ours. We have general elections to Parliament and the state assemblies; there are by-elections to these bodies; then we have periodic elections to rural and urban local bodies as well as by-elections for the same. It is thus probable that almost any outbreak of communal violence would be proximate, at any point in time and space, to some election or the other. But it may be too facile to assume that, because of such proximity, the two are necessarily related. There are many elections that are neither preceded nor followed by communal riots, as for instance in the state assembly elections of 2008, there was no rioting in the states of Jammu and Kashmir, Delhi, Rajasthan, Madhya Pradesh and Chhattisgarh. Therefore, just as Varshney has conceded that the relationship between civic engagement and riots is 'probabilistic and not lawlike', so is the relationship between elections and communal violence.

CONCLUSION

Having studied the different causes posited by different scholars, it would be more realistic to view Hindu-Muslim riots as overt manifestations of simmering tensions, which are prevalent wherever members of the two communities reside in proximity to each other. Feelings of antipathy towards the 'other' are ever-present in the minds of Hindus and Muslims. A belief in the stereotypical images of the 'other' gets ingrained in the psyche of individuals from both communities in the course of their upbringing and stays in their subconscious.

There are widespread stereotypes among Hindus about Muslims: a) they are 'dirty' because of their food habits; b) they are aggressive and religious fanatics, ready to begin jihad at the slightest pretext; c) they are lecherous, ready to pounce upon and rape Hindu women, who remain uncovered by purdah, etc. Besides this, orthodox Hindus particularly resent Muslims because they eat the meat of cows, which are considered sacred by most Hindus.

Among Muslims, on the other hand, Hindus are seen as: a) idol worshippers, whose religious practices are irrational; b) their liberal attitude toward interaction between the sexes borders on the promiscuous; and c) they are cowardly in comparison with Muslims, etc.

I believe these stereotypes result in fomenting distrust between the two communities and this represents an ever-present danger because it only needs a spark to ignite hostile actions among them. A holistic view of this phenomenon has been summed up well by Thomas Blom Hansen:

> Many of the communal riots in contemporary India, especially those occurring in what police records often term 'trouble spots' with a long record of such ritualized violent encounters with the other community, do not appear as pathological parentheses in a sea of normality. They are, rather, points of condensation where the everyday knowledge, events, and interactions that may take the form of 'joking relationships' or minor irritants which in themselves cannot constitute a major insult, suddenly coalesce with older myths and narratives of enmity and violence into chains of equivalence, re-constructing the perennial enmity and antagonism between the groups. The provoking event is often teasing girls, fighting among

> youths, or police brutality that in combination with a communally charged atmosphere built up over some time may ignite large-scale violence. In such areas, communal violence and enmities are regular features of their social and political organization, with local strongmen and political activists maintaining systems of organization and vigilance with pre-designed roles and choreography, ready for the next confrontation.[35]

Riots will continue to be an enduring phenomenon so long as the politics of identity predominates the public discourse in our country. Until we can achieve a consensus among political parties, leaders and opinion makers, from the national level down to the grass-roots level, to eschew such politics, the character of discourse will not be conducive to promoting harmonious relations among different communities.

It has been argued – though the proposition is not universally accepted – that equitable economic growth with the lowering of income disparities, can, over time, promote harmony among all members of a society and lead to the diminution of tension between individuals and communities (this aspect is covered in the chapter on economic reforms and Muslims). We do appear to have entered an era of unprecedented economic growth. If this is sustained and the growth is equitable, not only for individuals but also for different communities, the tensions among them that lead to violence, could gradually diminish and then disappear.

NOTES

1 Paul R. Brass, *The Production of Hindu-Muslim Violence in Contemporary India (New Delhi: Oxford, 2003)*, p. 10.
2 Varshney, *Ethnic Conflict and Civic Life*, pp. 2-18.
3 Ibid., p. 17.
4 Ibid., pp. 117-215.
5 Ibid., p. 180.
6 Ibid., p. 182.
7 Wilkinson, *Votes and Violence*, p. 6.
8 Ibid., p. 8.
9 Ibid., pp. 21-23.
10 Ibid., p. 25.

11 Ibid., p. 47.
12 Ibid., p. 49.
13 Ibid., p. 50.
14 Christophe Jaffrelot, *The Hindu Nationalist Movement and Indian Politics: 1925 to the 1990s* (New Delhi: Penguin, 1999), pp. 513-514.
15 Wilkinson, *Votes and Violence*, pp. 162-163.
16 Ibid., pp. 165-169.
17 Brass, *Production of Hindu-Muslim Violence.*
18 Ibid.
19 Ibid.
20 This has been elaborated in the chapter on Hindutva.
21 Brass, *Production of Hindu-Muslim Violence.*
22 Ibid., pp. 124-131.
23 Wilkinson, *Votes and Violence*, pp. 26-37.
24 Ibid., p. 27.
25 Ibid., p. 28.
26 Brass, *Production of Hindu-Muslim Violence*, pp. 208-216.
27 Wilkinson, *Votes and Violence*, p. 31.
28 Ibid., p. 33.
29 Ibid., pp. 33-35.
30 Ibid., p. 98.
31 Ibid., p. 100.
32 Ibid., p. 97.
33 Ibid., p. 106.
34 Ibid., pp. 97-136.
35 Thomas Blom Hansen, *The Saffron Wave – Democracy and Hindu Nationalism in Modern India* (Princeton (NJ): Princeton, 1999), pp. 205-206.

Is the State and Police Neutral and Even-handed?

The aftermath of a Hindu Muslim riot leads to inevitable stocktaking – reels of statistics are produced of the dead and injured, of properties damaged and looted, of the loss in manpower and business, loss to the national exchequer – and a blame game by politicians to denigrate other parties begins. Theories are propounded as to the cause of the outbreak of the riot, stories are told of the immense suffering of the families, striking photographs euphemistically called the 'face of the riot' are splashed all over the media and pious hopes are expressed that such an event should not occur again, which puts a blot on the fair image of the country. Rarely, if ever, cool minds get together to consider all the aspects of the riot, particularly the role played by the state and the police in curbing or exacerbating the riot and ways and means to be adopted for preventing such occurrences in the future.

Often the work to be done by the state machinery post-riot far exceeds the work done during the riot. It includes reviews of the intelligence gathering units and the role played by each individual partaker of the riot, and the action, if warranted, to be taken under the due process of law. Most of the time, once a riot is over, such introspection and postmortem is not done. We rarely learn from experience and are hence condemned to repeating our mistakes – we tend to begin with a clean slate every time a communal riot breaks out.

The responsibility to control violence and restore normalcy in most situations rests with the district administration and the police. The principal functionaries at the district level, responsible for the law and order, are the district magistrate (DM) and the superintendent of police (SP). The DM is assisted by executive magistrates and the SP by the entire hierarchy of the police department. It is the policemen who provide the interface between the administration and the public during a riotous situation. Thus, the neutrality of the police is of utmost importance to maintain people's belief in the system.

NEUTRALITY OF THE POLICE

In a secular state like ours there ought to be no discrimination against anyone on the basis of their religion or ethnicity. In the event of any conflict between members of two communities, it is expected that the state remain neutral and even-handed. When there is a clash between individuals or groups belonging to two communities, the police, acting on behalf of the state, have to intermediate to bring about a peaceful resolution. In doing so it should not take sides but act as an impartial arbiter, so that it retains the confidence of both communities.

A senior officer of the UP police, V.N. Rai has researched the record of the Indian police in handling communal riots and published his findings in the book *Combating Communal Conflict.*[1] He has studied ten riots in depth, which have occurred at different places and times in the country, beginning with riots in Kanpur in 1931 and ending with the riots in Bombay in 1992-93. The other riots studied by him had occurred in: Ranchi in 1967; Ahmedabad in 1969; Bhiwandi and Jalgaon in 1970; Banaras in 1977; Jamshedpur in 1979; Bhagalpur in 1989; Meerut in 1990; and in Ayodhya in 1992.

He has consulted certain archival material and reports of human rights activists like People's Union for Civil Liberties (PUCL) and People's Union for Democratic Rights (PUDR). He has also interviewed serving and retired police officers as well as victims of the riots. The sample size of his study is: 50 police officers; 200 'minority' riot victims; and 200 'majority' riot victims.[2] Certain relevant questions were posed to the victims of riots regarding the issue of neutrality of the police. Below are the results of some of the findings.

Research Question I

'How do you find police during communal riots? Friend ( ) Enemy ( ) Neutral ( )' This question was posed to the riot victims of both the majority and minority communities. Responses of 200 riot victims from both the communities were then analyzed.

Minority Riot Victims

Category	Frequency	Percentage
Friend	3	1.5
Enemy	194	97
Neutral	3	1.5

Majority Riot Victims

Category	Frequency	Percentage
Friend	143	71.5
Enemy	13	6.5
Neutral	44	22

Source: Combating Communal Conflict, *V.N. Rai, p. 100.*

Going by the nature of the responses, it is clear that Muslims perceived the police as an enemy rather than a friend, while the reverse was true of the Hindus.

Research Question II

'Will you approach the police for help during communal riots? Yes ( ) No ( ) Can't say ( )'

Minority Riot Victims

Category	Frequency	Percentage
Yes	32	16
No	147	73.5
Can't Say	21	10.5

Majority Riot Victims

Category	Frequency	Percentage
Yes	186	93
No	4	2
Can't Say	10	5

Source: Combating Communal Conflict, *V.N. Rai, p. 101.*

The normal reaction should be that when life and property are in danger during a riot, the police are approached for help. From these responses it is apparent that a majority of the Hindus would do so but the Muslims would not. Thus, according to this study, the Muslims affected by the riots do not have faith in the impartiality or the secular credentials of the police.

One reason could be that there is inadequate representation of Muslims in the police forces. In such a scenario, the largely Hindu police are prejudiced against Muslims and act accordingly in volatile situations. Usually, Hindus perceive Muslims as being aggressive and prone to violence; as those who engineer riots with a view to killing as many Hindus as possible. This attitudinal orientation, which may be influencing Hindus in the police force, is well summed up in the following words of V.N. Rai.[3]

> The attitude of the majority community or the Hindus towards riots is based on two pre-determined beliefs. They are convinced that it is the Muslims who start the riots and it is the Hindus who suffer more in the course of rioting. Behind these pre-determined beliefs are certain formulations that are deeply rooted in the Hindu psyche. The average Hindu is convinced that the Hindus are by nature liberal, spiritual, tolerant and nonviolent. As opposed to this, Muslims are by nature cruel, violent, treacherous and fanatic. Once both these formulations have become a part of the Hindu psychology, it is not difficult for a large number of the Hindus also to believe, that it is the Muslims who start riots and that mostly the Hindus suffer due to these riots. It is only natural to assume that a 'cruel and fanatic' community will start riots and that a nonviolent and tolerant community will be most harmed.

The all-India official statistics regarding casualties in communal clashes in the period 1968-80, however, are at variance with the general perception of the Hindus about their Muslim counterparts.

Details of Casualties in Communal Clashes from 1968 to 1980

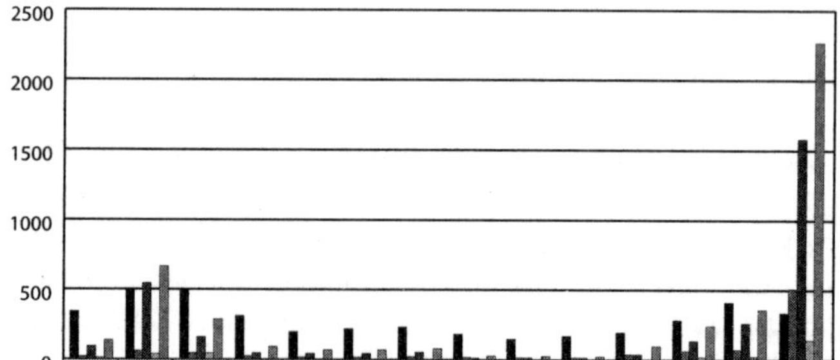

	1968	1969	1970	1971	1972	1973	1974	1975	1976	1977	1978	1979	1980	Total
No of Incidents	346	519	521	321	210	242	248	205	169	188	219	304	427	349
Killed: Hindu	24	66	68	21	21	26	26	11	20	12	51	80	87	530
Killed: Muslims	99	558	176	45	45	45	61	22	19	24	56	150	278	1598
Killed: Others/Police	10	49	54	3	3	1	0	0	0	0	1	31	10	159
Killed: Total	133	674	298	70	70	72	87	33	39	36	108	261	375	2289

By N.C. Saxena, LBSNAA, Mussoorie, based on government reports and Judicial Commission findings.

....

Details of Casualties in Communal Clashes from 1961 to 1980

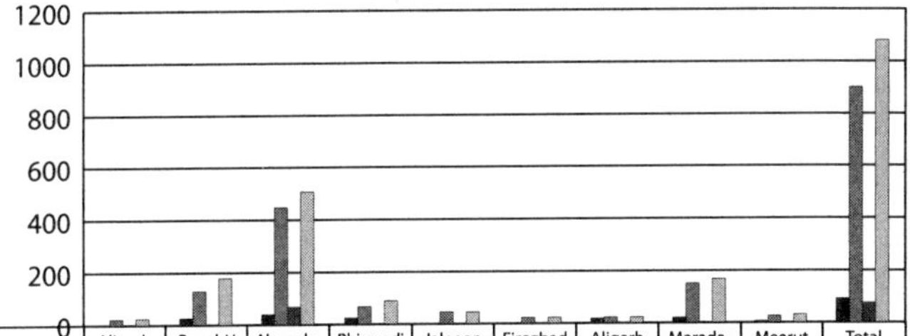

	Aligarh (1961)	Ranchi/ Hatia (August)	Ahmeda-bad (Sept)	Bhiwandi (May 1970)	Jalgaon (May 1970)	Firozbad (1972)	Aligarh (1978)	Marada-bad (Aug)	Meerut (upto 3rd Oct)	Total
Killed: Hindus	1	20	24	17	1	3	6	18	6	96
Killed: Muslims	12	156	430	59	42	16	19	142	21	897
Killed: Unidentified	0	1	58	2	0	2	3	0	2	74
Killed: Total	13	177	512	78	43	21	28	166	29	1067

By N.C. Saxena, LBSNAA, Mussoorie, based on government reports and Judicial Commission findings.

From these two graphs it is quite clear that Muslims suffer considerably more casualties in these riots than Hindus. In the period of thirteen years from 1968 to 1980, 1,598 Muslims (75 per cent) were killed compared to 530 Hindus (25 per cent).

In the riots at Jabalpur in 1961 and at Indore in 1969, of which I have first-hand experience, most of the properties damaged by arson and looting belonged to Muslims. In the riots in Bombay, in December '92–January '93, Wilkinson[4] has mentioned that an estimated Rs 9,000 crore was lost in production, tax revenues and property losses; and the export industries where Muslims accounted for a large share of the workforce, such as in leather, jewellery, bakeries and textiles, were particularly hard-hit. Mumbai's readymade garment industry, which largely employs Muslims from the northern states, cost the manufacturers more than US $ 3 million per day in lost production because of the migration of Muslims back to their hometowns and villages.

Since up-to-date figures were not available from published sources, invoking the RTI Act, I obtained some more information on the subject from the Ministry of Home Affairs. In the following chart, it becomes clear that in the macro-level picture, in the twenty-seven years between 1980 and 2006, 8,490 Muslims (63 per cent) were killed in Hindu-Muslim riots, in India, as against 5,021 Hindus (37 per cent). No firm estimates of the properties damaged during such communal incidents were available.

Number of Hindu-Muslim Communal Incidents and Number of Casualties from 1980 to 2006*

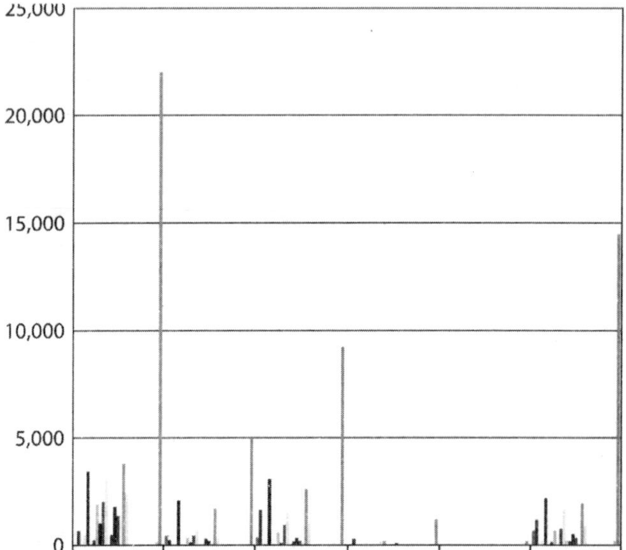

	Incidents	Hindu (killed)	Muslim (killed)	Others (killed)	Police (killed)	Total (killed)
Andhra Pradesh	1,270	318	341	2	5	666
Assam	383	178	838	133	2	1,151
Bihar	3,085	737	1,395	84	10	2,226
Delhi	337	43	64	2	2	111
Gujrat	2,979	1,110	1,798	28	20	2,956
Haryana	33	2	11	0	0	13
J&K	149	25	22	0	3	51
Karnataka	1,521	222	313	17	5	597
Kerala	527	59	69	7	0	135
Madhya Pradesh	1,591	256	363	0	7	625
Maharastra	2,658	529	923	85	11	1,548
Manipur	13	6	3	96	0	105
Orissa	443	30	47	1	1	79
Rajasthan	1,091	176	179	12	7	374
Tamilnadu	765	85	79	0	1	175
Tripura	29	2	7	0	0	9
Uttar Pradesh	3,188	988	1,641	38	23	2,690
West Bengal	1,491	229	355	16	2	602
Himachal Pradesh	9	1	2	0	0	3
Meghalaya	11	3	6	0	0	9
Punjab	7	1	0	0	0	1
Nagaland	0	0	0	0	0	0
Uttaranchal	13	3	3	0	0	6
Pondichery	3	0	0	0	0	0
Chhattisgarh	7	1	1	0	0	2
Mizoram	1	2	0	0	0	2
Goa	2	0	0	0	0	0

* *Compiled from information furnished by the Ministry of Home Affairs under the RTI Act.*

....

Unless we believe as Mark Twain did that 'There are three kinds of lies: lies, damned lies and statistics', the data does show that Muslims are at the receiving end of the riots. When such is the case, the entrenched belief in the Hindu psyche that Muslims are the aggressors who start the riots defies logic. Why should Muslims set in motion something knowing very well who would be the greater sufferers?

Not only do Muslims suffer more in terms of loss of lives and property in communal clashes, a majority of those killed in police firing are also Muslims as the following table illustrates.

Name of Riot	No. of Persons Killed in Police Firing	
	Hindu	Muslim
Bhiwandi (1970)	Nil	9
Firozabad (1972)	Nil	6
Aligarh (Sept-Oct 1978)	Nil	7
Meerut (1982)	Nil	6

Source: Combating Communal Conflict, *V.N. Rai, p. 115.*

The thorough study of the problem done by V.N. Rai also shows that though the majority of the victims in riots belong to the Muslim community, the police discriminates against them with regard to law enforcement as well. They arrest more people from the Muslim community, searches are conducted mostly in Muslim houses and curfew is imposed in a harsher manner in their localities.[5]

On the outbreak of violence, when the internal security scheme in the district is brought into operation, the list of antisocial elements maintained by police stations is reviewed; if deemed necessary, persons who are expected to create trouble are identified and preventively arrested by the police. At Indore I found that in the lists of such elements (referred to in common parlance as the '*goonda* list') the majority were Muslims. From discussions with police officers I have gathered that this is the case in most of the districts with a sizeable Muslim population.

I recall that in Indore most of the '*goondas*' identified for arrests could not be apprehended because they had gone underground, perhaps knowing that they would be targeted. When riots break out it is believed that these elements take advantage of the situation to indulge in arson and looting of properties. Since most of the properties damaged or vandalized belong to Muslims, it is fair to conclude that there is a bias in the preparation of the *goonda* lists. This kind of bias results in the antisocial elements of the majority community remaining free to indulge in looting and violence during riots.

The Hashimpura Episode

The macro-level statistics cited can be analyzed to prove the point but for reality to sink in it will be appropriate to briefly summarize an incident which stands out as a case exemplar of police prejudice and brutality. This incident took place at Hashimpura in the Meerut district of UP in May 1987. This tragic episode was preceded by a major communal riot in the district. It has been graphically described by V.N. Rai – at the time posted as SP, Ghaziabad, a neighbouring district of Meerut – and also by Harsh Mander.[6]

Since the violence and communal rioting which had broken out in Meerut was not coming under control, certain policemen, convinced that the riots could be ended only by 'teaching the Muslims a lesson', planned and executed a horrific crime against humanity.

A contingent of the armed wing of the UP police known as Provincial Armed Constabulary (PAC), on the evening of 22 May 1987, forced all the residents of Hashimpura (a predominantly Muslim locality) out of their homes onto the road. They invaded their homes and vandalized their property and belongings. Almost all the able-bodied Muslim men, totalling 324, were herded into trucks and driven to police lockups where they were beaten up. They were then shifted into jails where the prisoners attacked and killed five of them.

In Hashimpura, after the arrested persons had been driven away, nearly fifty teenaged and older men were rounded up by the PAC constables into a yellow truck. They were then driven up to a place on the banks of the upper Ganga canal in Muradnagar, Ghaziabad. These men were then pulled out of the truck, shot dead by the policemen, and their bodies were thrown into the canal. A handful of them managed to escape under the cover of darkness and gave their eyewitness accounts later.

SP, Ghaziabad, V.N. Rai insisted on filing police complaints even though there was pressure to suppress the story. In 1988, the UP CID was asked to investigate the offence, but its report submitted six years later in 1994 was not made public and no charges were framed initially. The matter reached the High Court, later the Supreme Court, and many years after this horrific massacre, charges were framed against the accused in May 2006. Sixteen PAC men were charge sheeted in the case. The kin of the victims still await justice.

This single episode of the brutal killing of so many Muslims of Hashimpura is emblematic of how the deep-seated prejudices of certain police personnel can result in a horrendous outcome. It cannot, however, be concluded that such prejudices are embedded in the minds of all Hindu police personnel across the many Indian states.

Paul Brass has documented the role of the UP PAC in acting as an anti-Muslim force during the riots in his book.[7] It is probable that such bias among the police is more in evidence in certain states such as UP, Gujarat and Maharashtra and not as much in the other states, especially those in South India.

Relative to the percentage of their population, Muslims are under-represented in the police forces in most states, including in Kerala and West Bengal. These two states, however, have witnessed very few incidents arising out of Hindu-Muslim discord or of an anti-Muslim police bias, even though both states have a high proportion of Muslim population. The available evidence shows that anti-Muslim bias among police personnel is not a country-wide phenomenon, but is prevalent only in certain states, mainly in northern and western India.

ROLE OF POLITICAL PARTIES AND THE POLITICAL EXECUTIVE

In our democratic setup, political parties, party functionaries and workers have important roles to play in influencing the dynamics of interreligious relations. Wilkinson's hypothesis is that electoral competition is the main causative factor for the occurrence or otherwise of communal riots in India.[8] This has been dealt with in detail in the preceding chapter but it can be said in brief that political parties in India take up 'ethnic wedge issues' for purposes of political mobilization of a certain community to garner votes and build a constituency on religious lines. In the chapter on Hindutva, there is a detailed account of the mobilization of Hindus over the Ayodhya temple issue, which has resulted in rich electoral dividends for the Bharatiya Janata Party (BJP). Thus, when political parties or state governments are not neutral, riotous situations emerge consistently.

On the other hand, when there is political will to act impartially and protect the minorities, the government can ensure that riots do not break out. This can be done even in a state like Bihar, which is generally considered to be poorly administered. In 1992, when riots broke out all over India after the destruction of the Babri Masjid, Bihar remained riot-free. When asked how this was ensured, the then chief minister, Lalu Prasad Yadav explained how his government had arrested the returning 'militants' (*kar sevaks*) from UP (the site of Ayodhya) before they could reach Bihar's towns and villages, and how he had threatened all the DMs and station house officers (SHOs) with the loss of their jobs if they allowed any riots to break out in their towns. 'The political will of the state government,' Lalu Yadav said, 'was clear.'[9]

A SULLIED IMAGE

In searching for an answer to the question posed in the title of this chapter, the overall picture that emerges does not show the state and its administrative machinery, especially the police, in a good light. The state government and political parties act even-handedly and protect minorities only when it suits their electoral purposes. At the other extreme, they are quite willing to create situations which result in communal clashes if it suits their party's agenda and results in consolidation of votes in their favour.

The Gandhi-Nehru construct of principled secularism[10] seems to no longer hold any meaning for the politicians of the day. Functionaries at the cutting-edge level, i.e. the magistracy and the police in the lower echelons of these departments are usually governed by their prejudices in dealing with the minorities. They can, however, be made to step in line if there is a clear-cut directive, as was the case in 1992 in Bihar.

This situation will prevail till a consensus can be evolved among all political parties not to exploit the 'ethnic wedge issues' for political gain. It is necessary to organize orientation and training programmes for policemen, particularly in the vulnerable states such as UP, Bihar, Maharashtra and Gujarat, to ensure that they overcome their personal prejudices and act fairly and impartially when dealing with communally charged situations. Recruitment policies also need to be reviewed so that Muslims can be better represented in the police forces in the states.

NOTES

1 Rai, *Combating Communal Conflict*, pp. 99-126.

2 Ibid., pp. 13-16.

3 Ibid., p. 66.
4 Wilkinson, *Votes and Violence*, pp 14-15.
5 Rai, *Combating Communal Conflict*, p. 114.
6 Harsh Mander, 'Brutalised, but not broken', *The Hindustan Times*, 18 December 2006.
7 Brass, *Production of Hindu-Muslim Violence*, pp. 119-123 and 328-330.
8 Wilkinson, *Votes and Violence*, pp. 137-171.
9 Ibid., p. 101.
10 Discussed in detail in the chapter on secularism.

Handling of Communal Riots

The underlying factors leading to Hindu-Muslim riots, occurring from time to time at various places in the country and on different occasions, are deep-rooted in the psyche of the communities and so complex in their origin that any attempt to identify the causative reasons for a specific riot proves to be a futile exercise. No paradigms can be set, no time frame delineated or any estimate made about the extent and severity of a Hindu-Muslim riot. What is certain is the fact that riots adversely affect everyone, irrespective of the community they belong to.

It is reasonable to assume that the socio-political factors, which create deep divides between the communities and are ever-present beneath the surface, are at the root of riots, rather than a conflict of economic interests, which may be merely surface manifestations of the underlying malaise.

In this perspective, it is evident that the administrative machinery in charge of law and order, including the handling of Hindu-Muslim riots, is not in a position to have a lasting impact on the social or political dynamics often responsible for such occurrences. The DM and the SP are usually the ones handling a communal riot at the district level (except in cities where the commissioner of police system is in place). The average tenure of such officers has become very short over time – generally lasting less than a year. This is also true of most other officials, who assist the DM and SP. Nevertheless, even if officers had longer tenures, considering the core competence of the field officers and their training, it is unrealistic to assume that they could have had any significant impact on the dynamics of Hindu-Muslim relations in a district.

PREVENTIVE ACTION

While recognizing these limitations, I feel it is useful to set out the steps the district officers in charge must take to prevent riots.

Situations vary and so do the steps taken to prevent violence or mitigate the consequences when violence does occur; thus an iteration of these should be useful and of some benefit to administrators.

Intelligence

Gathering of intelligence on simmering issues which can potentially result in conflict is of critical importance. If the police and the district authorities get timely information regarding such issues, action can be taken to effect compromises, resolve differences and defuse mounting tension.

The intelligence wing of the district police is usually called the 'special branch'. The special branch reports directly to the SP and sends weekly reports to the DM. Intelligence is gathered either by 'plain clothes' operatives or by 'informers', who are often given financial incentives for furnishing information. Besides the special branch, operatives of the IB also gather intelligence, which is at times informally shared with the DM and the SP.

The special branch has only skeletal staff at the district level and their operatives are often not in a position to get information about troubles brewing in the remote corners of a district. The SHO is the key functionary at the grass-roots level and if he is efficient, with an ear to the ground, very little can escape his attention. It is, therefore, important that SHOs are trained to not only be aware of their responsibilities but also keep their superiors informed of the problems in their jurisdiction that need to be resolved.

If the intelligence setup functions efficiently and the district authorities become aware of the nascent problems affecting the two major communities, they can intervene to prevent a conflagration. In my experience, the record of these agencies – in being able to provide timely information to the district authorities – is uneven. This is best substantiated through two instances cited later: the first about the riots averted in Chanderi; and the second about the riots that occurred in Indore, both in MP.

In the case of Chanderi, referred to in the Bhagalpur case study, the compromise we brought about between the two communities left behind an undercurrent of resentment among the Shia Muslims there. It was at best a makeshift solution. Nonetheless, we could intervene because we received timely information regarding the problem. This incident also demonstrates that while a clash can be averted, there are no quick fixes for restoring communal harmony.

The riots in Indore illustrate the other aspect of information gathering. About a year before this episode happened, a press reporter mentioned to me that there were whispers about communal tension developing between Hindus and Muslims in a particular locality, that is, Bombay Bazaar. Since this particular reporter covered the happenings in the city of Indore, I asked the SP to take necessary precautionary measures and followed it up with a written communication. A police picket was posted at Bombay Bazaar and the SHO was asked to keep a vigilant eye on developments and ensure regular police patrolling of the area.

With these measures, the area remained peaceful and there were no instances of breach of peace. Gradually, however, complacency crept in and after some time, without my knowledge, the police picket was withdrawn and redeployed elsewhere. I was not informed about this even though the picket had been posted on my advice. Thus, when trouble actually erupted in the locality in June the next year, no security was in place to prevent it from escalating.

My argument here is that besides official sources, sensitive information about brewing trouble is available from other quarters, provided the district authorities are receptive to such information. The DM in a district, in the course of discharging his multifarious responsibilities, has to meet, virtually every day, a cross section of people from all strata of society. Press reporters and local leaders can be sources of useful information. Evidently, all such information is not always reliable and may be even given with tendentious intent, but the DM should be willing to test its veracity and act on it if found to be correct. The authorities in a district should not depend entirely on official channels for intelligence but also develop informal channels by remaining accessible to the public, because occasionally they can get information which the official intelligence gatherers fail to obtain.

Intervention of Authorities

Once information is available of an impending problem, there are both formal and informal ways of tackling it. Informally, the district authorities may intervene with regard to a dispute to evolve a solution to the problem by bringing the warring parties together, as in the case of the Chanderi incident. Trouble can be nipped in the bud, if the authorities take action on the available information.

Apart from informal interventions, the police and executive magistrates can take recourse to certain legal powers available to them under the laws of the land, to prevent untoward situations. I shall briefly dwell on some of the key legal provisions which can be invoked for the purpose; first of all, action can be taken by the police under provisions of Section 153-A, 153-AA and 153-B of the IPC. Under these provisions of the IPC, when individuals or groups act in a manner that promotes religious animosity – through provocative speeches or by distributing literature of incendiary nature, etc. – legal action can be taken against them. Unfortunately, these provisions are rarely invoked, although they can be effective instruments for prevention of communal disturbance, if used in time against the potential mischief-makers.

There are certain preventive sections of the CrPC that can also be employed to pre-empt trouble. These provisions are contained in Sections 106 to 113 of the CrPC. Executive magistrates have been given powers, specially under Sections 107 and 110, to take action and ask potential offenders to execute bonds for good behaviour. Under proviso to Section 113 CrPC, the magistrate even has the power to order immediate arrest of a potential offender. If the police and the magistracy have credible information about the intention of offenders to commit acts that would lead to breach of peace, the powers under these sections can be judiciously used to prevent rioting and violence.

The police also have wide powers to arrest potential offenders, even without a warrant, under Section 151 of the CrPC, and the arrested person has to be produced before a magistrate within twenty-four hours of the arrest. This power given to the police can be utilized to arrest persons bent on creating trouble, without having to resort to the more draconian laws relating to preventive detention, like POTA (or Prevention of Terrorism Act), which have been enacted in certain states to combat terrorism.

Dealing with the Media

At the stage of prevention, prudent handling of the media is crucial. In our democratic setup, freedom of speech is guaranteed by the Constitution and freedom of the press is considered sacrosanct. In recent times, the role of the media has taken on larger-than-life dimensions. It is sad but true that the media does not always act responsibly, and at times, purveys information in a manner that can cause hostility among the communities. A case in point is the communal riot in Jabalpur in 1961, which started due to the publication of a news item in an inflammatory manner in a local newspaper. Another instance relates to the 1969 Indore riots, when a totally false rumour was spread about a large number of Muslims having gathered in a mosque, fully armed and preparing to attack Hindus in the neighbouring locality. On personal verification, this rumour turned out to be entirely unfounded. Brass too cites a glaring example[1] in his experience: an outright falsehood was printed in a leading Hindi newspaper in the midst of the largest riot in the history of Aligarh in December 1990. It stated that Hindus had been massacred in the Aligarh Muslim University hospital, which led to the prolongation of the violence and justified further killings of Muslims, already the principal victims of the riots.

In times when trouble is brewing, the district authorities must constantly liaise with media persons so that they do not publish distorted version of events. In fact they could play a positive role in squelching false rumours. The district authorities must keep the media fully briefed about the developments so that facts are publicized in the correct perspective and distortions are avoided.

In the course of the Indore riots, besides issuing daily press releases about the incidents, I had found it useful to hold an informal press conference every evening to provide the media with detailed information about the day's events and answer their questions. At these briefing meetings that I took as DM, all senior police officers and executive magistrates were also present. It is beneficial to have such an institutionalized system for interaction with the media, particularly when disturbances have occurred, so that the media plays a positive role in helping the administration control the situation.

Although I do not have first-hand experience of dealing with electronic media, because at that time television was non-existent, I find that officials usually avoid answering questions posed to them by television reporters or even resort to obfuscation. While it is a salutary practice for civil servants to avoid publicity, it is also incumbent on them to convey information clearly, especially to set the record straight about any false rumours or misinformation that may have been spread by persons with vested interests.

Processions

Many communal clashes have occurred when processions – parading religious symbols – have been taken out through the cities and towns. Many a time, the processionists shout provocative slogans to incite passions and, naturally enough, invite the ire of the other community. Sometimes, after a death occurs in controversial circumstances, the funeral procession carrying the body of the deceased may also generate tensions and lead to violence.

It is my experience that attempts by the authorities to dissuade community leaders from taking out such processions do not generally succeed. The so-called leaders are willing to give verbal guarantees of maintaining peace through and after the procession but such promises are rarely kept. The numerous riots that occurred in the wake of the Rath Yatra (a religious chariot procession) taken out by L.K. Advani from Somnath to Ayodhya (though it did not reach its destination) bear witness to this phenomenon.

Thus, if persuasion fails (as it usually does), it is prudent to prohibit such processions under Section 144 of CrPC. This provision is the single-most powerful instrument, available to executive magistrates and the police, for preventing a breach of peace. Under this provision, the assembly of five or more persons, taking out of processions, carrying of arms and weapons, etc., can be prohibited. An order imposing curfew in a designated area can also be passed under this provision. Usually this provision is invoked and orders issued after an outbreak of violence. It needs to be stressed that if breach of peace is apprehended in time, a judicious use of powers under this section can prevent a tense situation from deteriorating into violence and mayhem. However, the downside to imposition of curfew is that it can be misused by the police to target members of a particular community. This is discussed later in this chapter.

The central government introduced the Communal Violence Bill (Prevention, Control and Rehabilitation of Victims) in the Rajya Sabha in 2005. In Chapter III of this bill, extensive powers are proposed to be given to the DM to take various measures for preventing acts leading to communal violence. It is not necessary to dilate on the details since the bill is yet to be enacted into law. Meanwhile, the provisions of Section 144 CrPC remain the most effective legal instrument for the district authorities to prevent and control riots.

ACTION TO CONTROL DISTURBANCES

Despite the best efforts by district authorities, however, rioting and violence do occur; and when this happens, the authorities have to act quickly to control the situation and prevent it from aggravating.

In the towns and cities that have a history of violence, internal security schemes have been prepared, which are to be put into operation by the DM in consultation with the SP, on the occasion of such an outbreak. The different measures that may be undertaken are:

1. Intensifying the patrolling of the affected areas by the police.
2. Using Section 129 of the CrPC to disperse an assembly of five or more persons.
3. Using the powers under Section 151 of the CrPC to arrest antisocial elements.
4. Enacting appropriate prohibitory orders under Section 144 of the CrPC.
5. Using Section 130 and 131 of the CrPC for deploying the military.

Section 129 CrPC

If it is apprehended that the gathering of five or more persons, at any particular place, is likely to cause a disturbance of public peace, an executive magistrate or a police officer can use the power given to him under this Section to command such an assembly to disperse. In the event the direction is not obeyed, the official can use force to disperse them and also arrest them.

Thus, this Section can be utilized to prevent a gathering from turning violent. However, it can be effectively exercised only if adequate police force is available to assist the executive magistrate or police officer in charge. If the authorities are alert and prepared, this provision in the law can be used to de-escalate situations from getting out of control.

Section 151 CrPC

Each police station maintains a list of antisocial elements who take advantage of the situation when a town is engulfed in violence. The SHOs are given the discretion to arrest and detain such elements, generally under Section 151 of the CrPC. If the police are successful in detaining the *goondas*, much mischief can be prevented. This is an important element in the action to be taken by the police in controlling the situation in a strife-torn area.

Section 144 CrPC and Imposition of Curfew

If breach of peace is apprehended in any particular area, prohibitory orders under Section 144 CrPC may be issued, inter alia, prohibiting the assembly of five or more persons, the use of loudspeakers, taking out of processions, etc. If such measures do not prove effective in restoring peace and order, to prevent the riots from beginning, the scope of the prohibitory order under this Section can be extended to forbid persons from coming out of their houses to any public place, in specified areas during specified hours. Such an order, in common parlance, is termed as a 'curfew' order. If curfew has been imposed, its efficacy depends on proper enforcement. I have experienced in Jabalpur and Indore that effective enforcement of curfew goes a long way in bringing the situation under control. But it can be done only when adequate police and/or paramilitary forces are available with the administration.

It is widely believed that imposition of curfew means that the policemen on duty automatically have the powers or the orders to 'shoot at sight'. This perception is incorrect. Curfew orders always specify the acts which are prohibited; these orders are promulgated in certain designated areas or localities; and they generally ban the public from venturing out in the streets. Breach of the order by individuals usually results in the police either chasing away the offenders or arresting and detaining them. Shooting anyone would be a last resort, that too, only in self-defence.

There are some drawbacks of the curfew order, however, that do not always work in people's favour. Firstly, enforcement of curfew causes considerable hardship to the public at large, who have to remain confined to their homes. The poorer section of society suffers the most, particularly those who live in slums. Therefore, it should be resorted to only when absolutely necessary; however, once it is imposed it should be effectively and impartially enforced. Generally, it is not prudent to lift the curfew altogether; this should be done in stages by increasing the hours in which the period of curfew is relaxed.

Secondly, the prejudices and biases of the authorities against a certain strata or community may become pronounced during curfew. Paul Brass,[2] based on evidence collected in the riot-prone cities of Aligarh, Meerut and Kanpur in UP, has documented such instances. In enforcing curfew, the police often exhibit their bias against Muslims. It is more rigorously enforced in predominantly Muslim-populated areas, while Hindus are allowed to breach it with impunity and the police even overlook their transgressions, as they loot and plunder properties belonging to Muslims. Brass has singled out the UP PAC in this respect, since this force has, time and again, been guilty of such bias.

No doubt curfew is like a double-edged sword. If effectively and impartially implemented, it can help the authorities to control a deteriorating situation quickly. But excesses, as pointed out by Brass, can occur and must be guarded against. The study conducted by a UP police officer, V.N. Rai,[3] as documented earlier, brings out the bias in police behaviour against Muslims when handling communal riots. The study finds that in almost every respect, Muslims are discriminated against and they have to face the twin hazards of the fury of Hindu mobs and police brutality.

In recent times, the media has also highlighted numerous instances of such bias and brutality during the Gujarat riots in 2002 (see chapter for details). It must be mentioned that this bias is not confined to the police but often permeates the entire governmental machinery, including the political executive and the bureaucracy. In Gujarat, even though curfew had been imposed, the police and state government's bias against the minority community resulted in a huge death toll of Muslims.

Section 130 and 131 CrPC

These Sections concern the use of armed forces, that is, the military, in dispersing any unlawful assembly of persons. The armed forces are to be called in only when the police become ineffective in dealing with the situation. This brings me to the rather delicate issue of requisitioning the military in aid of civil power for controlling law and order situations. Apart from these Sections of the CrPC, there are executive instructions issued by the central government, regarding when and how the military can be deployed for this purpose.

At the district level, if the DM judges the situation to be such that the military should be called in, he can approach the military commander of the area and request for the military to be deployed under his jurisdiction. The army contingent then must be made available as soon as possible. The DM's requisition also has to be confirmed by the state government.

When necessary to control mob violence, the executive magistrate can hand over the situation to the officer in charge of the contingent of the armed force. Once the army is in place and no magistrate is available on the spot, the officer in charge can act on his own to disperse an assembly or arrest any persons involved in unlawful activities.

I have called this matter 'delicate' because police officers tend to view this action as a vote of no confidence in their ability to bring the situation under control. When I had called the military during the

Indore riots in 1969, I distinctly remember the unhappiness of the police officers at that time. At the departure of the military, they tried to convey to me the impression that calling the contingent was not required at all, despite the fact that it was the flag march that went a long way in bringing the situation under control.

The failure to properly deploy and utilize the army in controlling communal riots has been a matter of debate. Justice Srikrishna, in his report on the communal riots in Bombay in 1992-93, has adversely commented about the role of the state government in failing to utilize the armed forces properly in controlling the riots in the metropolis. Failure to deploy the army effectively and in time, during the Gujarat riots in 2002, has also been widely criticized in the media. In my view it is safer to err on the side of caution and deploy the armed forces to assist the civil administration. Experience shows that the very presence of the army in a disturbed area has a salutary impact in cooling down tempers and bringing a riotous situation under control speedily.

However, the role of the army in dealing with insurgency is altogether a different matter, such as in the case in Jammu and Kashmir or the Northeast, where the army is sometimes accused of excesses and human rights violations.

It needs to be mentioned in passing that under the Communal Violence Bill 2005, powers are proposed to be given to the central and state governments to declare certain areas 'communally disturbed'. Once any area is so declared, the authorities will have wide powers to take action to curb communal violence. The newly elected central government of 2009 will have to consider the matter afresh and then take steps to enact the legislation. Till it does so, however, it is a matter only of academic interest.

To conclude, incidents of rioting, other types of mob violence, arson and looting continue till law enforcement agencies are able to restore order by taking suitable measures as outlined above. Once adequate police forces are available and the administration has the will, peace and order can certainly be restored. If chaos continues to prevail for an unconscionably long time, as it did in Gujarat in 2002 for instance, the problem evidently lies elsewhere.

ROLE OF POLITICIANS

Although the political executive and politicians legally have no direct role in the handling of riots, they often interfere, thereby hampering the efforts of the district authorities. Chief ministers, ministers and even members of legislatures and political party functionaries jump into the fray with their own agendas. When the resources of the district administration and the police are already stretched, attending to the VIPs who descend on the scene, ostensibly to show sympathy to the victims of the riots, becomes a source of distraction as manpower has to be diverted to provide security and other facilities to them.

To be fair, it must be said that all politicians do not act irresponsibly. I recall that when the riots broke out in Indore in 1969 and I was posted as DM there, the then chief minister of MP, Shyama Charan Shukla rang me up and said he would like to come to Indore immediately to monitor the situation. I candidly told him that since the violence had not abated and with the limited police force we had to bring the situation under control, it would be advisable for him to defer his visit by a few days. Perhaps he did not expect such a reaction and my response was greeted with silence. He took a few moments to mull it over and then graciously agreed to change his plans and postponed his visit by several days. I believe there would be very few politicians today who would appreciate that kind of advice and abide by it. My reaction would usually be treated as impertinence and be very likely to invite a severe reprimand.

Apart from trying to hog the limelight, local politicians often interfere in administrative matters, such as asking for the transfer of an SHO against whom they are wont to make trumped-up allegations of bias in dealing with rioters. The district authorities, with the backing of the political executive, need to be firm in not yielding to such unreasonable demands.

THE AFTERMATH

In the case of Hindu-Muslims riots, well after normalcy has been restored, a tense situation tends to prevail due to the bitterness engendered between the two communities. The situation can be compared to a doused fire, whose embers have not been entirely extinguished and can erupt into flames any time, if fanned.

It is in the early period in the aftermath of riots that the administration and the police have to be extremely vigilant. As a precaution, therefore, appropriate orders under Section 144 CrPC may have to continue, to ensure that people do not gather with mischievous intent and the antisocial elements are kept in check.

The communal riots in Bombay in 1992-93 demonstrate how recurrence of riots can take place if ill will between the communities is allowed to persist and adequate precautions are not taken. After rioting had been controlled by 12 December 1992, tension continued to be built up through large-scale attendances at religious ceremonies and prayers that were accompanied by communally inciting speeches made by the leaders of both communities.

In the surcharged atmosphere, the spark was provided by the murder of Mathadi workers, who Shiv Sainiks alleged were killed by Muslims. This resulted in a second wave of riots in Bombay in January 1993, which happened after a lull of nearly three weeks (see chapter for details). This kind of recurrence represents a collective failure of the administration, since the initial outbreak of violence can be attributed to lack of anticipation and preparedness, but there can be no excuse for large-scale violence being allowed to recur, because by then the administration is expected to have become fully alive to the imperatives of the situation.

After normalcy has been restored, while the formal measures for maintaining peace and order continue, the administration has to make simultaneous efforts, through dialogue, to restore harmony between the two communities – just as they must do to prevent rioting. Depending on ground realities, peace committees can be organized comprising leaders of both communities in the areas affected during the riots, which should work actively to bring the two communities together. Sometimes, with the cooperation of local leaders, peace marches, joint prayer meetings, etc., can also be organized, since such events have symbolic value and provide a healing touch. This is the time when efforts should be made by the administration to encourage both communities to institutionalize the 'associational' forms of civic engagement, which, Varshney believes, can act as a bulwark against outbreaks of violence.

RELIEF AND REHABILITATION FOR VICTIMS OF RIOTS

A very important task for the state and local administration is to provide relief and rehabilitation to the victims of communal riots. Wherever large-scale rioting occurs, involving loss of life and property, relief camps have to be set up where the sufferers are temporarily located. Families who have lost earning members and their homes have been destroyed need to be suitably compensated. Arrangements should be made for tending to injured persons in the local hospitals.

These tasks of providing relief to the victims of riots have to be organized on a war footing; and the administration must deal with such issues with care and sensitivity. It becomes necessary to earmark administrative personnel, doctors, paramedics, etc., exclusively for this purpose. If the relief measures are adequate and delivered well in time to the sufferers, it helps to restore confidence in the population and over time, creates goodwill for the administration and the police.

This was done with some success in the aftermath of the Indore riots in 1969. In Indore, the relief and rehabilitation measures were of course required only on a small scale compared to say, what was needed to be done after the riots in Gujarat in 2002. In the case of the latter, the relief measures for the victims of the minority community were found to be wanting and have been criticized severely both in the media and by the Human Rights Commission.

The human face of the state and local administration has to be at the fore in dealing with the sensitive issue of Hindu-Muslim relations, particularly in areas and localities with a history of past animosity and clashes. Officers and personnel dealing with this sensitive matter should be given proper training and motivated to act in an even-handed manner, so that their impartiality is not questioned by members of either community. NGOs, human rights activists, etc., have a role to play at the sensitive locations and can be instrumental in keeping the agent provocateurs from either community in check.

NOTES

1 Brass, *Production of Hindu Muslim Violence*, pp. 124-126.
2 Paul R. Brass, 'Collective Violence, Human Rights, and the Politics of Curfew', *Journal of Human Rights*, ISSN: 1475-4835 pint/1475-4843 online, DOI: 10.1080/14754830600812324, pp. 323-340.
3 Rai, *Combating Communal Conflict*, pp. 112-114.

THE MUSLIM QUESTION

Religion and Population

GLOBAL PERSPECTIVE

In the context of his thesis that the late twentieth century has seen a global resurgence of religions around the world and that it has led to the intensification of religious consciousness and rise of fundamentalist movements, Samuel Huntington[1] has cited figures of the world population which adhere to major religious traditions. The relevant table on 'Proportion of World Population Adhering to Major Religious Traditions' is excerpted below:

in percentage

Religion/Year	1900	1970	1980	c. 1985	c. 2000
Western Christian	26.9	30.6	30.0	29.7	29.9
Orthodox Christian	7.5	3.1	2.8	2.7	2.4
Muslim	12.4	15.3	16.5	17.1	19.2
Non-religious	0.2	15.0	13.3	13.5	13.7
Hindu	12.5	12.8	13.3	13.5	13.7
Buddhist	7.8	6.4	6.3	6.2	5.7
Chinese folk	23.5	5.9	4.5	3.9	2.5
Tribal	6.6	2.4	2.1	1.9	1.6
Atheist	0.0	4.6	4.5	4.4	4.2

Huntington has expressed some reservations about the authenticity of the data; but assuming a certain veracity of the figures, he has commented that there has been an increase in the population of adherents of the two major proselytizing religions, Islam and Christianity. It can be seen from the table that in the space of a century, the percentage of Western Christians has gone up from 26.9 to 29.9 per cent and the proportion of Muslim population has increased more dramatically, from 12.4 to 19.2 per cent. Incidentally, the Hindu population has also increased, in this time span, though by just a little over 1 per cent.

Huntington has averred that Christianity spreads primarily by conversion and Islam by conversion and reproduction. Positing a declining trend in the Christian population in the years to come with a steady increase in the Muslim population, Huntington has projected that by the year 2025, Christians will probably approximate 25 per cent of the world population and Muslims 30 per cent. It is, however, debatable if this claim can be sustained on the basis of a systematic demographical study.

Huntington has speculated about the socio-political and economic consequences of this changing demographic balance but we need not pursue this matter further, and focus, instead, on the question of the growth of population of Hindus and Muslims in India. I have cited Huntington and the projection made by him only to deal with the subject in our own backyard, without losing sight of its global ramifications.

THE INDIAN SCENARIO

For long, Hindu communalists have targeted Muslims for their alleged propensity to proliferate with a view to achieving majority status by outnumbering the Hindus in this country. Public attention got focused on this issue when the *The First Report on Religion Data*, a monograph of the Census of India, 2001 was released on 6 September 2004 in New Delhi. This immediately generated controversy; the media played up the fact that the Muslim growth rate of population in the last decade was 36 per cent against the Hindu growth rate of 20.3 per cent. It was soon detected that a gaffe had been committed in working out these figures, since the figures did not take into account the fact that there was no census in Assam in 1981 and in Kashmir in 1991, due to ethnic turmoil. After the necessary adjustments were made, the figures showed that the growth rate of Muslims was indeed higher than the Hindus' but the gap was not so marked as indicated earlier.

In an article in the *Economic and Political Weekly*, Alaka M. Basu[2] has cited a glaring instance of distorted reporting of the facts in the media, like on 6 September on the website of the newsmagazine, *Outlook*: 'The first-ever census report of religion today showed a high growth of Muslims at 36 per cent in sharp contrast to the decline in the Hindu population to 23 per cent in the country.' This sentence is extremely misleading since it refers to a decline in the Hindu population, whereas in reality the population had grown substantially, and it was the decadal growth rate that had declined.

The then BJP president, Venkaiah Naidu, did his bit to add fuel to fire by saying that he was disturbed by the 'decline in the Hindu population'. What was really tendentious about the *Outlook* report was that it implied that the Hindu population in the country now constitutes only 23 per cent of Indians. This kind of reportage was powerful ammunition in the hands of propagandists to make the gullible believe that Hindu population was getting decimated in their 'motherland'. In reality, Hindus constitute as much as 81.4 per cent of the total population of the country as per the 2001 Census.

The proportion and the adjusted growth rate of population by religious community are given in the tables* below ('Religious Communities [Adjusted]' followed by 'Growth Rate [Adjusted]').[3] Note that the growth rate table compares population over a decade within a particular community, not vis-à-vis other communities.

in percentage

Religions/Year	1961	1971	1981	1991	2001
Hindus	84.4	83.5	83.1	82.4	81.4
Muslims	9.9	10.4	10.9	11.7	12.4
Christians	2.4	2.6	2.5	2.3	2.3
Sikhs	1.8	1.9	2.0	2.0	1.9
Buddhists	0.7	0.7	0.7	0.8	0.8
Jains	0.5	0.5	0.5	0.4	0.4
Others	0.3	0.4	0.4	0.4	0.7
Religion not stated	Neg.	Neg.	Neg.	Neg.	Neg.

in percentage

Religions/Decade	1961-71	1971-81	1981-91	1991-01
All Religious Communities	24.8	24.8	23.8	21.5
Hindus	23.4	24.2	22.8	20.0
Muslims	31.2	30.8	32.9	29.3
Christians	36.0	19.2	17.0	22.1
Sikhs	32.0	26.2	25.5	16.9
Buddhists	17.0	25.4	36.0	23.2
Jains	28.5	23.7	4.0	26.0

* *Exclude Jammu & Kashmir and Assam for all decades from 1961 to 2001.*

Notes:

1. The Census 2001 population figures for India and Manipur exclude those of Mao Maram, Paomata and Purul subdivisions of Senapati district of Manipur.
2. No Census conducted in Assam in 1981 and in Jammu & Kashmir in 1991.
3. Neg. = Negligible.

In the context of the Hindu right's projection of declining Hindu population vis-à-vis growing Muslim population, if we analyze the figures in the tables above, it emerges that in the decade 1991-2001, the Hindu population came down by 1 per cent. In the forty years since 1961, the percentage of Hindus has gone down by 3 per cent. Correspondingly, in the last decade of the previous millennium, the Muslim population increased by 0.7 per cent and in the forty-year time frame, it increased by 2.5 per cent. It is worth noting that in actual numbers, during both periods, many more Hindus have been added to the total population than Muslims, because of the higher base of the Hindu population. This fact gets obscured when we only look at the percentages.

Since the Hindu right also lashes out often at the alleged large-scale conversion to Christianity, it may be mentioned in passing that the percentage of Christians in the total population between 1961 and 2001 has actually declined by 0.1 per cent.

As regards the growth rate of Hindus and Muslims, while the decadal rate is higher in the case of Muslims at 29.3 per cent against 20 per cent for Hindus, the decline in the growth rate has been sharper in the case of Muslims which, in this period, has declined by 3.6 per cent against 2.8 per cent in the case of Hindus.

Two issues of the *Economic and Political Weekly* for 25 September 2004 and 29 January 2005 carried a number of excellent articles by scholars and demographers on subjects related to population growth and religions. It transpires that the paranoia about the Muslim population outnumbering that of the Hindus dates back to the beginning of the twentieth century. Successive censuses before Independence published data regarding population categorized by religion. When such data was published after every decennial census, it used to attract attention and generate controversy. The high priests of Hinduism made it an issue and propagated the theory that the Hindu race was in danger of 'dying out'. But far from 'dying', from less than 250 million a century earlier, Hindus are more than thrice that number today. At that time, the British clearly highlighted the differential growth rates in line with their divide and rule policy. Therefore, wisely, the practice was done away with after Independence.

As early as 1912, a pamphlet was published in Calcutta by U.N. Mukherjee titled 'Hindus – Dying Race'.[4] Jagatguru Shankaracharya, in a Hindu Mahasabha meeting at Nasik in 1925, claimed that at such rates it would take just one century for Hindus to disappear completely. Statistics from 1911 to 1921 Censuses were used to wrongly publicize the increasing number of Muslims and decline in the Hindu population. Newspapers, magazines, pamphlets, etc., were published to perpetuate these myths under catchy titles such as '*Hinduon ka Bhayankar Haas*'.[5]

In the earlier decades of the twentieth century, highlighting the prevalence of widow remarriage among Muslims, the practice of polygamy, and religious conversions was central to the scheme of Hindu propagandists fanning fears about the unbridled growth of the Muslim population. So many decades later, these sedulously propagated myths stand disproved, when the 2001 Census showed that even now Hindus comprise more than 80 per cent of the total population of the country. Nevertheless, the hoary rhetoric continues to figure in public discourse, with claims still being made that the number of Muslims would exceed that of Hindus by 2050.

The reason for reintroduction of the practice in the 2001 Census is not clear, although it can be safely assumed that it was done by the ruling government to gain political mileage. The hasty release of the data in a well-publicized manner, without making the necessary adjustments, creates doubts about the intention and motives of the then ruling party.

As such, these fulminations need not be given any weightage, except for the reason that they promote communal discord, resulting in pernicious demands like ethnic cleansing. Yet, since it is important to discuss some of the information relating to this issue, let us examine dispassionately the factors affecting Hindu and Muslim population growth rates and the dynamics thereof. Central to this debate is the issue of fertility differentials between Hindus and Muslims. Alaka M. Basu[6] explains that population growth rates are not the same as birth rates and are determined by various factors besides fertility rates. Bearing that in mind, she discloses from the National Family Health Survey (NFHS) report of 1998-99 that the difference in the Hindu-Muslim total fertility rate (TFR) is as low as 0.81, with that of Muslims being marginally higher. Also, there is enough proof that both Hindu and Muslim fertility rates are declining, with that of the Muslims falling faster.

Basu says, 'population growth is a function of births as well as deaths. So if two populations have the same birth rates, the one with a lower death rate will show a higher rate of growth. And at least a part of the higher growth rate of Muslims in India can be attributed to their lower mortality rates.' Thus the other important determinant affecting population growth rates is the infant mortality rate (IMR), that is, the number of babies per 1,000 births who die within a year of birth. As per NFHS 1998-99, the IMR among Hindus was higher than that for Muslims. This difference is repeated in the mortality rate of children between the ages of one and five. These differentials are significant, particularly because the Muslim community is considered to be subject to greater economic deprivation than Hindus.

So, it is for the Hindus to introspect about the lapses in healthcare for their children, which result in a lower growth rate in comparison to Muslims. Of note is the fact that the juvenile sex ratio (number of girls per 1,000 boys till the age of six years) for Hindus is significantly lower than that for Muslims, which means that among infants and children, there are more number of female deaths among Hindus than among Muslims. This throws light on the fact that discrimination against females is more prevalent among Hindus.

According to demographers, when the population growth rate of a country begins to decline steadily, it enters a phase described as 'fertility transition'. The experience of developed countries in the West shows that such a transition is irreversible once it sets in. In fact, it gains momentum and does not stall till the process is complete, when the population reaches the 'replacement level'. Replacement level is an approximate measure where one generation replaces the next thereby resulting in a stable population. Thus, it can also be seen as a stage where population growth comes to a standstill since the mortality rates balance the birth rates, and migration into the country is down to negligible.

In India, fertility transition began in the 1970s and accelerated from the 1980s across all religious groups. While the fertility rates among Muslims are marginally higher than those of the other communities, this does not affect the overall situation. There is an ongoing debate in the West as to whether the transition gets over once the replacement level is reached or it continues even afterwards. For us this issue is not of much interest at present as the replacement level in India is not expected to be attained till at least the middle of the twenty-first century.

Despite the evidence about fertility transition having set in, there are still certain allegations regarding the resistance of Muslims to adopt family planning practices and their encouragement of polygamy, which need to be addressed.

Muslims scholars and writers have asserted that there is no injunction in the Qur'an against family planning. Asghar Ali Engineer[7] mentions that that the holy Prophet himself commended *azl* or coitus interruptus to prevent conception. Other eminent Islamic thinkers such as Imam Ghazali in the twelfth century and Maulana Abdul Aziz in the eighteenth century have permitted *azl* and even abortion, under certain circumstances. The Muslim Personal Law Board has also declared its intention to promote family planning among Muslims on the pattern of Iran, which has reached the goal of zero-population growth rates.

The fact that under the Shariat law, a Muslim man can take up to four wives is repeated ad nauseam in the Hindu communal discourse. It is also highlighted in the context of a vociferous demand for adoption of a Uniform Civil Code (dealt with in the following chapter) by Muslims in India. Quoting certain studies, R.B. Bhagat[8] has observed that polygamy is not directly related to high fertility. On the contrary, it is found that women in such marriages have lower fertility. As per the 1971 Census of India, it is also not true that the prevalence of polygamous marriages is higher among Muslims compared to Hindus.

Besides the fertility rate, the migration of Muslims into the country and conversions are the other factors cited for the increase in Muslim population. However, there is no authentic data about the extent of such migration impacting population growth. Moreover, as Basu points out in her article, the rate of migration from Bangladesh has lessened significantly over the years.

To counter the bigoted propaganda of the Hindu right that within a few decades the Muslim population will overtake that of Hindus, demographers have attempted to make projections regarding the Hindu-Muslim population, till stabilization is reached. In their article, Mari Bhat and Francis Zavier[9] have done this projection on what is termed the 'cohort component' method. The assumptions of the method are quite transparent and the mathematics is stated to be simple yet unassailable. This method of forecasting population growth has a good track record. According to this projection, India's population would stabilize at about 1.7 billion at the end of the twenty-first century, with the percentage of Muslims in the total population being limited to 19 per cent. It is also important to note that the net addition to the population during the next hundred years is estimated to be more than twice for Hindus than that for Muslims.

While this projection may be credible, I am more inclined to accept the view of certain demographers who have forecast India's population stabilizing at a level of 1.5 billion rather than 1.7. If this happens, perhaps the Muslim population would stabilize at around 16-17 per cent of the total instead of 19 per cent. In any event, there can be no question of Muslims ever outnumbering Hindus in this country.

The issue of unbalanced population growth of Hindus and Muslims keeps cropping up periodically in our public discourse. This happens because of the nature of the politics of identity practised by the religious leaders and political parties in our country. In a modern and developed society, matters relating to religious affiliations should be relegated to the background; the dominant themes in public discourse should revolve around the socio-economic concerns of all, especially of the disadvantaged and deprived sections of the population. Politics of identity, centred on religious affiliations vitiate the atmosphere and create tensions leading to conflict.

Experts have contended that riots result in stalling the rate of fertility decline by communal polarization, instilling fear and perpetuating insecurities. Riots can also affect the delivery of health care and family planning services and prevent many Muslims from going to health centres, where the bulk of staff are from the Hindu community.[10]

It should be clear that it is in the long-term interest of adherents of all religions, particularly Hindus and Muslims, to steer clear of contentious issues such as growth of population; and those who play a leadership role for these communities must desist from the temptation of making political capital by purveying misinformation, through deliberate distortion of facts and figures.

With more accurate statistical information available to the common public due to the RTI Act, we can reasonably hope that in future the public domain will be free from the acrimony centred on the contentious population question.

However, it needs to be said that viewed in a broader perspective the whole controversy is rather pointless. As a civilization matures, the religious identities of its constituent peoples lose relevance in the arena of public discourse. The Hindu right is concerned with the population issue because it believes that India is essentially a 'Hindu civilization'. This is an exclusivist approach that needs to be shed in our societal interest. This issue has been addressed in the chapter on the clash of civilizations under the subheading 'Is India a "Hindu" civilization?'.

Notes

1 Samuel P. Huntington, *The Clash of Civilizations and the Remaking of World Order* (New Delhi: Penguin, 1997), p. 65.
2 Alaka M. Basu, 'The Squabble that Never Ends', *Economic and Political Weekly* 39 (39), 25 September 2004, p. 4294.
3 Population Religion-wise Census 2001, Office of the Registrar General, India, Statement 1a, 'Proportion and growth rate of population by religious communities, India' (1961-2001).
4 Charu Gupta, 'Census, Communaism, Gender and Identity', *Economic and Political Weekly* 39 (39), 25 September 2004, p. 4302.
5 Ibid., p. 4303.
6 Basu, EPW, p. 4295.
7 Asghar Ali Engineer, 'A Handy Tool for Anti-Minorityism', *Economic and Political Weekly* 39 (39), 25 September 2004, p. 4304.
8 R.B. Bhagat, 'Fact and Fiction'. *Economic and Political Weekly* 39 (39), 25 September 2004, p. 4292.
9 P.N. Mari Bhat and A.J. Francis Zavier, 'Role of Religion in Fertility Decline: The Case of Indian Muslims', *Economic and Political Weekly* 60 (5), 29 January 2005, p. 399.
10 R.B. Bhagat and Purujit Praharaj, 'Hindu-Muslim Fertility Differentials', *Economic and Political Weekly* 60 (5), 29 January 2005, p. 412.

Uniform Civil Code

Article 44, one of the directive principles of the Constitution of India lays down that the state shall endeavour to secure for the citizens a Uniform Civil Code throughout the territory of India. The directive principles, under the Constitution, are 'fundamental in the governance of the country' but are not enforceable by any court.

This particular directive principle, among others, remains unimplemented till date. The Hindu right ascribes the failure to enact a common civil code by the Parliament to the resistance by the Muslim community and the alleged policy of 'appeasement' towards Muslims followed by successive governments. It is interesting to note that the BJP-led NDA government too, which remained in power for six years, like its predecessor governments was unable to take any steps to enact such a legislation.

The Supreme Court too has, from time to time, expressed itself in favour of a Uniform Civil Code and commented adversely on the government's and the legislature's inability to bring it into being. These observations have been in the nature of *obiter dicta* (incidental remarks by judges) in the course of certain judgements passed in cases that came before it.

HISTORICAL DEVELOPMENTS AND HINDU PERSONAL LAWS

After the Constitution had been adopted in independent India, certain bills to reform the Hindu code were introduced in Parliament. The reform was opposed by sections of the Hindu community, including leaders such as Acharya Kripalani and even President Rajendra Prasad, for singling out Hindus for reforming their personal laws. In an article, former chief justice of India P.B. Gajendragadkar[1] has quoted the following averment of Acharya Kripalani on the subject:

> If they (members of the legislature) single out the Hindu community for their reforming zeal, they cannot escape the

> charge of being communalists in the sense that they favour the Hindu community and are indifferent to the good of the Muslim community or the Catholic community in the matter of divorce. Do we want one community to be in advance of other communities in India, simply because it happens to be in the majority? The charge levelled against Hindu communalists is that they want their community to be in a more advantageous position than other communities.

Prime Minister Nehru who had pushed for this reform was of the view that if all the steps could not be taken at once, it was better to take the first essential step by secularizing the personal laws of the Hindus who constitute over 80 per cent of the population of the country. This view, which prevailed, was based on the logic that as a result of the efforts of many social reformers Hindus were prepared to accept reform in their personal laws; and once the step was taken the ground would be prepared for enacting similar laws for other communities, who would then be more ready to accept reforms.

At this stage, however, it is necessary to critically look at the prevailing Hindu laws and evaluate whether the laws have actually been secularized and whether there really is a Uniform Civil Code in existence even for Hindus.

Mani Shankar Aiyar has analyzed this issue[2] and pointed out that India already has a voluntary civil code, viz., the Special Marriage Act 1954 and certain other pieces of legislation, not based on religion, notably the Indian Succession Act 1925, which provide a comprehensive legal framework for all matters of marriage, divorce, maintenance and succession for any Indian who wishes to eschew religion-based jurisprudence. Most Hindus, however, do not subscribe to these secular laws. The clutch of personal laws adopted by the legislature for Hindus are the Hindu Marriage Act of 1955, the Hindu Succession Act, the Hindu Adoption and Maintenance Act, and the Hindu Minority and Guardianship Law, all enacted in 1956.

While Hindu laws have been reformed to the extent that practices such as polygamy are no longer valid, a number of provisions of these laws cannot be deemed to be uniform or secular since there exist provisions, which are not uniformly applicable to all Hindus or have a gender bias. In fact there is a bewildering diversity in the personal laws for Hindus, applicable in different regions and to different castes. In several regions of the South, a Hindu man may marry his niece under the Marumakkathyam law but it would be decreed as a voidable marriage for a Mitakshara Hindu in the North.

The Hindu Succession Act prevents daughters from seeking partition of joint family property and prohibits them from objecting to sons undertaking such partition without their consent. The law also grants a son share in his father's property as a matter of birthright but imposes various constraints on the daughter, who has to demand and secure these rights within the ambit of certain restrictions. In contrast, Islamic laws have no such gender bias and a daughter acquires unfettered and total rights to her father's property on his demise. In Islamic law, the daughter remains an integral part of her father's family, with all the legal rights over property whether she is married, unmarried or divorced, whereas in Hindu law a daughter leaves her father's family on marriage and becomes a part of her husband's family.

Hindus also enjoy special treatment regarding taxation through the tax-saving entity called the Hindu Undivided Family (HUF). Under the Income Tax Act 1961, a HUF is to be regarded as a distinct unit of assessment. It is noteworthy that once a family has been assessed as HUF it would continue to be identified as an undivided entity even after its partition. It is difficult to envisage a situation being acceptable to Hindus wherein they would lose such privileges were there to be a Uniform Civil Code.

In this backdrop it is extremely doubtful if Hindus, who have various shades and schools of personal laws, with diverse provisions favouring traditional practices and preserving certain privileges, would willingly switch over to a Uniform Civil Code. While the Hindu right uses the failure to subscribe to a Uniform Civil Code as an issue to critique the Muslims, their bluff would surely be called if they were to be asked to follow only the existing secular personal laws such as the Special Marriage Act 1954, the Indian Succession Act 1925, etc., instead of the specific laws adopted for Hindus.

REFORMING MUSLIM PERSONAL LAWS

As in the case of Hindus, the Sharia principles, which govern the personal laws of Muslims, are not uniformly applicable to all Muslims. There are nearly six schools of jurisprudence among Muslims, four among Sunnis and two among Shias. While most Indian Muslims follow the Hanafi branch of Sunni law, the Muslim personal law in India does not cover a large number of Muslims, who prefer their own interpretation of Sharia law.[3]

The contentious question of reform of Muslim personal laws thus primarily relates to three issues where the Sharia laws, as interpreted by clerics, are deemed to be archaic and discriminatory against women. These pertain to verbal or triple divorce, the legality of polygamy and the right of maintenance for divorced women.

Triple Divorce (*Talaq*)

Triple *talaq* is a Sunni Islamic procedure wherein a husband divorces his wife by repeating the word *talaq* ('I divorce you') three times. The procedure is considered to be controversial and a latter-day innovation. It is not a part of the Holy Qur'an and was introduced in the times of Caliph Hazrat Umar. It is also not used in Shia jurisprudence.[4]

Asghar Ali Engineer,[5] who has written extensively on these matters, has affirmed that triple divorce is not a Qur'anic injunction. The Qur'an prescribes divorce through arbitration. Engineer has commented that it is highly unfortunate that many Muslims in India ignore a clear Qur'anic injunction and practise a form of divorce disapproved by the holy Prophet. Triple divorce in one sitting is not in vogue in most of the Islamic countries; even Pakistan and Bangladesh have changed their laws in this respect. The All-India Muslim Personal Law Board (AIMPLB) should follow suit and opt for doing away with this pernicious form of divorce.

The issue of triple divorce has regularly featured in disputes in the courts and there have been several pronouncements by judges disfavouring it. In January 2007, the Bombay High Court in the *Dilshad Begum* case held that the pronouncements of *talaq* by the husband or merely declaring his intentions or his act of having pronounced the *talaq* was not sufficient and did not meet the requirements of law.[6] The Supreme Court had also given a similar landmark pronouncement in the case of *Shamim Ara vs State of Uttar Pradesh* in 2002.[7]

A new monograph on Muslim personal law recently prepared by the AIMPLB states: 'The Shariat regards divorce as a permissible but undesirable act ... Uncontrolled use of divorce without regard to the restrictions imposed by the Shariat is a *gunah* (crime). To divorce the wife without reason only to harm her and in violation of the procedure prescribed by the Shariat is *haram* (prohibited).'[8]

It is evident that the secular judiciary and the liberal stream among Muslims do not approve of triple divorce. However, some ulamas (Muslim clerics or a body of Muslim clerics), who represent rigid orthodoxy, contest such an interpretation of the Sharia. The pot keeps boiling because of lack of unanimity of views among the Muslims, though it is a reasonable assumption that the vast majority amongst them do not subscribe to triple *talaq*.

Polygamy

With regard to polygamy, Islamic scholars have clarified that the permission to take more than one wife was given in the special and exceptional historical circumstances when, due to frequent tribal wars, many of the menfolk were losing their lives and the women, widowed or otherwise, who outnumbered the men, needed to be protected. The conditions under which polygamy is allowed are rigorous and difficult to fulfil; and hence, even in earlier Islamic periods, they were believed to be as good as banned.

In actual practice, a minuscule number of Muslim men take more than one wife and that too after fulfilling certain conditions. Therefore, this is really a non-issue. But there is a case for prohibiting polygamy altogether, through a voluntary process, for which the initiative should come from the conscience-keepers of the Islamic religion.

Maintenance of Divorced Women

The third issue of maintenance of divorced Muslim women has become inextricably linked to the celebrated *Shah Bano* case. The developments in this case, alongside the movement to construct a Ram temple at Ayodhya, at the site where the Babri Masjid was situated (and later demolished), have become an integral part of the communal discourse from the 1980s onwards. The basic facts of the case and the related developments are, therefore, worth recounting here.

Shah Bano, an elderly woman from Indore in Madhya Pradesh, was divorced by her lawyer husband, whom she sued for maintenance under Section 125 of the Criminal Procedure Code (CrPC). Under this provision the former husband of a divorced woman, without means to support herself, has to pay for her maintenance till she remarries or dies. But taking refuge under Sharia law her husband refused to pay her maintenance beyond the period of Iddat, which is a three-month period after divorce and before which she cannot remarry. According to the Qur'an, this 'waiting period for a divorced woman is with the basic purpose of ascertaining her condition with reference to pregnancy as well as to provide the divorcing couple adequate time to review and, if possible, to revise their decision'.[9]

The High Court and later the Supreme Court, however, ruled in her favour and granted maintenance for life under Section 125 CrPC.

This judgement created a furore and had the Muslim ulamas up in arms who attacked the court judgement as being untenable and contrary to the tenets of Islamic laws. The government of the day, headed by Prime Minister Rajiv Gandhi, evidently considering it politic not to antagonize the orthodox sections of the Muslim populace, enacted the Muslim Women (Protection of Rights on Divorce) Bill, which exempted Muslim women from application of Section 125 CrPC. This was criticized by liberal Muslims and of course, by the Hindu right.

For most commentators the enactment of the law was interpreted as a surrender to the forces of obscurantism. It was believed that in getting this law enacted Rajiv Gandhi was trying to perform a balancing act for the action taken to open the Babri Masjid to Hindu devotees for worship of the idols that had been surreptitiously placed there in an earlier era. Such speculations, which got a great deal of media coverage at the time, only helped in keeping the controversy alive.

Engineer[10] has pointed out that though the law enacted by the Parliament restricted the payment of maintenance after the period of Iddat, later the Calcutta and Bombay high courts have, through a liberal interpretation of the law, decreed that a Muslim husband must make 'fair and reasonable provision' by a paying an adequate lump sum amount for his divorced wife, within the Iddat period, till such time that she remarries or incurs any other disability under the Muslim Women (Protection of Rights on Divorce) Act, 1986. Unlike the judgement in the *Shah Bano* case, this liberal interpretation given by the courts has not come under fire from Muslim fundamentalists; and with the liberal interpretation of Islamic law prevailing, the travails faced by divorced Muslim women have been mitigated to a considerable extent. This item can, therefore, perhaps be dropped from the agenda for reform of Muslim personal laws.

Besides the *Shah Bano* case, the Supreme Court has also made *obiter dicta* observations in the *Sarla Mudgal vs Union of India* and *John Vallamatton vs Union of India* cases, which have been reported in the *All India Reporter* (AIR) 1995 and AIR 2003 respectively, for the need to enact Uniform Civil Code, in pursuance of the directive principle under Article 44 of the Constitution. The *Sarla Mudgal* case pertained to conversion of the husband to Islam to enable him to take another wife. The *John Vallamatton* case related to the legality of the Section 118 of the Indian Succession Act 1925. This section is applicable only to Christians and it prohibits the making of a will for religious purposes, in certain situations, in the last moment in one's life. This was challenged in the court by a Christian religious functionary resulting in the provision being struck down by the Supreme Court. The observation of the then chief justice V.N. Khare, made in passing about the *John Vallamatton* case, which reignited the debate regarding the delay in having a common civil code, is reproduced below:

> We would like to state that Article 44 provides that the State shall endeavour to secure for all citizens a Uniform Civil Code throughout the territory of India. It is a matter of great regret that Article 44 of the Constitution has not been given effect to. Parliament is still to step in for framing a common civil code in the country. A common civil code will help the cause of national integration by removing the contradictions based on ideologies.

The observations of the Supreme Court regarding the need to give the citizens of India a Uniform Civil Code, be it in the *Shah Bano*, *Sarla Mudgal* or *John Vallamatton* cases, were not really germane to the issues raised in these cases before the apex court. These were passing observations and perhaps ought to have been avoided, since the proponents of majoritarian politics are prone to cite them to berate the minorities. The Supreme Court should appreciate that in a democratic polity such as ours, it is impractical to enact a common or Uniform Civil Code until a consensus develops among all communities to accept it.

CONSTITUTION AND THE COMMON CIVIL CODE

Another aspect of this matter which needs to be discussed is whether the Freedom of Religion granted to citizens of India under Articles 25 and 26 of the Constitution comes in the way of the state in implementing a uniform or common civil code. The orthodox among Muslims have maintained that the imposition of a common civil code would be violative of the spirit of Article 25. Although there has been no authoritative pronouncement on the subject by the apex court, it is generally accepted that there is no necessary correlation between religious and personal laws in a society. Hence marriage, succession and like matters of a secular character cannot be brought within the guarantee of Right of Freedom of Religion.

However, these issues have become emotive due to the way they have been raised by a certain section of the majority population.

Even though the enactment of a Uniform Civil Code would be in pursuance of a directive principle of state policy under the Constitution, it ought to be done only after a broad consensus among most religious bodies and communities in the country has been arrived at.

THE ROAD AHEAD

The foregoing discussions lead to the conclusion that the issue of enacting a Uniform Civil Code is complex. It is invidious to blame any particular community for the failure of successive governments to bring about a legislation to achieve this objective. Personal laws, whether for Hindus, Muslims or Christians, as they exist today, are many and varied. A Uniform Civil Code cannot be implemented, for all practical purposes, unless there is consensus on the provisions of such a code among the leaders and followers of all the different religions. In the prevailing milieu, this would be hard to achieve.

Where personal laws are iniquitous or permissive of outdated practices, these need to be reformed from within; the leaders of the respective communities should take the initiative to reform such laws and practices. Since some of the personal laws of Muslims have been the main target for attention in this respect, the All-India Muslim Personal Law Board is the appropriate authority to take action to change these practices, especially to make their interpretation less discriminatory against women.

There should also be a consensus to take this issue out of the domain of communal discourse so that passions are not aroused, causing damage to the secular fabric of the nation.

NOTES

1 P. B. Gajendragadkar, 'Common Civil Code – A Must', *Bhavan's Journal* (Glimpses from the Past, 1971), http://bhavans.info/periodical/bj_selection25.asp
2 Mani Shankar Aiyar, *Confessions of a Secular Fundamentalist* (New Delhi: Penguin, 2004), pp. 89-94
3 Tariq Ansari, 'Why I Support the Uniform Civil Code', *Mid Day*, 25 July 2003.
4 'Triple Talaq', http://en.wikipedia.org/ wiki/Triple_talaq.
5 Asghar Ali Engineer, *Communal Challenge and Secular Response* (New Delhi: Shipra, 2003), p. 208.
6 Tahir Mahmood, 'Quranic Justice', *The Times of India*, 1 February 2007.
7 Ibid.
8 Ibid.
9 'Iddah', http://en.wikipedia.org/wiki/Iddah.
10 Engineer, *Communal Challenge and Secular Response*, pp. 198-199.

Muslim Deprivation and the Communal Divide

With the Sachar Committee Report[1] serving as the backdrop, the issue of the deprivation and backwardness of the Muslim community in India has been the subject of much discussion and debate in the media. Since it is often said that the frustration among Muslims – particularly Muslim youth – resulting from denial of equal opportunities in access to education and employment sometimes impels them to violence, it would be apposite for us to examine how the Muslim community fares compared to others, in relation to certain key paradigms of development.

According to the 2001 Census, Muslims comprise 13.4 per cent of India's population. A little over 52 per cent of them reside in the states of Uttar Pradesh, West Bengal and Bihar. The four southern states of Kerala, Karnataka, Andhra Pradesh and Tamil Nadu account for about 20 per cent of the Muslim population and Muslims constitute about 30 per cent of the population of Assam.

LITERACY RATES

The following table shows the gap in the literacy levels between the Muslims and non-Muslims in India.

Literacy Gap (All-India literacy levels)*

Muslim Men	55
Non-Muslim Men	64.5
Muslim Women	40.6
Non-Muslim Women	45.9

Source: Census 2001. India Today, *14 August 2006.*[2]

* *As a percentage of their population.*

Although the disparity between Muslim and non-Muslim literacy rates is prevalent in all the states, it is considerably lower in the economically advanced states of West and South India compared to Uttar Pradesh, Bihar, Assam and West Bengal. But, unfortunately, the latter group of states account for a much larger percentage of the Muslim population.

Access to Education

The Sachar Committee has observed that the 'popular perception that religious conservatism among Muslims is a major factor for not accessing education is incorrect'.[3] Recognition of their educational backwardness is present among a large section of Indian Muslims and they are keen to remedy the situation, according to the report. The committee has identified poverty among Muslims as the main reason for their educational backwardness. Abject poverty is a major cause forcing children to drop out from school. This is particularly true for girls. Moreover, small children are expected to work in establishments or as domestic helps to contribute to the family income. This is a reason why the prevalence of child labour is higher among Muslims than other communities.

The general perception among many Muslims is that education does not necessarily translate itself into formal employment. The low levels of representation of Muslims in the public and private sectors and the perceived discrimination in securing salaried jobs make Muslims attach lesser importance to formal education compared to other communities.

The third reason is said to be that very few good quality schools, especially government schools, are found in Muslim-dominated areas. This forces Muslims to either go to private schools, which are expensive, or drop out. The committee has also expressed the view that many schools are culturally hostile to Muslim students, who experience marginalization and discrimination.[4]

Some of the reasons advanced by the Sachar Committee for the educational backwardness of Muslims may be debatable but the fact remains that since Independence, the system and the circumstances have conspired to prevent Muslims from accessing education to the same extent as the other communities, excepting perhaps the Dalits, who may be worse off.

The mean of the years of schooling (MYS) of Muslims is the lowest (three years and four months) when compared with other socio-religious communities. The MYS of Muslim children is 83 per cent of the MYS of all children; and the disparity is highest in the case of rural boys, closely followed by rural girls. This is also true of enrolment, attendance and dropout rates in schools. As many as 25 per cent of Muslim children in the six to fourteen years age group have either never attended school or have dropped out. This is higher than that of any of the other socio-religious communities considered by the Sachar Committee.

According to its findings, once children complete primary education, the proportion of children completing middle school is the same (65 per cent) for Muslims, SCs and STs, but it is still lower than the average of all other communities completing middle school (75 per cent). The next transition from children who have completed middle school and are likely to complete secondary school also shows a similar pattern. With regard to transition from secondary school to college education the percentage is 26 per cent for Muslims and 34 per cent for other groups.

The number of Muslim students enrolled in institutions offering quality technical or management courses such as IITs and IIMs is very low. For instance, Muslims constitute only 1.3 per cent of students studying in all courses in all IIMs in India. In the case of IITs, the share of Muslims in postgraduate courses was found to be about 4 per cent and in undergraduate courses even lower at 1.7 per cent. The representation of Muslims in the top medical colleges is about 4 per cent.

Without detailing all the statistics provided by the Sachar Committee, it may be stated that the percentage of Muslims who gain access to higher education, including engineering, medical and management, is lower than that of other socio-religious categories, sometimes even lower than SCs, STs and OBCs, who fall under the most backward classes in the country. It is in this context the Sachar Committee has made the recommendation that 'relative deprivation in education of Muslims vis-à-vis other socio-religious communities calls for a significant shift in the policy of the state, along with the creation of effective partnership with private and voluntary sectors'.[5]

Late S.S. Gill, who was the secretary, Mandal Commission, has pointed out an anomaly in the recommendations of the Sachar Committee in an article,[6] which should be mentioned, so that a balanced picture is presented with regard to the education deficit of Muslims. The Sachar Committee report has treated Muslims as a single monolithic community but breaks up Hindus into four segments, which are SCs, STs, OBCs and Hindu upper castes. Comparing the entire Muslim community only with upper caste Hindus is not appropriate as Muslims too should have been divided into the two well-known categories of Ashraf and Ajlaf; these categories come close to the Hindu caste system and only the well-off Ashrafs can be compared to upper caste Hindus. This distinction, which has been overlooked by the Sachar Committee, should be kept in view when comparing the status of Muslims vis-à-vis other socio-religious groups with respect to participation in education and also employment. Gill has rightly observed that while the relative deprivation of Muslims is an established fact, this misplaced overstatement of a strong case lends it no additional strength.

Madrasas

Before adverting to the question of employment opportunities for Muslims, it is relevant to consider the role of madrasas in the education of Muslim children. References to madrasas in the media are generally made only in the narrow framework of security concerns as madrasas are branded as the breeding ground of terrorists, especially by the Hindu right-wing groups.

Influential clerics defend the madrasa system of education. For instance, Maulvi Rabe Hasani Nadvi, rector of the Nadwat ul Ulama Madrasa, Lucknow, and president of the AIMPLB describes madrasas as representing the ideal system of education, which is in no need of any substantial change. He insists that 'far from producing terrorists, madrasas are devoted to training students who possess high morals, nobility and humaneness'.[7] He dismisses 'the modern secular system of education as a leftover from colonial times, critiquing it for ignoring the higher goals of moral life and being, in one sense, opposed to these'.[8] It may incidentally be mentioned that, ironically enough, the Hindu right also holds similar views about the modern system of education in India being a hangover of the colonial times.

As Yoginder Sikand points out, Nadvi has clearly gone overboard in his defence of madrasas and orthodox Islamic teaching methods. There is no admission of the fact that 'in many madrasas sectarian prejudice is actively cultivated, a fact which is lamented by Muslim modernists. … With almost every madrasa being associated with one or the other of the competing schools of Islamic thought, one of their main functions is to rebut the claims of their competitors to represent normative Islam'.[9] Such an approach can only serve as a prescription for promoting sectarianism.

Defenders of madrasas such as Nadvi do not recognize the fact that 'madrasas often promote narrow insular mindset. These madrasas generally focus on the nitty-gritty of medieval *fiqh* or jurisprudence on a host of issues that have completely lost relevance (in this day and age)'.[10] While there is no hard evidence about madrasas in India propagating terrorism, they are certainly responsible for contributing to backwardness among the Muslim community because they have not been amenable to reforming their curriculum to modernize their system of education.

It should be pointed out that the negative perception of madrasas contributing to religious indoctrination and of denying the benefits of modern education to Muslim children, may be rather exaggerated, because the Sachar Committee finds that only 4 per cent of the Muslim children attend madrasas. This figure may, however, be only of the madrasas recognized by the state education boards and not the ones attached to mosques. In many instances, Muslim children have been found to be simultaneously enrolled in two schools – secular schools teaching English and science and in *maktabs* (madrasas attached to mosques) where they read the scriptures.[11]

Thus it is imperative that the education imparted through madrasas is modernized rather than envisaging their abolition altogether.

Strategy to Address Educational Backwardness of Muslims

A multi-pronged strategy needs to be adopted for addressing the problem of educational backwardness of the Muslim community. This was indeed promised in the statement made by the Ministry of Minority Affairs in both houses of Parliament, on 31 August 2007, in the follow-up action on the recommendations of Sachar Committee. It was stated therein that 'the outreach of upper primary schools will be expanded, particularly for Muslim girls, and where necessary, with "girls only" schools, more Kasturba Gandhi Balika Vidyalayas (KGBV) will be opened in areas with substantial Muslim population; priority would be given to the opening of secondary and senior secondary schools in areas of Muslim concentration, a special literacy drive will be taken up in districts with a substantial population of Muslims, Block Institutes of Teacher Education (BITEs) would be established to impart pre-service and in-service training to primary, upper primary and secondary level teachers in such areas, additional allocation will be made for opening women's hostels in schools and universities, the Madrasa Modernization Programme will be revised to enhance the components eligible for assistance, the mid-day meal scheme will be extended, especially in educationally backward Muslim concentration blocks and the question of equivalence of qualifications from madarsas for subsequent access to higher education will be addressed'.[12]

MUSLIMS' SHARE IN EMPLOYMENT

In terms of share in employment, particularly in government jobs, Muslims do not fare well. The following table serves to illustrate this point:

Name of States	Muslim Population (%)	Share in State Jobs
Assam	30.9	11.2
West Bengal	25.2	4.2
Kerala	24.7	10.4
Uttar Pradesh	18.5	5.1
Bihar	16.5	7.6
Jharkhand	13.8	6.7
Karnataka	12.2	8.5
Delhi	11.7	3.2
Maharashtra	10.6	4.4
Andhra Pradesh	9.2	8.8
Gujarat	9.1	5.4
Tamil Nadu	5.6	3.2
Sum of 12 States	Muslims 15.4%	In Govt. Jobs 6.4%

Source: Compiled from Sachar Committee findings, The Indian Express, *1 October 2006.*[13]

The Sachar Committee has found that as far as All India Services are concerned, only 3 per cent IAS officers are Muslim. The percentages in the IFS and IPS are 1.8 per cent and 4 per cent respectively. The Muslim community has a representation of only 4.5 per cent in the Indian Railways. Although data may not be accessible as far as the armed forces are concerned, it can safely be stated that the representation in these is even lower than in the civil sector.

Issue of Caste-based Reservations for Muslims

In order to address the problems of lack of access to higher education, jobs under the central and state governments, etc., leaders of the Muslim community have, at various times, advocated affirmative action or reservations for Muslims. Though there appears to be no constitutional bar to using religion as a criterion for selecting backward classes for the purposes of reservation, this has not found favour with the governments or the courts. In British India, reservations had been provided on religious lines to minority communities in elected bodies and in jobs under the government. After Independence, however, this policy was not favoured because i) it was deemed to be incompatible with secularism; ii) in the absence of a caste system among Muslims, there was no overt social discrimination suffered by them to justify special measures; and iii) it would undermine national unity.[14]

Though Muslims and Christians have remained beyond the pale of caste-based reservations, in 1956, this benefit was extended to the Sikhs and later on to Buddhists and Jains as well. Not only has this benefit been denied to Christians and Muslims but conversions to these faiths legally disqualified Dalits from the benefits given to the scheduled castes. In giving the benefits of caste-based reservations to Sikhs, Buddhists and Jains these religions have been treated as off-shoots of Hinduism. In the discrimination made in this respect, we can see the shades of Vinayak Damodar Savarkar's view who pontificated that 'Every person is a Hindu ...' who regards India as 'the land of his religion and cradle of his faith'.[15]

Mandal Commission

While Muslims have been denied caste-based reservations, the exception to the pattern of exclusion has been the Mandal Commission that had declared over eighty Muslim groups to be backward, which constituted half the Muslim population. According to the findings, Muslims constitute a little over 8 per cent of the 27 per cent OBC population. The Mandal Commission made provisions for reservations of the identified backward Muslim groups. Muslim OBCs have thus been included in the backward lists in the central and state levels.

Representation of Muslims in Elected Bodies

In a democratic polity, the extent of representation in elected bodies of members of any community has a relationship with the existing political empowerment of that community. Like members of other communities, Muslims can articulate their concerns through their elected members in the union Parliament, state legislatures, district *talukas* and village-level elected bodies such as panchayats. But it appears that the representation of Muslims is quite low in such bodies across the country. While it is not feasible to give detailed statistics, the following table gives an indication of Muslim members in the Lok Sabha from 1952 to 1999.[16]

Year	Total	Muslim Members	% of Muslim Members
1952	499	22	4.4
1957	499	23	4.6

contd.

Year	Total	Muslim Members	% of Muslim Members
1962	496	23	4.7
1967	520	29	5.5
1971	520	29	5.5
1977	544	34	6.2
1980	531	49	9.2
1984	517	45	8.7
1989	531	29	5.4
1991	533	27	5.6
1996	545	27	4.9
1998	545	29	5.3
1999	545	31	5.6

In the absence of reservation for Muslims in elected bodies, their numbers have consistently been much lower than representation in proportion to their population. No doubt there is a case for a higher level of representation in elected bodies for Muslims. Reservation, however, is not the answer to this problem. The representation of Muslims will gradually increase through the implementation of reforms – as promised by the government based on the recommendations of the Sachar Committee – wherein Muslims would get better access to education, employment and other facilities that the state provides to its citizens.

MUSLIM DEPRIVATION, SOCIAL DISCRIMINATION AND GHETTOIZATION

Clearly, Muslims have suffered from deprivation, to an extent, in the areas relating to access to education and employment and also with regard to representation in elected bodies. This unnecessarily results in their faring worse than other socio-religious communities in indices such as income and health.

Ascension of Muslims to high positions such as those of the president and vice president of India, the chief justice of the Supreme Court, or even chief of the air force, does not hold more than a symbolic value. When it comes to hard numbers, Muslims are indeed under-represented, relative to their population, in the armed forces, paramilitary forces, the police and sometimes even in corporate fields.

The well-regarded actor Shabana Azmi, former Rajya Sabha member and a social activist, equally respected for her thespian qualities as well as her intellect, recently bemoaned the fact that builders in Mumbai, her city of residence, had refused to sell her property because she was a Muslim. This brought in a torrent of letters from similarly discriminated Muslims wishing to buy or rent property in Mumbai. Subsequent media attention to this episode brought to light the expected fact that this happens in other metro and non-metro cities with clockwork regularity.

This underscores the social discrimination Muslims have to contend with, even when they are celebrities, in the cities and towns where they live. Such discrimination leads to the 'ghettoization' of Muslims, wherein they have to restrict themselves to certain areas in a town or city. In these areas, property is almost exclusively owned by and given out to Muslims. Its fallout can occur in terms of reverse discrimination in the sense that non-Muslims cannot find place in Muslim-dominated areas.

That prejudice against Muslims exists becomes quite evident in times of communal tension, which sometimes persists for a long duration after the communal disturbances have been controlled. The continued discrimination against Muslims and their resultant ghettoization, subsequent to the 2002 Gujarat riots, is an instance in point.

IMPACT OF ECONOMIC REFORMS ON MUSLIMS

This discussion has so far been somewhat overly concerned with the government's role in providing and/or denying access to education, jobs and other benefits to Muslims. In a recent article, M.J. Akbar[17] has perceptively pointed out that the ongoing economic reforms have altered the culture of business, easing, unintentionally, a few genuine reasons for Muslim anger, like discrimination in private sector jobs. The explanation for this is that when products were protected from competition and capital was available through cosy deals, businessmen in the closed economy could afford to be biased in hiring employees. In the relatively more open economy of today, where competition is fierce and profit is the main motive, private limited companies have to hire on the basis of merit and pay salaries according to the worth of the individuals. With the expansion of the market, Muslims have also got the opportunity to make and sell their products in a competitive environment.

Akbar also speculates that the reforms are apparently having their impact in terms of de-escalation of Hindu-Muslim violence. After the initiation of economic reforms in 1991, there have been only two outbursts of Hindu-Muslim conflagration, both connected to old wounds. These were the riots in 1992-93 in Bombay, after the Babri

Masjid episode, and in 2002 in Gujarat. Thereafter, since the reforms began to have a real, visible impact on the overall growth rate, the incidence of Hindu-Muslim violence appears to be declining.

GLIMPSE OF THE FUTURE

If, as projected by the Planning Commission, economic growth is sustained at a level of 9 per cent in the 11th and subsequent Plan periods, Muslims would also prosper along with the other communities. If Akbar's hypothesis is right, economic growth, in the wake of reforms, will be 'secular' in nature. It is really too early to prognosticate and we do not have enough evidence yet to be able to say so, but there is certainly a sliver of hope that with the widening and deepening of economic reforms, the communal divide may gradually disappear and riots become history.

NOTES

1 Rajindar Sachar, 'Social, Economic and Educational Status of the Muslim Community of India: A Report' (November 2006).
2 Onkar Goswami and Kabir Malik, 'A Shocking Divide', *India Today*, 14 August 2006.
3 Sachar, *op. cit.*, p. 15.
4 Ibid., pp. 15-16.
5 Ibid., p. 84.
6 S.S. Gill, 'Sachar Report Flawed', *The Times of India*, 23 January 2007.
7 Yoginder Sikand, 'Beyond Terror', *The Times of India*, 8 November 2006.
8 Ibid.
9 Ibid.
10 Ibid.
11 Abusaleh Shariff and Zakir Husain, 'Stuck in Shallow Waters', *The Times of India*, 26 January 2006.
12 'Action Taken Report: Follow-up Action on the Recommendations of the Sachar Committee', Ministry of Minority Affairs, Govt. of India.
13 Seema Chishti, 'Even if Govt. is Employer, Muslims Fall off Job Map', *The Indian Express*, 27 October 2006.
14 Zoya Hassan, 'Reservation for Muslims' (2005), http://www.india-seminar.com/2005/549/549%20zoya%20hassan.htm.
15 Aiyar, *Confessions of a Secular Fundamentalist*, p. 18.
16 Qurban Ali and Arshi Khan, 'Status Paper on Muslims', http://www.dalitminorityinternationalconference.com/muslimpaper.html.
17 M.J. Akbar, 'Are Economic Reforms the Solution to Communal Riots?', *The Sunday Times of India*, 22 June 2008.

IN A WIDER PERSPECTIVE

Fundamentalism vs Liberalism: The Struggle Within Islam

Within Islam, the world over and in India, there has long been a struggle for supremacy between elements who are committed to a liberal ethos and those subscribing to a doctrinaire version of the religion. In the past decade with the Al-Qaeda and, at one remove, the Taliban being perceived as a threat and an ever-present danger in many parts of the world, including the West, the Middle East and South Asia, the spread of Islamic fundamentalism has become a major concern virtually across the globe. It may not be an exaggeration to say that future world peace is critically dependent on the outcome of the struggle between liberalism and fundamentalism within Islam. In India, the country with the second-largest Muslim population in the world, we are increasingly becoming aware of the face-off between the liberal and the jihadi elements since it has now become an integral part of the public discourse.

HISTORICAL BACKGROUND: THE ISLAMIC WORLD

To be able to appreciate the dichotomy between liberalism and fundamentalism in Islam, we need to delve into some history. The holy book of Islam, the Qur'an, actually began to be compiled only after the death of Prophet Mohammad in AD 632. It was in AD 666 that the third Caliph Othman announced the authoritative Madina version of the holy book. Since the *surahs* (chapters) of the Qur'an did not provide answers to all questions of a changing society, the necessity was felt for further scriptural authority to interpret Islamic law. Two centuries after the death of Prophet Mohammad, Al-Bukhari compiled the Hadith, which is based on examples from the life of Prophet Mohammad and his sayings.[1]

Those who portray Islam as a religion of peace, as one that decries bigotry and violence, often quote from Qur'an in support of the liberalist interpretation of their religion. For instance, the Qur'an acknowledges the existence of various religions. *'Li kulli gaumin hadd*'[2] (There have been spiritual guides for all peoples). Further, it proclaims the principle of '*La ikraha fi al-din*' (Let there be no compulsion in the matter of faith). '*Lakum dinukum wa liya din*' (For you, your faith; for me, mine) is the principle of peaceful coexistence enjoined in one of the closing chapters of the Qur'an. Dr Rafiq Zakaria,[3] well-known for his secular and liberal orientation, has cited many verses from the Qur'an to show that Islam believes in pluralism and respect for all religions. Thus the Qur'an categorically states in *surah al-Nam*, in verse 108:

> Do not revile those who
> Worship other gods
> Lest in their ignorance
> They revile your God.
> Each people adhere to
> Their beliefs,
> They act as they please.
> But in the end
> All shall return to their Lord
> And will be told of the
> Wrongs they did.

However, it needs to be stated that scriptures (of almost any religion) provide enough material for being selectively cited in support of the case the writer concerned wishes to make. Numerous works and articles have appeared (a la Arun Shourie) in which Islamic scriptures have been quoted to show how Islam promotes jihad and an intolerant attitude towards other religions.

The first schism in Islam occurred when the Shi'ite sect split from the dominant Sunnis. Shi'ite faith was adopted extensively in Persia (Iran). While Shi'ites remained faithful to the Qur'an, they developed their own Hadith. Numerous other sects also came into being with their own interpretation of Islam. In the eighteenth century, Abd Al Wahhab (1702-1793) began the Sunni Wahhabiya movement that accepted the Qur'an and Hadith as fundamental texts, but opposed all innovations and insisted on a narrow, puritanical interpretation of the texts. Although Wahhab did not himself wish to start any specific school of Islamic thought, the term 'Wahhabism' is derived from his name.

The Wahhabi ideology was rooted in the politics of extremism and terror. However, it had only a fringe following in the Islamic world till it was promoted by the Wahhabi Al Saud dynasty that came to power in 1924. They captured Mecca and Madina and thus took control of the Haj.[4] The Wahhabi Al Saud dynasty used its financial muscle, acquired through the exploitation of oil resources, to propagate an orthodox and even intolerant version of Islam where listening to music, celebrating the annual birth anniversary of the Prophet (Milad-e-Nabi) and death anniversaries of the Sufis (Urs) are deemed to be unlawful (against the Sharia).[5]

Freely using their resources and wealth, the Wahhabiya movement was able to spread its influence across many countries among the Muslims. This was done through construction and repairs of mosques, opening of madrasas and other means of proselytization. The madrasas were then utilized to preach a revivalist brand of Islam. This led to radicalization of many Muslims living in countries such as Bangladesh and Indonesia, where the populations earlier followed a moderate and pluralist version of their religion. Intolerance of the Wahhabis is evident from their concerted attacks on other less puritanical sects like the Bahais and Ahmadiyas. Though they succeeded in radicalizing the Islamic societies in many parts of the world, they gained only a limited following in India.

The continuing struggle between the Palestinians and the Jews, the events post 9/11 including the war in Afghanistan and Iraq and America's declaration of the 'war on terror' has created a major confrontation between radical Islam and the West. The Al-Qaeda and the Taliban, steeped in Wahhabi ideology, are spearheading this confrontation with the West.

INDIAN TRADITIONS

In India's civilizational history, there is a long tradition of both the orthodox and the liberal versions of Islam (the latter represented by the Sufi *silsilas* or orders), having their own following and propagating their beliefs and philosophy. The core beliefs of these two opposing tendencies in Islam are well summed up by William Dalrymple in the following words:

> In orthodox Islam, the object of creation is the worship of God – a relationship of subordination in which God is the master and the devotee is the slave. This relationship is a very straightforward one; if you worship God in the proper way you will be rewarded – on the Day of Judgement you will go to paradise – and if you do not, you will go to hell. The Sufi-minded poet-princes of the Mughal court and their

> circle in the Delhi ashraf elite completely rejected this idea. They argued instead that God should be worshipped not because he had commanded us to it, but because he was such a lovable being. As a result all traditions were tolerated; anyone was capable of expressing his or her love for God, and that ability transcended religious associations, gender or indeed one's place in the social order.[6]

In our history there are numerous instances when the indigenous population was made a victim of Islamic bigotry. There was Sultan Mahmud of Ghazni, who repeatedly invaded North and West India in the eleventh century, ruining and plundering many cities and temples. In the seventeenth century, there was Mughal Emperor Aurangzeb, who imposed a discriminatory tax (*jeziya*) on Hindus.

On the other side of the spectrum, stands Akbar – the Mughal emperor of India in the sixteenth century – who had great interest in Hindu philosophy and culture as also in other religious traditions. He even tried to introduce a new religion (*Din-i-Ilahi*) in which he attempted to synthesize the best traditions of all religions. He was a great patron of arts and letters and his court was filled with Hindu and Muslim artists, musicians, painters, scholars and writers. 'Indeed, Akbar was a major theorist in the direction of toleration, and was a pioneering leader in the world in arranging inter-faith dialogues involving scholars from different religious backgrounds.'[7]

Writing about these two divergent trends, referring again to medieval times, Asghar Ali Engineer writes that in a multicultural society it is not possible to maintain 'pure' religious or cultural traditions in any community.[8] Nevertheless, the Muslim ulama and the Brahmins were determined to maintain this purity. But the Sufi and Bhakti saints were trying their best to evolve composite trends. While the Brahmins and the ulama wrote in Sanskrit and Arabic respectively, the Sufis and Bhakti saints wrote and spread their word orally in local languages and dialects.

Baba Farid, Kabir and Sant Tukaram, who wrote in dialects, are examples of this struggle for multiculturalism. At this time, Mujaddid Alf Sani, a contemporary of Jahangir, strove for the purity of religion and culture. He attempted to purge Islam of all Hindu influences but his writings found no recognition and he was barely known among the common people. Meanwhile, the Sufi saints who blended Hindu and Muslim customs, practices and beliefs, enjoyed immense popularity.

Sufi traditions date back to the thirteenth and fourteenth centuries or even earlier. Khusrau, the celebrated disciple of Nizamuddin Auliya, the great Sufi saint, was the poet laureate of the Sultanate period and a great upholder of composite traditions. The Muslim poets Ras Khan and Rahim wrote in Awadhi (a local dialect), expressing their devotion to Lord Krishna and their ballads were equally popular among Muslims and Hindus.

In the present scenario, the paying of homage at numerous *dargahs* of Sufi saints, most notably of Salim Chisti and Moinuddin at Fatehpur Sikri and Ajmer, by millions of Hindus and Muslims, is emblematic of our composite culture.

These examples illustrate that the puritanical and eclectic versions of Islam have coexisted from historical times and, at least in the period before the modern era, the latter had greater salience among the people.

THE SPLIT BETWEEN THE FUNDAMENTALISTS AND LIBERALS

In India, the split between the fundamentalist and the liberal elements among Muslims can be traced back to the events immediately following the famous revolt against British rule in 1857. After that revolt, 500 years of Muslim rule came to a conclusive end with the last Mughal emperor, Bahadur Shah Zafar being exiled to Burma. This was a big blow to Muslim society in India, which quickly went into a state of deprivation from one of dominance. English was imposed as the official language replacing Urdu and other vernaculars. Muslims were ousted from existing administrative jobs and very few from the community were enrolled in British-run educational institutions.

This situation gave rise to two rival movements within the Muslims. The revivalists attributed their downfall to the deviant ways of the Mughal durbar in its later days and the failure to follow the teachings of the Qur'an by Bahadur Shah Zafar. They thus advocated a return to more puritanical forms of Islam. This orthodox version of Islam found expression in the now famous institution of Dar Uloom at Deoband in western Uttar Pradesh (UP). Though the Deobandis deny it, the Dar Uloom did come under Wahhabi influence. It has been a centre for teaching and propagation of an orthodox Sunni version of Islam.

The other group of Muslims which emerged at the time were interested in shedding orthodoxy and sought advancement of their community through modern science and Western education. Sir Sayyid Ahmed Khan was one of the pioneers of this kind of movement. He founded a college at Aligarh, which later became the Aligarh Muslim University. It was established with the aim of being a secular educational institution for teaching science, languages and philosophy, leaving the preaching of religion to the mosques.

The setting up of these two institutions in close proximity with each other, at Deoband and at Aligarh, both in Uttar Pradesh, in some ways demonstrates the historical split that occurred in Muslim society in India at the time – between the liberals and the orthodox.

Orthodox elements among the Muslims in India today, however, no longer stand on a common platform. The Barelvis, the largest sect of Sunni Muslims in India will have no truck with the Deobandis. These differences are particularly acute in the state of Uttar Pradesh, which has the largest population of Muslims in the country. The Shi'ites have deep differences with the Sunnis, whether they are Barelvis, Deobandis or owe allegiance to any other sect.

These differences within the Muslim community have spilled over into the political arena. In order to unify their respective communities to be able to gain political salience, some clerics have organized forums such as the Shia cleric, Maulana Kalb-e-Jawwad's Peoples' Democratic Front (PDF) and Imam Ahmed Bukhari's United Democratic Front (UDF).[9]

It is a tad unfortunate that while the orthodox elements have organized themselves to make their voices heard, sometimes through violent means, the liberals among Muslims generally remain a silent, unorganized majority.

EMOTIVE ISSUES: FEMALE ATTIRE AND FATWAS

Two issues that have usually stirred strong emotions and brought differences between the liberals and the orthodox to the fore are related to female attire (wearing of the hijab, the niqab and the burqa) and issuance of fatwas by religious clerics.

The wearing of the hijab (headscarf) has quite often become a confrontational issue in the Western world. In October 2006, 'an Afghan woman carrying a baby in her arms and wearing a headscarf was shot in the head by an American Latino while walking on a street in Fremont, California (USA). She died leaving six small children behind.'[10] This resulted in the women of Fremont observing a 'Wear a Hijab to Work Day' to mark their protest against the shooting.

Sadia Dehlvi makes the pertinent point that in these times when Muslims are associated with terrorism in most of the Western world, and are subjected to hate crimes, Muslim women take to wearing of the hijab as an assertion of their identity.

According to scholars, the Qur'an emphasizes the importance of the modesty of women and the need for safeguarding it but does not specifically prescribe any particular type of garment. The two oft-quoted verses of the Qur'an in this context from *Surah Noor* are: i) 'Say to the believing men that they should lower their gaze and guard their modesty; that we will make for greater purity for them; and Allah is well acquainted with all that they do' (Qur'an 24:30); and ii) '... and say to the believing women that they should lower their gaze and guard their modesty; that they should not display their beauty and ornaments except what appear thereof; that they should draw their veils over their bosoms and not display their beauty except to their husbands, their fathers, their husband's fathers, their sons ...' (Qur'an 24:31).[11]

Today, we are witnessing contrasting attitudes towards female attire in different segments of the Muslim world.[12] Turkey and Tunisia ban female civil servants and students in state schools from covering their heads. But in Saudi Arabia and Iran, women cannot appear in public with more than their face and hands exposed. The Taliban regime in Afghanistan had ended up mandating the burqa, an extreme form of the veil for women. In present-day Iraq a section of the Sunnis warn women to wear gloves and niqab (which differs from the burqa only in having an opening for the eyes). In 2006, in Pakistan, a provincial minister was shot dead as her sheer head covering was not considered Islamic enough.

Two broad trends have emerged in the Muslim world with regard to the question of appropriate attire for women. One is the movement towards more overt signs of piety, including 'Islamic attire'. These include the wearing of hijab, niqab and burqa, as the case may be. The contrasting trend is the undercurrent of rebellion against these dogmatic restrictions. Even in countries like Saudi Arabia and Iran, there are women who are bucking the trend and show defiance, from time to time, against the rigid orthodoxy, which insists on them keeping their bodies covered according to the dictates of the conscience-keepers of their societies. There are instances of women who drive cars or go out in the company of men other than their husbands or siblings and put up similar kinds of protests. This development is symbolic of the disputations occurring – across countries in the Islamic world – regarding the values to uphold in these societies.

Though India has the second-largest number of Muslims, there is no discernible trend towards orthodoxy and assertion of identity through the observance of stricter dress codes or changing of behavioural mores in other ways within the community. This may happen as a reaction if the polity were to tilt towards majoritarianism and away from the secular ethos India embodies.

Fatwas

Perhaps for the first time worldwide attention came to be focused on the question of fatwas when Ayatollah Khomeini issued one against Salman Rushdie for *The Satanic Verses*, which was perceived as a heretical book against Islam and the Qur'an. In India, in recent times the media has given much prominence to the case of Imrana, a Muslim woman who was raped by her father-in-law. Though the father-in-law was convicted for the offence, a cleric issued a fatwa according to which Imrana was commanded to leave her husband and marry her father-in-law.

Islamic scholars aver that a fatwa is nothing more than an opinion of a deemed scholar or authority on a specific question of Islamic law.[13] There may be varying interpretations of Islamic law but the fatwas that gain attention are usually the outcome of an orthodox interpretation. In India, which is not an Islamic state, compliance to such a dictate is voluntary and failure to abide by it cannot invite stoning or imprisonment, as might happen in say, Saudi Arabia. Nevertheless, because the media often hypes and even ridicules some of the fatwas issued by clerics, much heat is generated and this contributes to the Muslim community being perceived as obscurantist. Some of the fatwas do appear to be outrageous in the present-day societal milieu.

The fatwa or the ruling given in the Imrana case referred to above, is based on the Hanafi Sunni school which most Deobandi ulama adhere to.[14] It is derived from a finding given by Imam Abu Hanifa, founder of the Hanafi school, 'that when a woman has sex after marriage with her husband she becomes the mother of all his children and so cannot marry his son, even though that son may be from a previous marriage. The ruling includes the possibility that a daughter-in-law and her father-in-law may have an illegal sexual relationship, in which case also her marriage to the man's son would be invalid. It is on the basis of this argument that the Deoband mufti issued his fatwa annulling Imrana's marriage to her husband'. This fatwa was widely criticized not only by rationalists and non-Muslims, but even by Islamic scholars and Muslim women's organizations, who heaped scorn on it. For instance, Yawar Baig, an Islamic scholar, argued that Abu Hanifa's ruling applies to a case of consensual sex and not of rape and was therefore inapplicable to this instance.

A ruling given by Darul Uloom in Deoband, which has a separate department for fatwas, holding co-education of Muslim girls as un-Islamic is another example of a fatwa rightly criticized as regressive.

Mufti Abdul Ahad Falahi of the AIMPLB, an Islamic lawyer and judge who works from a small setup in Mumbai, has dispensed hundreds of fatwas on marriage, divorce, inheritance and business. He even addresses a number of queries regarding the community's interest in the stock market. '"Don't buy the shares of investment companies and mutual funds as they deal in *sood* (interest). There's no harm, however, in going for shares of established, honest business houses like Reliance, Tata and Birla," replied the mufti who probably knows nothing about business at all. Shares of a company like Kingfisher cannot pass Falahi's muster simply because its primary business is breweries.'[15]

In yet another instance, the Darul Uloom of Deoband issued a fatwa stating that 'life insurance is an un-Islamic act and should be avoided at all costs'. The logic given is that 'life insurance is not permissible because there is interest income in it and the act involves gambling as well, both of which are illegal under Shariat'.[16] Interestingly, acquiring any income from interest on capital is considered un-Islamic by some because such income is not earned through hard work. This fatwa was also ratified by the AIMPLB. However, the Shi'ite clerics do not agree with this ruling and Maulana Kalbe Sadiq said that he saw nothing wrong in taking an insurance policy.

After the episode involving Salman Rushdie, another case that made headlines the world over and led to demonstrations and even violence in a number of countries relates to the publication of a drawing of the Prophet by a Danish cartoonist. A minister in Mulayam Singh's UP government offered a reward for the head of the cartoonist. The fact that he continued to remain a minister even after this announcement speaks volumes for our secular political ethos.

Islamic scholars, such as Asghar Ali Engineer, have argued that unlike Christianity, Islam is not governed by a church and therefore no maulvi (cleric and teacher) can ostracize a Muslim for not heeding a fatwa. A fatwa, which appears to be illogical and offends the sensibilities of most liberals, results in antipathy being generated against the Muslim community as a whole, who are perceived to be caught in a time warp and are unable to come out of it. Again, forward-looking Islamic scholars argue in favour of *ijtihad*, which is the creative re-interpretation of Islamic jurisprudence in order to meet contemporary concerns. The Prophet was in favour of *ijtihad*. Until this is done, we will continue to hear of fatwas stemming from obscurantist ideas about the Sharia.

MOVEMENT TOWARDS LIBERALISM

There are certain welcome signs that even the tradition-bound Muslim clerics are now taking note of present-day realities and shedding dogma in their approach to the burning issues of the day. A mammoth rally was held in Delhi's Ram Lila ground on 31 May 2008, in which an estimated 3 lakh Muslims gathered and took a pledge against terrorism. In response to a query by a Rajya Sabha MP, Mehmood Madani, Darul Uloom of Deoband issued the following fatwa, which was read out at the aforementioned rally in Delhi: 'Islam is a religion of peace and harmony. In Islam, creating social discord, breach of peace, rioting, bloodshed, pillage or plunder and killing of innocent people anywhere in the world are all considered the most inhuman crimes.' The fatwa concluded by saying that 'Islam was born to wipe out all kinds of terrorism and spread the message of global peace. Allah knows best'.[17]

The same fatwa was endorsed by a very large gathering of Islamic clerics at a conclave in Hyderabad in November 2008. The occasion was the 29th annual convention of the Jamiat Ulama-e-Hind. The ringing endorsement of the fatwa is indicative of the stance now being taken even by the orthodox sections of Muslims against terrorism. It could also mean that they are moving away from strict adherence to a revivalist brand of Islam that primarily emanates from the Arab world.[18]

Interestingly enough, on being challenged by the Vishwa Hindu Parishad (VHP) to issue a fatwa declaring India as Dar al-Aman (country friendly to Islam) the Darul Uloom, Deoband, did precisely that on Sunday, 1 March 2009. The fatwa was read out at a well-attended rally in Bhubaneshwar, where Chief Minister Naveen Pattnaik and other bigwigs were present. The fatwa said: 'The Indian Constitution guarantees equal protection and rights for all communities. Therefore, for Muslims, India is Dar al-Aman or a Muslim-friendly country.'[19]

As the article informs us, 'In Islamic theology, geographical areas are often divided into Dar al-Islam (country where Islamic law prevails), Dar al-Harb (country hostile to Islam) or Dar al-Aman. In Dar al-Harb territory, jihad is legitimate. The fatwa added that India had ceased to be a Dar al-Harb with the end of colonial rule.' In the meeting, a resolution was also passed condemning the 26/11 attack on Mumbai.

It is evident that even the traditionally orthodox Muslims in India are seriously attempting to distance themselves from the fanatic jihadi elements. Such fatwas and resolutions definitely result in weaning away the vast majority of Muslims in India from supporting or even sympathizing with the fringe, who resort to mindless violence to achieve their ends. It of course needs to be said that irrespective of such fatwas, an overwhelming majority of Muslims in India have never had anything to do with jihadis.

THE OUTCOME

While the saga of the long-standing and continuing struggle between the liberals and the orthodox in the Islamic world will continue to play out due to the differing interpretations of the verses in the Holy Qur'an and other scriptures, at least in India the outcome of these ongoing dialectics will depend on the role to be played by leaders of the Muslim community, state policy and the media.

The state policy has to be so tuned that it does not pander to anachronistic views and actions for fear that religious sentiments would be hurt. In this respect, a consensus among all political parties, and other influential civil organizations, is needed to not act in a manner that would be prejudicial to fostering a harmonious relationship between the different communities.

The media too must act responsibly and not give undue attention and publicity to obscure cases that can lead to stereotyping a community in the public mind. Currently, the electronic media seems to be more concerned with 'viewership' (Television Rating Points or TRP ratings) and the print media with its circulation numbers. Freedom of the press is a cherished value guaranteed by our Constitution. But the single-minded pursuit of profit through increased readership or viewership, by sections of the print and electronic media, militates against the public interest. The media, sometimes referred to as the 'fourth estate', should self-regulate to avoid reporting incidents in a manner that could prove to be inflammatory.

In fact, in recent times, the media (particularly television news channels) attracted considerable flak for their coverage of 26/11 in a manner that was helpful to the militants in planning their moves while the Indian security forces were struggling to fight them. In response, the Indian News Broadcasters Association issued certain guidelines on 18 December 2008, which are being characterized as the first major step towards self-regulation. These guidelines provide for self-imposed restraint on the media, such as not to disclose details of hostages, the withholding of sensitive information on rescue operations, to exercise judgement in not airing details of identity and the number of hostages, etc.[20]

This is a welcome initiative and next time around (heaven forbid!) if an incident like 26/11 recurs, observance of the guidelines should ensure that media coverage would be consistent with security imperatives.

If only the community leaders, the state authorities and the media act in concert, can we expect to see a movement towards the development of a harmonious society, where frictions resulting from heightened awareness of differing religious identities become minimal. This is the outcome we must look forward to.

Notes

1 Murad Ali Baig, 'Islam hijacked', *The Times of India*, 5 October 2006.
2 Tahir Mahmood, 'Pluralism and Unity in Islam', *The Hindustan Times*, 13 November 2007.
3 Rafiq Zakaria, 'Hindus & Muslims – Their Bond Inspires Unity', *The TAJ* (Jan-Mar 2005).
4 Baig, *op. cit.*
5 Sadia Dehlvi, 'Ideology of Intolerance', *The Hindustan Times*, 26 July 2007.
6 William Dalrymple, *The Last Mughal: The Fall of a Dynasty, Delhi, 1857* (New Delhi: Penguin Books, 2007), p. 77.
7 Amartya Sen, *The Argumentative Indian: Writing on Indian History, Culture and Identity* (London: Allen Lane, 2005), pp. 59-60.
8 Engineer, *Communal Challenge and Secular Response*, p. 73.
9 Haidar Naqvi and Zia Haq, 'Muhammad's Divided Men', *The Hindustan Times*, 6 August 2006.
10 Sadia Dehlvi, 'Hijab and the Truth Behind', *The Hindustan Times*, 5 November 2006.
11 Ibid.

12 'Muslim and the Veil: The Meaning of Freedom', *The Economist* 383 (8528), 2007, pp. 59-60.
13 Mohammed Wajihuddin, 'Inside the World of Fatwas', *The Times of India*, 29 August 2007.
14 Yoginder Sikand, 'Brouhaha Over a Fatwa', Asia Times Online Community and News Discussion, 21 July 2005.
15 Wajihuddin, *op. cit.*
16 Amita Verma, 'Fatwa Issued Against Life Insurance', *The Asian Age*, 31 August 2006.
17 Saba Naqvi Bhaumik, 'Ayatollahs All', *Outlook*, 10-16 June 2008.
18 Zia Haq and Ashok Das, 'No Terror Please. . . We're Muslim, say 6,000 clerics', *The Hindustan Times*, 9 November 2008.
19 Zia Haq and Soumyajit Pattnaik, 'Fatwa Declares India as Being Islam-friendly', *The Hindustan Times*, 2 March 2009.
20 'Post-Mumbai, Self-regulation Guidelines for Media Unveiled', http://www.thaindian.com/newsportal/uncategorized/post-mumbai-self-regulation-guidelines-for-media-unveiled-lead_100132599.html.

Terrorism and the Indian Muslim

Terrorism stands on a footing of its own and need not feature in a work focused on communal riots. The aspects concerning terrorism are many and complex. I recognize it is rather ambitious on my part to even attempt to deal adequately with the complexities involved and offer credible analyses and solutions to overcome this menace. Nevertheless, since people often tend to perceive outbreaks of communal violence and acts of terrorism as two sides of the same coin, it is appropriate to cover the subject of terrorism in its various facets. This should, inter alia, be helpful for the reader in appreciating the dividing line which exists between communal riots and acts of terrorism.

Whenever a terrorist strike takes place in India – and unfortunately, this has been happening with increasing frequency in recent times – the authorities usually put the blame on certain Islamic terrorist outfits such as Jaish-e-Mohammad (JeM), Lashkar-e-Toiba (LeT) and Harkat-ul-Jihad-al-Islami (HUJI). It is also given out that these organizations, based in and operating from the soil in neighbouring countries, especially Pakistan and Bangladesh, infiltrate into India with the backing and support of foreign intelligence agencies, in particular Pakistan's Inter-Services Intelligence (ISI). It is alleged that these nefarious designs are carried out with the active participation of 'sleeper cells', generally manned by members of Students Islamic Movement of India (SIMI) set up in strategic locations in the country. The term sleeper cell refers to a cell, that is, isolated grouping belonging to an organization. The cell 'sleeps' or lies dormant inside a target population and acts only when it receives specific orders from its handlers.[1]

The role of an organization styled as Indian Mujahideen has also of late been linked to these incidents. While these assertions, based on information available with our intelligence agencies, may be true, concrete evidence of the involvement of these outfits has not been, generally speaking, submitted in courts of law. In most of the terror-related incidents, the culprits have not been apprehended and prosecuted.

There has been a paradigm shift in the perception of terrorism in India after the attacks in Mumbai on 26 November 2008 (popularly known as '26/11'). For the first time perhaps, the terrorists involved in the attack were specifically identified and one of them, Ajmal Amir Kasab, was apprehended. The other nine involved in the attack were killed, but not before they had created mayhem and held the commercial capital of India to ransom for close to three days.

Such incidents often lead to profiling of Indian Muslims in a way that every single member of the community is viewed as a suspected terrorist. This happens despite the fact that a vast majority of Muslims in India have nothing to do with terrorist activities; and quite often many members of the minority community also are killed or harmed during a terrorist attack.

It may be recalled that the victims in the terrorist strike at a mosque in Malegaon in Maharashtra in September 2006 were all Muslims. Even in the serial bomb blasts aimed at commuters travelling in local trains in Mumbai's Western Railway corridor (July 2006), a number of those killed or injured were Muslims. The face of the terror strike in Jaipur on 13 May 2008 has come to be a little Muslim girl, Shubhana Khan. In the Mumbai attack of 26 November 2008, of the 173 persons believed to have died thirty-three were Muslims. Though rationalists often say that terror has no religion, this truism cuts no ice with many Hindus, who view every Muslim with thinly veiled hostility and are always ready to brand him or her as a potential terrorist.

Another linkage between communal riots and terrorist attacks is that some of the attacks targeting places of religious significance are carried out with a view to create or exacerbate the communal divide. The terrorist attacks in Akshardham Temple in Gujarat in September 2002, at temples in Varanasi in March 2006, at the mosque in Malegaon in September 2006, in Hyderabad in 2007 and at Ajmer Sharif in October 2007, are cases in point.

TERRORISM – NOT A MUSLIM MONOPOLY

After the cataclysmic events on 9/11 in the USA, the subsequent terrorist strike in the London metro and the failed one at the Glasgow airport, certain statements made by political leaders and commentators in the Western world have given currency to the view – which has become a popular opinion worldwide – that 'while all Muslims are not terrorists, all terrorists are Muslims'. To cite one instance, Senator John McCain, the Republican candidate who lost the presidential election in the USA to Barack Obama, averred that America needs a leadership 'to confront the transcendent challenge of our time: The threat of radical Islamic terrorism'.[2]

In other words, in non-Islamic countries, mainly as a result of how terrorist strikes have been portrayed in the media, terrorism per se has come to be strongly identified with Islamic terrorism.

In an article, Swaminathan Aiyar[3] has documented the numerous acts of terrorism and details of individual organizations that have indulged in terrorist activities, both in the past as well as in recent times, to show that terrorism is not a Muslim monopoly. In Sri Lanka, the Tamil Tigers, one of the most vicious and formidable terrorist groups in the world, were the first to train children as terrorists. They are Hindus.

Suicide missions as a tactic were not first invented and practised by Muslim Palestinians, as is widely believed. Much before that, in the concluding phase of the Second World War, Japanese kamikaze pilots intentionally crashed their aircraft – laden with explosives, bombs, torpedoes and full fuel tanks – into the Allies' ships. More recently, the Tamil Tigers have carried out suicide bombings, sometimes targeting political leaders (Rajiv Gandhi, Premadasa), whom they have viewed as enemies of their cause. Though the Tamil Tigers were on the run, on 20 February 2009 they launched a kamikaze-like attack on Colombo with two airplanes – causing heavy loss of lives and damage to government property.

In the hoary past, anarchists killed Russian Czar Alexander-II and twenty-one bystanders in 1881. The First World War started when Archduke Ferdinand of Austria was assassinated by anarchists. The terrorists in these instances were not Muslims. Many would remember how in 1995 members of Aum Shinrikyo, a Buddhist cult, tried to kill thousands in the Tokyo metro using poison gas. The instances where non-Muslim terrorists have perpetrated acts of terrorism are too many to be recounted here.

In India, freedom fighters such as Bhagat Singh, Chandrasekhar Azad, Khudiram Bose and many others, used methods akin to tactics adopted by terrorists of today to eliminate some of their British oppressors. None of them was Muslim. Currently, we have the United Liberation Front of Assam (ULFA) – a united terrorist group comprising Hindus – which targets Muslims. Christians, Nagas and Mizos have also been carrying out insurrections through militancy, using methods not very different from those used by terrorist outfits, Islamic or otherwise, in different parts of the world.

In recent times, Punjab witnessed terrorism in the garb of the Khalistan movement, which was brought under control through counterterrorism measures, successfully implemented by the state administration and police. The 'terrorists' in this instance were Sikhs. While Operation Blue Star[4] perhaps marked the beginning of Khalistani terrorism, Operation Black Thunder[5] marked the beginning of its end, though Khalistan-related terrorism did continue for some more years, till it was decimated by the firm actions taken in the mid-1990s by Director General of Police K.P.S. Gill, under the leadership of Chief Minister Beant Singh. It was tragic that Beant Singh, who oversaw the demise of terrorism in Punjab, paid the ultimate price, being assassinated at the hands of the remnants of a movement he was instrumental in rooting out.

The recent investigations by the Anti-Terror Squad (ATS) of the Maharashtra police have revealed a new dimension of terrorism in India. The media has been quick to brand it 'Hindu Terror'.

According to reports which have appeared extensively in the national press, an organization named Abhinav Bharat has been responsible for the bomb blast of 29 September 2008 at Malegaon in Maharashtra. The bomb was kept on a bike that went off at Bhikku Chowk, a predominantly Muslim locality in Malegaon. Six persons were killed and eighty-nine injured. For their alleged role in the blast the police initially arrested one Sadhvi Pragya Singh Thakur and four of her associates, including a retired major of the Indian Army. The arrested persons are said to belong to the outfit Abhinav Bharat. Subsequent investigations led the ATS to arrest a serving officer of the Indian Army, one Lt Col Srikant Purohit. A certain Swami Dayanand Pande, alleged to be involved in the conspiracy, has also been arrested.

It has been reported in the media that the ATS is investigating the possible involvement of other serving persons in the Indian Army in the conspiracy. Leaks in the media suggest that Lt Col Purohit is suspected of providing the RDX, which was used in the Samjhauta Express train blast at Panipat on 29 February 2007, in which sixty-seven persons were killed, including Pakistani nationals. The case, currently under investigation, is being labelled as an instance of 'Tit for Tat Terrorism'.

At the time of writing, it is too early to say anything definitively about this case of so-called 'Hindu Terror' since the matter is under investigation and charge sheets are yet to be filed in any court of law. The case has been greatly politicized, with senior party functionaries, belonging to different political parties, making statements in line with their own predilections.

The point to be made is that it is invidious to associate terror with any religion, for no religion sanctions terrorism. Ideally, expressions such as 'Islamic Terror' or 'Hindu Terror' should not figure in public discourse. Unfortunately, however, we do not live in an ideal world.

In India again, Maoists, who do not have allegiance to any religion, have spread terror across 150 districts, popularly known as the Naxalite belt. Clearly, the terrorism practised by Maoists is a much greater threat and ever-present danger than that posed by Islamic jihadi outfits, which are largely confined to the major cities and towns across India.

For many years the Western world, particularly America, remained cocooned in the belief that they were immune to the threat of terrorism and that it was a phenomenon confined to the 'less civilized' regions of the world such as the Middle East, Africa and South Asia. The event of 9/11 shattered this illusion and, therefore, has been a defining moment in history. But at the same time it had the unfortunate consequence of terrorism per se being equated to Islamic terrorism within the developed world and even in non-Islamic developing countries.

After 9/11, in the West and particularly in the US, paranoia about Muslims led to the incarceration and torture of Muslim youth suspected – unjustifiably in many cases – of being terrorists. They were transferred to the infamous Guantanamo Bay prison and subjected to inhuman treatment. Certain feature films, *Khuda Ke Liye* produced in Pakistan and *New York*, a recent Bollywood release, have succeeded in focusing attention, at least in South Asia, on this regrettable consequence of terrorist attacks perpetrated by some misguided elements, who happen to be Muslims.

Aside from certain historical events, which have brought Islamic terrorism in the forefront of the discourse on the subject, grist for the mills has been provided for academics and intellectuals by Samuel Huntington's treatise, *The Clash of Civilizations*. Huntington's averment that 'the underlying problem for the West is not Islamic fundamentalism, IT IS ISLAM' sums up, in essence, his Weltanschauung (or world view). The validity of Huntington's thesis is indeed questionable and we shall examine this matter separately. But recent events have given Huntington's view salience and fed the paranoia about the dangers of Islamic terrorism.

Before dealing with this problem in the Indian context, it would be appropriate to look at it in the global perspective. Those who have carefully studied the phenomenon have concluded that terrorism defies preconceived notions and assumptions. The reality of terrorism is that it adapts, mutates and constantly challenges preconceptions. Therefore, counterterrorism strategies should do the same thing. That is the best way to limit damage which terrorism can inflict and it would ultimately reduce the supply of new recruits.

TERRORISM IN ISLAM THROUGH THE AGES

It would be interesting to delve, albeit briefly, into the evolution of terrorism and the methodologies adopted by terrorists to achieve their goals over a somewhat extended time frame. At the outset it may be stated that no religion sanctions the right to any individual to kill any other human being. According to conventional monotheistic belief of both Christianity and Islam, only God may decide who will live and who will die. Consequently, individuals or groups who undertake missions to kill others in the name of religion, have been indoctrinated to believe in certain verities that are against the basic tenets of their own religion.

The origin of terrorism among the followers of Islam dates back to the battle of Karbala (in modern-day Iraq) in the seventh century, in which Ali's party (Ali was the son-in-law of Prophet Mohammad) was defeated by the forces of Abu Bakr, a member of Mohammad's circle, who had taken power after Mohammad's death. The battle of Karbala was fought for establishing succession to Prophet Mohammad and it ended in the defeat of Ali's faction. This was the origin of the split between the Shi'ites and Sunnis. The term Shia derives from Shiat Ali or partisans of Ali. 'The defeat at Karbala became a focal point for the oppressed and the subservient, and established a tradition that produced the assassins as well as the Islamic revolution of Imam Khomeini and the current, ongoing Islamic reformation.'[6]

With the weakening of the Abbasid dynasty in Baghdad from the eleventh century onwards, various schisms and factions appeared on the scene. Among them was a radical sect called 'Assassins'. This sect was led by their founder, Hassan-i-Sabbah.

The name given to the sect 'Assassins' is thought to be derived from '*hashshashin*' or 'hashish users'. The legend, much popularized by Marco Polo's travel writings, runs thus: 'when Hassan-i-Sabbah was living in his mountain stronghold of Alamut, he sparked the yearning for death in his young disciples with a running ruse. The men were given hashish – so much hashish that they fell into a stupor, whereupon Hassan-i-Sabbah had them taken to a garden hidden in the grounds of the fortress. No sooner had they woken up than they found they were no longer wearing the same old rags as before, but robes made of silk interwoven with gold threads; they were lying on lush green grass and cushions; servants handed them elegant carafes of water and wine. The virgins of Paradise were there, ready to do their bidding, and there was more hashish, too. Completely off their heads, they eventually lapsed into a stupor once again, whereupon they were carted off and put back in their normal clothes. On waking up, presumably with a hangover, they asked their master what on earth had happened to them. Paradise, replied the self-appointed imam; or, more precisely, a foretaste of Paradise, a trial visit. Anyone who wanted to return there on a permanent basis would have to sacrifice himself as one of the Fedayeen, as an assassin eager to die.'[7]

Though parallels have been drawn by writers between Osama Bin Laden and Sabbah, especially since 9/11, mainly in terms of their followers retreating into inhospitable mountainous terrain and their readiness to sacrifice their lives, Bin Laden unlike Sabbah, belongs to the Sunni orthodox tradition. The followers of Laden, who are now known as the Al-Qaeda, attack not only Christians and Jews but also the Shi'ites, who are vilified as unbelievers, heretics and hypocrites. Therefore, the parallel drawn between Sabbah and Bin Laden is valid only in a limited sense.

Christoph Reuter finds the real connection between Hassan-i-Sabbah and Osama Bin Laden to be more complicated and which takes a rather circuitous route – via Khomeini, the Islamic revolution in Iran, and the genesis of suicide attacks as such. Khomeini certainly drew upon the common roots of the Shi'ite revolt against the rank injustices of the prevailing regime which also influenced Hassan-i-Sabbah's ideology. And 'among the Sunnis, too, the readiness to become a suicide assassin spread from the Iranian war volunteers and the first "martyr operations" by a process of direct influence and imitation'.[8]

During the Iraq-Iran war, which began in September 1980, with Iraq invading Iran, in the initial phase the Iraqis overran large swathes of Iranian territory and the onward thrust of the Iraqi Army was countered by 'human wave' attacks by thousands of young Iranians, who were the followers of Ayatollah Khomeini. The defining characteristic of the young Iranians comprising the 'human wave' was their willingness to die. The young recruits, who constituted Iran's suicide battalions, went into battle 'with the key to paradise around their necks'. The Khomeini regime persuaded the young Iranian recruits to the army into believing that the best thing that could possibly happen to them would be that they die fighting the eternal Sunni enemy. 'Can anyone who believes in the world beyond be afraid?' asked Khomeini, without the least doubt as to what constituted the right answer: 'We must thank God if He confers on us the honor of dying in the Holy Battle. Let us thrust our way into the ranks of the martyrs in our hordes ... if we have been afraid, this means that we don't believe in the world beyond.'[9]

It is paradoxical that Islam does not sanction suicide, yet paradise is the prize held out for those who die fighting for their cause. The belief in the attainment of paradise is leveraged as a device to circumvent the taboo against suicide. The attackers, mostly of impressionable age, are indoctrinated into believing that 'the prospect of paradise means that the attacker doesn't really take his own life, nor does he want to do so; he simply lives on, but in another place'.[10]

PROFILE OF MODERN-DAY TERRORISTS

These generalizations about the motivation of those who willingly die in suicide missions cannot be applied across the board to many who have taken part in terrorist attacks in recent times. A number of those who perpetrated the destruction of the Twin Towers of the World Trade Centre in Manhattan and attacked the Pentagon were well-educated and trained youths, familiar with the Western environment, who could not have become attracted to the idea of attaining martyrdom through the holding out of visions of paradise, where seventy-two vestal virgins would wait upon them and treat them to the pleasures of unending sex. In fact, the leader of this group, Mohammad Atta was known to be a misogynist, and was averse to the company of women.

It is interesting to note that the profile of many of the terrorists, who have indulged in acts of terrorism in recent times, is very different from the teenaged Iranian recruits, who were virtually plunging to their deaths while engaged in jihad against the Iraqi

Sunnis. For instance, five of the eight suspects arrested in the car-bombing cases, which occurred in the UK in 2007, were doctors. One of them, Kafeel Ahmed from Bangalore, was the Indian connection to these bombers in the UK. Kafeel was a qualified engineer, who on 30 June 2007 dowsed himself in petrol and drove the Jeep Cherokee, loaded with gas canisters, into the front façade of the Glasgow airport. He was exposed to a fire so hot that his mobile phone melted into his flesh. After a prolonged struggle for life in the hospital, he succumbed to injuries. A number of others involved in recent terror attacks were engineers or doctors. Khalid Sheikh Mohammad, who planned the 9/11 and other attacks, has a degree in chemical engineering from a university in the US. Ayman al-Zawahiri, Osama Bin Laden's top deputy, is a doctor as well.

In fact, a study by sociologists Diego Gambetta and Steffen Hertog of the Oxford University points to an intriguing correlation between those who study engineering and terrorism. These two scholars have theorized that it is possible that the study of engineering subjects may produce a mindset which makes one prone to radicalization.[11] Though this scholarly study is of interest, it need not be accepted as conclusive. It is only a good pointer for those engaged in counterterrorism to not profile possible terrorists based on metrics like education or income – even those with high education and good income can turn towards terrorism. Nevertheless, it is important to examine and ascertain how persons who have gone through the process of education can be so radicalized that they are willing to participate in the planning and execution of terrorist acts.

We shall take up the issue of the sources of radicalization later, along with the measures which need to be taken to prevent the recurrent acts of terrorism.

SPREAD OF TERRORISM FROM THE MIDDLE EAST TO SOUTH ASIA

The shift of the focus of terrorism to South Asia from the Middle East can be traced back to 1979 when the Soviet Union, with a view to increasing its influence in the area, set up a puppet regime in Afghanistan. The United States masterminded a plan to check the ambitions of the Soviets. It armed the militias of the Afghanistan overlords and financed them to fight the Soviets in the name of jihad. Pakistan was brought into the picture as a conduit for supply of arms to the fighters. Besides the militias, thousands of mujahideen from all over the Islamic world were armed, financed and trained to reinforce Afghanistan for the confrontation with the Soviet war machine.

General Pervez Musharraf, in his somewhat self-congratulatory autobiography, titled *In the Line of Fire*,[12] has very candidly admitted to the role of Pakistan in creating mujahideen and the Taliban, who, after the end of Soviet occupation of Afghanistan, became loose canon for spreading terrorism in the region. He blames the earlier regimes in Pakistan, particularly the one headed by General Zia ul-Haq, for colluding with America in creating a Frankenstein monster.

The mujahideen involved in the jihad against the Soviet forces in Afghanistan, who were armed to the teeth with sophisticated weaponry, had to find other outlets, once this particular jihad had ended in victory. While withdrawing in a hurry, the Soviets also left behind large cache of heavy weapons, including tanks, guns and even aircraft with a huge stock of ammunition.

General Musharraf writes that the upheaval in Afghanistan resulted in 4 million refugees coming into Pakistan and it also sparked off the emergence of Taliban in 1995. It further led to the coalescing of international mujahideen into the Al-Qaeda, with reinforcements coming from the Central Asian Republic, discontented Chechens and from several Arab countries.

Although Musharraf nowhere admits it, the mujahideen, since the mid-nineties, turned their attention to aid the militants in Jammu & Kashmir. They were instrumental in organizing training camps for the militants and infiltrating into the Indian territory to perpetrate acts of terrorism.

The incumbent president of Pakistan, Asif Ali Zardari has come out with an even more candid confession regarding Pakistan's involvement in nurturing terrorists. He recently told a gathering of civil servants that 'Militants and extremists emerged on the national scene and challenged the state not because the civil bureaucracy was weakened and demoralized but because they were deliberately created and nurtured as a policy to achieve short-term tactical objectives. Let's be truthful and make a candid admission of the reality'.[13] He also stated, 'The terrorists of today were heroes of yesteryear until 9/11 occurred and they began to haunt us as well.'[14] Earlier Zardari, in the same vein as Musharraf, had also blamed the US for fomenting militancy in Pakistan. He wrote in the *Washington Post*:

> The West stood by as a democratically elected government was toppled by the military in the late '70s. Because of the

> Soviet invasion of Afghanistan, the West used my nation as a blunt instrument of the Cold War. It empowered a (Zia) dictatorship that brutalized its people, decimated political parties, murdered the PM who had founded Pakistan's largest political party, and destroyed the press and civil society.[15]

After 9/11, Pakistan was virtually coerced into becoming an ally of the United States in the so-called 'war against terror'. It had to publicly disown the Taliban, which had till then flourished with Pakistan's support. In fact, it had to lend support to the United States and allied forces in the invasion of Afghanistan to oust the Taliban regime.

While Pakistan remains overtly committed to assisting the United States in the drive to eliminate the Al-Qaeda and root out the Taliban, in reality there are serious reservations regarding Pakistan's commitment to these objectives. Till today, Osama Bin Laden with his Al-Qaeda followers and Mullah Umar, the Taliban leader, are believed to be safely ensconced in Pakistani territory. The Pakistani armed forces have been singularly inept in dealing with the insurgents and warring elements operating from the difficult mountainous terrain of the Waziristan region. In fact, large tracts of the country, including the fabled Swat valley, have now been occupied by the Taliban. However, in May 2009, Pakistan's armed forces, after the goading of the US administration, finally mounted an offensive to drive out the Taliban from the valley. But Pakistan has never been sincere about its efforts to bring down infiltration into Indian territory by the mujahideen and also with regard to putting an end to the training of Kashmiri militants, who perpetrate acts of terrorism on our soil.

That Taliban insurgents are receiving shelter and support from Pakistan's intelligence services and its paramilitaries has been revealed in a study by the RAND Corporation,[16] commissioned by the US Department of Defence. According to the study, the insurgents find refuge in Pakistan's federally administered tribal areas, the North-West Frontier Province and Baluchistan province. The report also says that the insurgents regularly ship weapons, ammunition and supplies into Afghanistan from Pakistan. It has also been reported that a number of suicide bombers have been infiltrated into Afghanistan from Afghan refugee camps based in Pakistan.

The involvement of the ISI in promoting terror has attracted international attention, especially after the suicide-bombing attack of the Indian Embassy in Kabul in July 2008. President Hamid Karzai alleged that the Taliban elements in Pakistan, with the support of the ISI, were responsible for the attack. It has been reported extensively in the media[17] that top officials of the CIA travelled to Islamabad to confront their Pakistani counterparts about information regarding their ties with militants operating from tribal areas in Pakistan. The media has also reported that senior US State Department officials are interacting with their interlocutors in Pakistan on the question of ISI's hand in assisting Taliban militants, who are trying to destabilize the present regime in Afghanistan, which is backed by the US and its allies.

At the SAARC conference at Colombo in the first week of August 2008, the heads of government of both India and Afghanistan took up this issue with Prime Minister Gilani of Pakistan. The latter had to concede that an enquiry would be conducted into the question of alleged Pakistani involvement in the acts of terror perpetrated in Afghanistan, specifically into the bombing episode at the Indian Embassy in Kabul. Having individuals within its personnel who have close links with the Taliban, the ISI is seen, by some analysts, as a rogue organization, which is intent on creating mayhem in the neighbouring countries through acts of terror. An attempt by the civilian regime in Pakistan to bring the ISI under its control seems to have been foiled.

TERRORISM IN INDIA

For long, majority of Indians have been proud of their secular identity. Prominent political analysts, such as Thomas L. Friedman, have argued that though India houses the second-largest Muslim population in the world, it has not allowed Muslim fundamentalism to take root and grow. There is no Indian Muslim in the Al-Qaeda and no Indian Muslim has been found fighting alongside the jihadis in Iraq. The reason Friedman gives is:

> This is because of context – and in particular the secular, free-market, democratic context of India, heavily influenced by a tradition of nonviolence and Hindu tolerance. The Indian Constitution is secular and provides a real opportunity for economic advancement of any community that offers talent. The Indian democracy is not perfect. Nevertheless, to

> have sustained a functioning democracy with all its flaws for more than 50 years in a country of over a billion people, who speak scores of different languages, is something of a miracle and a great source of stability for the world. Two of India's presidents have been Muslims, and its current president, A.P.J. Abdul Kalam, is both a Muslim and the father of the Indian nuclear missile program. While a Muslim is a part of India's Supreme Court, no Muslim woman is allowed even to drive a car in Saudi Arabia. The Indian Muslims live in a context that empowers and protects them.[18]

With terrorist attacks occurring with increasing frequency, these assumptions are coming in for review. Although there still may be no evidence linking Indian Muslims directly with the Al-Qaeda, the bugbear of the West, there is reason to believe that other militant organizations based in Pakistan and Bangladesh, like the LeT, JeM and HUJI, have been able to infiltrate into our territory and recruit Muslims in India to act at their behest.

Among Muslims, there is, at the ideological level, conflict between the liberal and the orthodox, some of whom are turning into fundamentalists. Thus it would be meaningful to look at the incidence of terrorism in India in recent years.

Incidence of Terror Attacks in India

In earlier years, terrorism in India was identified almost entirely with the activities of militants from Jammu & Kashmir. With the rise of militancy in that state, a number of attacks began to take place against the armed forces, including the paramilitary and police forces in the state of Jammu & Kashmir. Occasionally, there were attacks against certain targets in other states, which were also the handiwork of Kashmiri militants. The perception that terrorism in India was a fallout of the militancy in Kashmir has since changed.

The defining moment was perhaps 12 March 1993, when serial bomb blasts ripped through thirteen different places in the city of Mumbai killing 257 people and injuring 713. This was the first blast in which RDX was used. It is believed that these blasts, masterminded by Dawood Ibrahim, were carried out by the members of his gang and associates. These blasts had nothing to do with the militancy in Kashmir but people believe these were in retaliation against the killing of Muslims in the communal riots which had rocked the city of Mumbai in December 1992–January 1993. Thus, this is one instance where a terrorist attack may be directly linked to a communal outbreak. Since 1993 there have been numerous terrorist attacks at different locations and targets in India, both before and after 9/11.

The second-largest number of incidents involving terrorism and number of persons killed in such incidents, next to Iraq, have occurred in India as the following graph prepared from a report published in the *Times of India*, 27 August 2007, shows:[19]

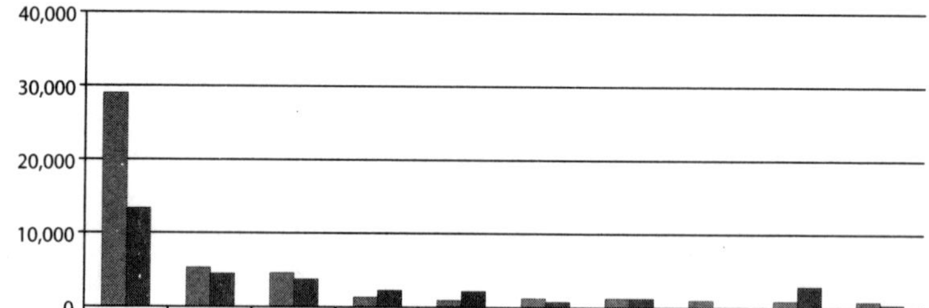

	Iraq	India	Afghanistan	Colombia	Thailand	Russia	Pakistan	Chad	Nepal	Sudan
■ Death	29070	3674	2405	1550	1324	1206	1121	1096	1059	1057
■ Incidence	12718	3032	1682	1721	1959	660	1112	32	2989	155

While it is not feasible to recount the details of all major terrorist attacks in India in recent times, it is relevant to mention a few of them over the last decade. This would enable us to draw certain conclusions regarding the nature of these strikes and ways to pre-empt them.

20 March 2000: Massacre at Chattisinghpora in J&K

'On the eve of President Clinton's visit, militants massacred thirty-five Sikhs in the village of Chattisinghpora. The militants were dressed in Indian Army uniforms, a tactic which is now commonly used by the insurgents. No group claimed responsibility for the attack.'[20]

1 October 2001: Attack on J&K State Legislative Assembly

'A car bomb exploded near the state legislative assembly in Srinagar killing thirty-eight people. The bomb was followed by an armed assault in the assembly premises by three armed terrorists.' (IPCS Report, 2006)

13 December 2001: Attack on the Indian Parliament, New Delhi

'Militants attacked the Indian Parliament in which nine policemen and Parliament staffers were killed. All five terrorists involved were also killed. They were identified as Pakistani nationals. The militants used AK-47 rifles and grenades for the attack. They wanted to kill political figures and create chaos in the Indian Parliament. Their designs were foiled because of the alertness of the security personnel.' (IPCS Report, 2006)

22 January 2002: Attack on American Cultural Centre, Kolkata
'Militants attacked the American Cultural Centre in Kolkata, killing at least four police officers and injuring twenty-one. Police arrested at least fifty suspects in the aftermath of the incident. The government accused Pakistan of involvement in the attack.' (IPCS Report, 2006)

24 September 2002: Akshardham Temple Attack
An attack on Akshardham Temple occurred when two heavily armed terrorists reached the monument in Gandhinagar. They entered the premises after scaling the perimeter fence. They then opened fire killing a woman and a volunteer instantly. Thereafter, they started throwing grenades at the devotees, creating mayhem in the temple.

'The siege of the Akshardham Temple complex of the Swaminarayan sect ended after a commando operation. The two terrorists who had stormed it the previous evening were killed. A total of twenty-nine individuals, including sixteen women and four children, were killed in the terrorist attack and seventy-four were injured, a few of them seriously.

'A National Security Guard commando was also killed and one critically wounded in the operation. Two state police commandos lost their lives while rescuing the people trapped in the complex before the NSG men took position. The Prevention of Terrorism Act court awarded death sentence to three persons in the 2002 Akshardham Temple terror attack case on 1 July 2006.' (IPCS Report, 2006)

29 October 2005: Blasts in New Delhi
'At least seventy persons were killed and several injured in three powerful serial explosions on the evening of 29 October 2005. While two bombs went off at busy marketplaces (Paharganj and Sarojini Nagar), one exploded inside a Delhi Transport Corporation bus (near Govindpuri).' (IPCS Report, 2006)

These blasts are believed to have been carried out at the instance of Pakistan-based terrorist organizations. Charge sheets were filed in the case against one Tariq Ahmad Dar and one Rafiq Shah.

28 December 2005: Attack on the Indian Institute of Science, Bangalore

'A senior scientist from New Delhi was killed and at least five persons were injured when assailants opened fire and lobbed grenades at the Indian Institute of Science. Suspected terrorists of the Lakshar-e-Toiba barged into the prestigious IIS campus and opened fire indiscriminately, killing a retired professor of IIT Delhi and injuring four others.' (IPCS Report, 2006)

7 March 2006: Serial Blasts in Varanasi

'The first explosion occurred in Sankat Mochan Temple near Banaras Hindu University. Many pilgrims were in the temple, as Tuesdays are considered particularly holy by devotees of Lord Hanuman.

Two other explosions occurred at the cantonment railway station – one in the Shivganga Express bound for Delhi and another in a waiting hall. At least 100 people were injured. Six bombs were found from other areas in the city, including a restaurant frequented by foreigners.

The mastermind of the Varanasi blasts and five of his accomplices were arrested on 6 April 2006 by the Uttar Pradesh Police. A module of the Bangladesh-based Harkat-ul-Jihad-al-Islami (HUJI) was also discovered. Wali Ullah and his associates were arrested from different parts of the state and a large quantity of arms and ammunition recovered from them.' (IPCS Report, 2006)

11 July 2006: Mumbai Train Blast

The toll in the serial blasts which took place in the city that July rose to 190. Police said 625 people had been injured in the blasts that took place in the first class compartments of trains at Mira-Bhayandar, Jogeshwari, Mahim, Santacruz, Khar, Matunga and Borivli on the Western Railway line on 11 July 2006 between 6 and 6.40 p.m. Unofficial sources indicated a higher number of casualties.

Over 200 suspects had been rounded up as a result of the ongoing investigations; with no group claiming responsibility, suspicion fell on the LeT and the Indian organization, SIMI. A possible hurdle to the ongoing peace process was created with both India and Pakistan exchanging acrimonious comments over the incident. National Security Adviser M.K. Narayanan in fact accused Pakistan of complicity in the blasts. (IPCS Report, 2006)

13 May 2008: Serial Blasts in Jaipur, Rajasthan

Eight bomb blasts were detonated within twelve minutes in a

crowded area in the historical city of Jaipur. Eighty persons are believed to have been killed in these blasts and over 200 injured. One of the bombs was detonated near the eighteenth-century Hawa Mahal (Palace of the Wind) and another targeted the famed Johri Bazaar, which is usually crammed with jewellers. The death toll would have been higher had not three more bombs been defused.

Police sources said that the bombs had been planted in plastic bags and attached to nine new bicycles. These were then placed with the aim of causing 'maximum damage'. Bicycles have been used in at least two other terrorist attacks in India during the past two years. Three groups – HUJI, SIMI and the LeT – top the list of suspects.

The attackers appeared to have targeted Hindus, with two of the bombs placed near temples. They were also timed to coincide with the weekly gathering of Hanuman devotees. The blasts also coincided with the tenth anniversary of India's nuclear bomb tests which took place in Pokhran, also in Rajasthan. (IPCS Report, 2006)

While I have given details of some these terrorist strikes, there have been, of course, several other major ones, including the one at a restaurant in Hyderabad on 18 May 2007 and in Ajmer Sharif on 11 October 2007, resulting in many casualties.

Other Recent Incidents in Cities

More recently there were serial blasts in the last week of July 2008 in Bangalore and then in Ahmedabad. The damage suffered in Bangalore was less in comparison to Ahmedabad where, on 26 July 2008, twenty-one bomb blasts occurred, in which fifty-six persons were killed and more than 200 injured. The blasts in Ahmedabad were of low intensity and they had been planted on bicycles. The pattern was similar to that of the Jaipur blasts of May 2008. A couple of days after the serial blasts at Ahmedabad, two explosive-packed cars and eighteen bombs were discovered across Surat in Gujarat. Fortunately, these bombs and explosives were defused.

Thereafter it was the turn of Delhi, where on 13 September 2008, within a matter of a few minutes, there were five bomb blasts in crowded localities and prominent shopping areas in which at least thirty were killed and more than 100 injured.

A large number of bomb blasts occurred in the state of Assam on 30 October 2008. At least eighteen bombs went off causing eighty-four deaths and 470 injuries. It was feared that the casualties could be higher. The explosions ripped through certain densely populated localities and shopping areas in Guwahati. There were also explosions in Kokrajhar, Bongaigaon and Barpeta. In Guwahati, forty-eight people were killed, in Kokrajhar twenty-one and in Barpeta fifteen. Subsequently, some more persons succumbed to their injuries. The perpetrators of the blasts in Assam have not been identified although according to police sources, the ULFA, in collusion with Bangladeshi Islamic militants, was responsible for these blasts.

Mumbai Attacks (26/11)

There were a series of terrorist attacks in Mumbai, beginning on 26 November 2008 and ending on 29 November, in which 173 people were killed and a larger number wounded. The prominent locations attacked by the terrorists were Chhatrapati Shivaji Terminus (CST), Oberoi Trident Hotel, Taj Mahal Palace and Tower Hotel, Leopold Café, Cama Hospital and the orthodox Jewish-run Nariman House (also known as Chabad House). Ten well-armed terrorists were involved. Of them nine were killed in gun battles with the police, naval commandos and commandos of the National Security Guard (NSG). Terrorist Ajmal Amir Kasab was captured alive. Before the other terrorists were killed, they held to ransom the largest metropolis of India for close to seventy-two hours, creating enormous panic and mayhem in the process.

After being in denial for quite some time, the authorities in the Pakistan government had to accept that Kasab was of Pakistani origin. It transpired that it was a well-planned operation and the terrorists came via the sea route from Pakistan to Mumbai.

A voluminous charge sheet was filed by the Mumbai police in the court of the metropolitan magistrate in Mumbai on 25 February 2009 and the case against Kasab is now under trial.

The Mumbai attacks represented a departure from the terrorist attacks described earlier in certain significant ways. As B. Raman has put it, this was a case of 'individualized brutality'. In such cases there is face-to-face brutalization of the targeted individuals. According to Raman, there have been past instances of individual brutality in Jammu & Kashmir but not in the Indian territory outside that state. Most of the other terrorist attacks have involved 'collective brutality' in the form of planting improvised explosive devices (IED) in public places, throwing hand grenades into crowds, etc.[21] In the Mumbai attacks, barring the CST, the attackers chose locations which mostly the rich and the famous frequent such as the seven-star hotels and the Leopold Café. Consequently, among those killed and wounded were several prominent personages.

The attack on the Nariman House revealed the anti-Semitic motivations of the terrorists. Jews have been subjected to an attack of this nature perhaps for the first time within India.

The locations such as the Taj and Oberoi hotels were also apparently chosen because they are patronized by a large number of foreigners. Among those killed were citizens of the USA, the UK and European and East Asian countries. This resulted in the attacks getting worldwide coverage and attention. None of the previous terrorist attacks in India had received so much attention in the developed world.

According to reports in the media, the Pakistan-based LeT and its front organization, the Jamaat-ud-Dawa are said to be behind the 26/11 Mumbai attacks.

The 26/11 episode has exposed certain systemic weaknesses in our intelligence gathering apparatus and in our preparedness to deal with such attacks, which are grave concerns.

LESSONS AND POINTERS

These incidents have, however, changed certain perceptions about acts of terror in India. A hitherto unknown organization styled as Indian Mujahideen claimed to have been responsible for many of these blasts. A few minutes before the blasts occurred at Ahmedabad a warning was sent over the internet of the impending attack. This may mark the beginning of a new phase in crime in the world as this powerful tool of the information age is being used by terrorist organizations while hitting targets in India.

Earlier incidents of terrorist attacks did not take place in such quick succession. Evidently, after one strike, terrorists took time to regroup before planning and executing another strike. It now appears they have been able to spread their tentacles far and wide, acquiring capability to strike at targets in different locations almost simultaneously. The 'sleeper cells' have apparently multiplied undetected across the states and can be activated almost at will, by their handlers, to strike at the designated locations. This is indeed a dangerous portent and underscores how inept our intelligence organizations have been in carrying out their mandate of detecting and destabilizing the terrorist networks in our country. It also appears to signal that radicalized Islam has gained a foothold in India.

The description of these several terrorist attacks, during the past few years, is enough to emphasize the fact that India has now become extremely vulnerable to attacks by terrorists. It is also clear that for quite some time terrorism in India has not been confined to being a fallout of the militancy in Jammu & Kashmir.

Soft Targets

It is relevant to note that barring a few of these episodes, such as the attack on the Jammu & Kashmir state assembly in Srinagar on 1 October 2001, the attack on the Indian parliament in New Delhi on 13 December 2001 and the attack on the American Cultural Centre in Kolkata on 22 January 2002, attacks took place against what are best described as 'soft targets'. Such targets are not under surveillance or round-the-clock protection and are frequented by the public. Intelligence expert B. Raman, while writing on this subject, has observed that attacks on such targets cause many human fatalities and demonstrate the capability of the terrorist group to operate without being detected by intelligence and counterterrorism agencies.[22]

Analyzing attacks on such targets, B. Raman has further observed that a long period of preparation is not required to attack these soft targets. All that is needed is creation and infiltration of 'sleeper cells' to carry out such attacks and deliver the weapons and explosive devices to the cell.[23]

When such incidents occur, since the police do not have leads to the real perpetrators, they indiscriminately arrest a large number of suspects belonging to the minority community. This also subserves the objectives of the terrorists, who want the communal divide to be perpetuated; thus hostility is generated against the administration and the police.

Some of the attacks targeting places of worship, such as temples or mosques, are specifically aimed at arousing communal animosity among the local population belonging to different communities.

While certain establishments like important government buildings, encampments of armed forces and security personnel, key installations such as power stations, airports and important sports stadiums can be guarded round the clock, numerous other places frequented by the public, such as places of worship, shopping centres and even railway stations, call centres, etc., cannot be well protected. It is necessary for the intelligence agencies to obtain information about intended attacks on such targets, if these are to be prevented. In order to assess how these 'sleeper cells' operating in India can be infiltrated by our security agencies and neutralized, we may pause and take a look at this problem in a global context, since terrorism has now become a worldwide problem.

Protected Targets

It is difficult to have foolproof protection against terror strikes even for buildings and installations protected by security personnel. Experts say that governments tend to focus much of their time and money on the last line of defence – deployment of guards around the clock, installation of CCTVs, and explosive-sniffers at airports, railway lines, and so on. But gadgetry alone has proved to be inadequate. In June 2006, Glasgow airport installed high-tech license plate recognition system. The system activates a barrier at the entrance to the inside lane around the airport. Taxis and buses can get through the barrier only with a registered number. However, this security system failed when Kafeel Ahmed and his accomplice were able to enter the protected area of the Glasgow airport, because they simply followed a registered car and sped past before the barrier closed.[24] The point is that terrorists can hoodwink their way past even very sophisticated security systems to create mayhem.

A former French counterterrorism official has been quoted to say that 'Unless you can arrest terrorists before they get to execution stage, your chances of averting bloodshed and death come down to luck'. It is also worth quoting Richard Pildes, a co-director of New York University's Center on Law and Security: 'Terrorism prevention is about information gathering and intelligence. It's not about defensive measures.'[25]

It is thus quite evident that there is no failsafe method to prevent destruction and bloodshed even in well-protected buildings and installations, when clever and determined terrorists target such places. As for 'soft targets', they can be hit almost at will. Intelligence, therefore, remains the key to pre-empt terrorist attacks.

WHY WE FAIL WHEN OTHERS SUCCEED

In this backdrop we need to assess why in India we have failed to prevent terrorist strikes time and again, while in the United States there has been no major strike for approximately seven years since 9/11 happened. The New York Police Department (NYPD) offers a model, which perhaps the intelligence and counterterrorism agencies elsewhere can emulate. The NYPD has officers based in cities around the world, including London, Tel Aviv, Amman, Paris, etc. The objective is to build relationships with other police forces to gather information about threats before they show up in New York City.[26]

An important task is also to infiltrate terrorist groups. We understand that Israel has managed to set up a web of Palestinian collaborators.

These examples have been cited to show what the intelligence and counterterrorism agencies of the state and central governments in India can do to be able to perform better in preventing terrorist attacks, which our country has been subjected to with such regularity. The way terrorist attacks have been handled by the authorities in the UK too stands out in sharp contrast to our own record. On 7 July 2005 (popularly referred to as 7/7), three bomb blasts occurred almost simultaneously at different locations in the London Metro. At the same time a blast also took place in a double-decker bus. In this incident, fifty-two commuters and the four suicide bombers were killed and 700 people were injured. While this attack could not be prevented, it was immediately investigated by the police, the conspirators were apprehended and brought to trial.

In August 2006, a terrorist plot to detonate liquid explosives, carried onboard several airliners travelling from the UK to the USA and Canada, was discovered by the UK police before it could be carried out. The sixteen persons arrested in connection with this failed attempt to blow up transatlantic aircraft were charged with terrorism offences and are facing trial. Interestingly enough, the FBI and the Scotland Yard began to investigate links of these alleged bombers with Kashmiri terrorists. It was reported in the UK press that they were funded by a 'charity' intended to help the victims of the 2005 Kashmir earthquake. The Pakistani and international press also reported that Rashid Rauf, the key player in the plot, had links with the JeM, a Kashmiri terrorist group.

Both the UK and the USA, which are in the front line of targets for attacks by terrorist outfits, have been able to organize their counterterrorism machinery to ensure that, as far as possible, terrorist attacks are prevented or their investigating agencies are able to uncover the plots of successful attacks and arrest the conspirators.

The record of the Indian investigative and counterterrorism agencies, in contrast, has been dismal. These agencies have not succeeded in preventing any of the numerous terrorist attacks that have taken place in different parts of India in recent years. While a large number of suspects have been arrested in connection with a number of terrorist attacks, in majority of the cases the real culprits have not been apprehended and very few cases have come to the trial stage.

In the case of the 1993 serial bomb blasts in Mumbai, the perpetrators of the crime were identified, arrested and brought to trial. But it took as long as fourteen years before the trial court could complete the trials, convict and sentence the accused persons.

It is clear that not only our intelligence and counterterrorism agencies are proving to be ineffective in dealing with terrorism, even our criminal justice system is not well geared to ensure speedy trial of those few who are brought to book for being involved in terrorist activities. The rate of conviction for terrorist crimes in India is also abysmally low.

Unless there is sea-change in our approach and methodology to tackle terrorism, people living in our cities and towns would continue to remain exposed to the possibility of terrorist attacks, causing death and destruction, as has been happening periodically at different locations in recent years. A slew of measures need to be undertaken to effectively deal with this grave threat, to which our people, particularly those living in the urban centres, are exposed.

Importance of Intelligence Gathering

The agencies in the central government which are most crucially involved in gathering intelligence pertaining to terrorist activities are the Intelligence Bureau (IB) and Research and Analysis Wing (RAW). The state governments have their own intelligence departments known under generic nomenclatures such as the 'special branch', etc. It does need to be stressed that our intelligence setup is undermanned. The IB has only about 3,500 operatives in the country, which is a minuscule number relative to our population of over a billion. This is a severe limitation. The special branches of the states too are similarly handicapped, with their operatives very thinly spread across the districts. It is also true that those assigned to the special branch consider it to be a punishment since they are deprived of certain perks – legitimate and otherwise – which the uniformed personnel enjoy.

These agencies obviously need to be strengthened and overhauled, and their operatives retrained so they are equipped to pre-empt and uncover terrorist plots. It may be beneficial to involve experts from foreign intelligence agencies in the UK, the USA, etc., in giving advice regarding the restructuring of our intelligence agencies and training their operatives.

The standard of investigations into incidents of terrorism in India needs to be drastically improved. The investigations are generally carried out by the state government's police forces, which are ill-trained and ill-equipped. They are also not given a free hand and are subjected to political interference at every step. The skills of these investigating agencies need to be upgraded and they should be immunized from political interference as far as possible. Successive police commissions have made recommendations in this regard, which have remained unimplemented due to lack of political consensus and will. The implementation of certain directives of the Supreme Court also remains stalled.

Use of the Internet, the Media and Mobile Telephony in Aid of Terror

Before taking up this matter further, it is apposite to reflect on how emerging technologies are being harnessed for spreading hate and terror.

The person who led the charge of jihad on the internet called himself 'Irhabi007' – a play on the Arabic word for 'terrorist' and the codename of popular literary figure, James Bond. He was a central figure in enabling the Al-Qaeda to reconstitute itself after the fall of the Taliban and its eviction from Afghanistan. 'Al-Qaeda and its followers moved to cyber-space, which has been described as the ultimate ungoverned territory, where jihadists have set up virtual schools for ideological and military training and active propaganda arms.'[27]

The internet has given jihadists a vehicle for propaganda, providing access to large audiences free from censorship, while preserving their anonymity. All kinds of propaganda material is purveyed through the internet and it becomes a means of getting disparate jihadi groups together and creates a sense of a global Islamic movement against their so-called enemy. Ayman al-Zawahiri, the second-most senior figure in the Al-Qaeda, regularly circulates video statements through the internet.

'In short, the hand-held video camera has become as important a tool of insurgency as the AK-47 or the RPG rocket-launcher. As Zawahiri himself once put it in an intercepted letter to Abu Musab al-Zarqawi (leader of the Al-Qaeda in Iraq till he was killed in June 2006), "More than half of this battle is taking place in the battlefield of the media."'[28]

The internet carries military manuals and other literature giving instructions on subjects like the use of weapons, assassination techniques, methods for manufacturing poisons and explosives.

The internet is fast becoming a source for radicalization of the youth. For instance, a twenty-three-year-old young Muslim woman, Samina Malik was convicted of a terrorism offence in Britain, when she was found guilty of collecting a library of jihadist manuals from the internet. Malik was working at an airport bookstore and called herself the 'lyrical terrorist' in online forums. She was found downloading the documents, '*The Al-Qaeda Manual*' and '*The Mujahideen Poisons Handbook*' among other titles from the internet.[29]

Abu Musab al-Suri, a close associate of Zarqawi, wrote a 1,600-page tract called 'The Call to Global Islamic Resistance'.[30] Suri has been described as the Al-Qaeda's leading theorist. The intention of drawing up this tract was that the new jihadis entering the movement should be properly instructed in Islamic doctrine. 'For him, someone who kills in the name of Islam without understanding the principles of Islam (that permit him to kill) is not a proper jihadi. Like the communist cadres that fought in the Cold War, being willing to fight is not enough. The fighter must also be properly introduced in the ideology of the group so that he is fighting and dying for the right reasons.'[31]

'The Call to Global Islamic Resistance' is a manifesto that 'has been referred to as a combination of Adolf Hitler's *Mein Kampf* and Vladimir Lenin's "What Is to Be Done?". Since its publication in 2005, it has attracted substantial media attention and is available for download in Arabic and on dozens of jihadist websites'.[32] Thus this veritable minefield of incendiary literature is easily accessible to impressionable young minds prone to radicalization.

The Western intelligence agencies trawl the internet to look for evidence of terrorist plots but even these are half-hearted attempts in checking the spread of terror. With the ever-expanding number of internet users, the internet will be increasingly used for radicalization and in aid of terrorist activities.[33] It is necessary for our intelligence agencies to get started on policing the internet – effectively – so that even if the material cannot be censored, the information relevant for detecting terrorist plots can be accessed and regularly monitored.

Attention has come to be focused on use of the internet by terrorist organizations even in India, when a warning was received via e-mail minutes before the serial bomb blasts at Ahmedabad on 27 July 2008. Though the e-mail address from which it had been sent could be identified, those who actually sent the mail could not be apprehended or even located.

An insider who has worked in a senior position in the RAW, Maj. Gen. V.K. Singh,[34] recounted the details of the desultory manner with which the issue of policing the internet has been handled so far by the intelligence agencies. Innumerable problems were encountered in operationalizing the facilities required for carrying out interception of the internet. Internet service providers (ISPs) were required to bear the cost of the monitoring equipment to be installed on their routers. The then president of NASSCOM (National Association of Software and Service Companies) expressed various reservations in this regard. The Centre for Development of Telematics (C-DOT) was tasked to develop monitoring software for carrying out the interceptions (although the software was available in the market). Maj. Gen. V.K. Singh describes how four years were lost because the software could not be properly operationalized. The traditional rivalry between IB and RAW also surfaced as the IB sought to replace RAW for monitoring the internet.

It is unfortunate that monitoring of the internet, which has become so crucial for counterterrorism operations, has been derailed because of the bureaucratic wrangling among various agencies as described by V.K. Singh. It needs iteration that, in the context of recent events, which underline the importance of monitoring the internet as a vital tool in the war against terrorism, all the issues among the concerned agencies should be speedily resolved so as to enable effective intelligence for the security of the country.

Mobile phones too are known to be used by terrorists who seek to hide their identity by using SIM cards obtained abroad. Intelligence agencies need to become so techno-savvy that they stay a step ahead of the terrorists; till that happens the phenomenon of terrorism will be difficult to contain in the modern era.

Coordination of Intelligence

Although the IB and the RAW are the most important agencies involved in intelligence gathering, there are as many as sixteen other intelligence agencies dealing with security and another three with economic intelligence. Incidentally, the proliferation of governmental organizations, which continues to happen unchecked, is a bane of our system of public administration.

Prem Shankar Jha has described how and why there is lack of coordination among these numerous agencies.[35] The Joint

Intelligence Committee (JIC) – the third tier of the National Security Council (NSC) – has to perform the function of collating the information collected by the various intelligence agencies. Earlier, the meetings of the JIC were presided over by the national security adviser (NSA) and they were attended by senior persons from the concerned intelligence organizations. In recent years, however, the meetings are chaired by the secretary of JIC, who does not have the required status to be able to get proper responses from the intelligence organizations that are expected to furnish the collected information. The role and effectiveness of the JIC has got further diluted with the appointment of two deputy NSAs.

In an interview given in the aftermath of 26/11, the chairman of the Administrative Reforms Committee (set up by the Government of India), Veerappa Moily, commenting adversely on the coordination of information gathered by intelligence agencies, said, 'all intelligence agencies, whether it's the Research and Analysis Wing or the Intelligence Bureau or the state intelligence bureaus, seem to be working in isolation. There is no convergence of intelligence or information at any level. After each terror attack, each agency passes the buck to the other when questioned about intelligence failure'.[36]

Maj. Gen. V.K. Singh has cited concrete instances as to how the rivalry between the three major intelligence agencies, RAW, IB and Military Intelligence (MI) 'has done incalculable damage not only to the agencies themselves but also the nation'.[37]

In the absence of an effective coordination mechanism, turf wars rage among these agencies, preventing the sharing and collation of the crucial information gathered by them. It has been learnt that in recent times the leadership of the two premier agencies, the IB and RAW, has also been lacklustre. As a result, the personnel are demoralized and their output is below par.

The terrorist strike of 26/11 in Mumbai brought into focus certain systemic weaknesses and the adverse consequences of the lack of coordination among official agencies. Information was leaked to the media that RAW and IB had earlier given a warning of a possible terrorist attack – through the sea route on Mumbai – with the Taj Mahal Hotel being one of the probable targets. However, according to reports in the media, the Mumbai police, the navy and the coast guard denied having received any such information. The naval chief purportedly said that there was no 'actionable intelligence' available about the Mumbai attacks.

It is evident that restructuring of all the intelligence agencies is required so that these systemic flaws can be eliminated. One possible solution could be the creation of the post of an intelligence czar, who would be vested with the necessary powers and wherewithal to put together all the important information collected by the various agencies and be in a position to issue timely 'alerts' to whomsoever required to prevent untoward incidents. The person appointed to such a position should outrank all the other players in the different agencies and report directly to the prime minister.

Politicization of Terror

Every time a terrorist attack takes places, politicians and political parties in India, almost invariably, try to exploit the situation to extract mileage in political terms. In recent times, with the UPA coalition in power at the centre, the Opposition repeatedly accused the ruling government of being soft on terror and brought up the issue of the UPA having scrapped POTA. As a riposte the UPA cited the handling of the Kandahar hijacking episode as a chink in the armour of the BJP-led government at the time of the incident.

The state and the central governments, too, tend to shift the blame on each other, more so when the parties in power in the two assemblies are not on the same side of the political divide. This happened in the case of Rajasthan, after the serial bomb blasts in Jaipur, which occured in May 2008. The state government of Rajasthan blamed the central government for not allowing it to firmly deal with Bangladeshi immigrants, some of whom could have been involved in terrorist activity. However, both the central government and the state government have proved to be ineffective in detecting the 'sleeper cells' operating in the state of Rajasthan.

This blame game between the ruling and Opposition parties, and between the state governments and central government, only diverts attention from what should be the aim of all agencies, which is to jointly deal with the menace of terrorism. It needs to be pointed out that the reaction of our political parties in the aftermath of terrorist attacks, including the one on 26/11, stands out in sharp contrast to the broad-based support, cutting across party lines, which was given to the US administration when it launched its 'war on terror' after 9/11. Besides the need of evolving some kind of political consensus to deal with terrorism, there are certain other dimensions of the problem that have to be taken care of.

POTA, UNPA and NIA

The repeal of POTA has been a contentious issue between the ruling United Progressive Alliance (UPA) government (May 2004 to May

2009 and June 2009 onwards) and the National Democratic Alliance (NDA). The government has defended its action based on the argument that POTA was a draconian law liable to be misused, particularly for victimizing the minorities. However, subsequent to 26/11, the government brought in the Unlawful Activities (Prevention) Act (UNPA) in 2008, indirectly bringing back some of the most stringent provisions of POTA. These include the period of pre-trial imprisonment of suspects up to 180 days, increasing the minimum period of police custody to thirty days (from the earlier fifteen days), denial of bail to the suspects if a prima facie case exists, and no bail to be granted to foreigners. Very importantly, in these cases, the accused is presumed to be guilty instead of being innocent.

A National Investigative Agency (NIA) has also been set up after the enactment of the National Investigation Agency Act, 2008. Under this enactment, special courts are also to be set up 'to investigate and prosecute offences affecting the sovereignty, security and integrity of India'.[38] The NIA is empowered to investigate an offence in response to a request from a state government or on a suo moto direction of the central government.

The NIA is believed to have been created on the lines of the FBI in the USA. However, its effectiveness will be revealed only over time. It may also open up a can of worms because law and order comes under the jurisdiction of state governments, who may not always be willing to cooperate with the centre. This in turn could be detrimental to the smooth functioning of the NIA.

THE CURRENT SCENARIO IN INDIA

In the current scenario in India, while certain international militant groups are invariably held responsible for a terror attack, the Students Islamic Movement of India (SIMI) is also generally identified as an organization through whose help these attacks are carried out in India. Since SIMI is the one homegrown organization allegedly involved in terrorist acts, it would be relevant to briefly dilate what it is all about.

Students Islamic Movement of India (SIMI)

SIMI's genesis lies in the Jamaat-e-Islami. The Jamaat has been functioning as a cultural organization committed to propagating neoconservative Islam among Muslims. In 1956, it set up a students' wing, the Students Islamic Organization (SIO). In April 1977, SIMI was formed to revitalize the SIO as a response from the hardliners to the reformism of the Jamaat mainstream. The SIO, initially operating in Uttar Pradesh, spread its influence in other states, such as Andhra Pradesh, West Bengal and Kerala. It is believed that SIMI established links with the LeT, JeM and HUJI; and the members of SIMI attended training camps across the border, set up by these organizations.

SIMI was banned by the central government in 2001 for two years and the ban has been extended thereafter. After being banned, SIMI has managed to continue its activities in the country mainly through subterfuge and creating front organizations. In recent times, many members of SIMI, including a prominent leader, Safdar Nagori, alleged to be plotting terrorist attacks, have been detained by the police at Indore and some other places. It has also been alleged that SIMI received political support from the erstwhile government in Uttar Pradesh, headed by Mulayam Singh Yadav. The Uttar Pradesh government, in September 2006, withdrew cases of treason from a Bahraich court against SIMI ex-president, Shahid Badr Falahi and twelve of its members, thereby undermining the efforts of the security forces in bringing terrorism under control in India.

SIMI draws members of its cadre from radicalized Muslim youth and represents the hardline militant face in Islam in India. On 5 August 2008, a tribunal passed an order lifting the ban on SIMI for want of adequate evidence to justify the continuation of the ban. On the following day, the Supreme Court intervened and issued a stay order and hence, at the time of writing, the ban continues.

LONG-TERM SOLUTION

In the long term, it is necessary to reach out to the youths in the Muslim community, who are prone to radicalization, by identifying the causes of their discontentment and eradicating those. There are many things that can be done to extend the benefits of modern education to the students studying in madrasas. They should also be provided better employment opportunities. In short, all possible actions should be taken to ensure that all the possible reasons due to which this segment of population may be providing recruits for terrorist activities are negated, so that they no longer remain alienated from the mainstream of our society.

In the words of an expert, 'Foreign-sponsored terrorism cannot make much headway if the internal environment in the country does not support it. A sense of insecurity among the minorities provides terrorism an opening in which to take root. It is important to win the confidence of minority groups. But more than anything else it is economic policies that will determine the future of these movements. A thriving economy, which gives hope to people, is more likely to defeat all types of extremist movements than any other strategy. Violent extremist movements grow more easily under conditions of poverty and misrule. Corruption and nepotism have provided the bedrock for the growth of terrorist movements in India. This has been true of all the affected areas in the country – Jammu and Kashmir, Punjab, the Northeast, Bihar and Andhra Pradesh.'[39]

✪

NOTES

1 'Clandestine cell system', http://en.wikipedia.org/wik/Clandestine_cell_system.
2 John Power, 'World View', *The Statesman*, 9 May 2008.
3 Swaminathan S.A. Aiyar, 'Terrorism is not a Muslim Monopoly', *The Times of India*, 23 July 2006.
4 This operation was ordered by Prime Minister Indira Gandhi in June 1984 against well-armed Sikh separatists ensconced in the Golden Temple at Amritsar. It was militarily successful but resulted in the deaths of eighty-three army personnel and 492 civilians. The operation caused widespread anger among the Sikh community and eventually led to the assassination of Indira Gandhi. Online reference: http://en.wikipedia.org/wiki/Operation_Blue_Star
5 About two years after Operation Blue Star, armed Sikh separatists were again holed up in the Golden Temple at Amritsar. Unlike the earlier operation, this time blockade tactics were used to wear out the militants. On 30 April 1986, NSG commandos stormed the temple and the militants surrendered. This time there were no casualties and this operation virtually broke the back of the separatist movement. Online reference: http://en.wikipedia.org.wiki/Operation_Black_Thunder
6 Christoph Reuter, *My Life is a Weapon: A Modern History of Suicide Bombing* (New Delhi: Manas Publications, 2004), p. 22.
7 Ibid., pp. 25-26.
8 Ibid., p. 27.
9 Ibid., p. 44.
10 Ibid., p. 148.
11 Shashi Tharoor, 'Why Some Engineers Become Terrorists', *The Times of India*, 30 March 2008.
12 Pervez Musharraf, *In The Line of Fire* (New York: Free Press, 2006), p. 275.

13 'Pak Nurtured Terrorism: Zardari', *The Times of India*, 9 July 2009.
14 Ibid.
15 Ibid.
16 'Pak Elements Aiding Taliban Insurgents Against US', *The Times of India*, 11 June 2008.
17 Mark Mazzetti and Eric Schmitt, 'ISI Backing Taliban, US tells Pak, CIA says Bombing of India's Kabul Mission Handiwork of this Nexus', *The Times of India*, 31 July 2008.
18 Thomas L. Friedman, *The World is Flat: A Brief History of the Twenty-first Century* (US: Farrar, Straus and Giroux, 2005), pp. 63-64.
19 Shankar Raghuraman, 'India Loses More Lives to Terror than Any Other Country in the World Except Iraq', *The Times of India*, 27 August 2007.
20 'IPCS Special Report', 27 July 2006, Institute of Peace and Conflict Studies, New Delhi. Hereafter cited in text.
21 B. Raman, 'Mumbai: Q&A' (2008), http://sify.com/news/columns/fullstory. php ?id=14814315&acid=13180904.
22 B. Raman, 'Striking at Will: We Must Ensure Security for Soft Targets', *The Times of India*, 15 May 2008.
23 Ibid.
24 'Terrorism', *Time*, 16 July 2007, p. 21.
25 Ibid.
26 Ibid.
27 'A World Wide Web of Terror', *The Economist*, 14-20 July 2007, p. 25.
28 Ibid.
29 'The Lyrical Terrorist: Be Careful What You Google', *The Economist*, 8-14 December 2007, p. 67.
30 Jim Lacey, ed., *A Terrorist's Call to Global Jihad: Deciphering Abu Musab Al-Suri's Islamic Jihad Manifesto* (Annapolis, Maryland: Naval Institute Press, 2006), p. viii.
31 Ibid., pp. ix-x.
32 Ibid., p. ix.
33 'A World Wide Web of Terror', *The Economist*, 14-20 July 2007, p. 27.
34 V.K. Singh, *India's External Intelligence – Secrets of Research and Analysis Wing (RAW)* (New Delhi: Manas Publications, 2007), pp. 130-140.
35 Prem Shankar Jha, 'How a Plot was Lost – The Tower of Babel', *Sunday Times of India*, 7 December 2008.
36 Apurva, 'Picking up the Pieces – RAW, IB Pass the Buck: Moily', *The Indian Express*, 3 December 2008.
37 Singh, *India's External Intelligence*, p. 157.
38 'Unlawful Activities (Prevention) Act', http://en.wikipedia.org/wiki/Unlawful_Activities_(Prevention)_Act.
39 Ved Marwah, 'Combating Terrorism', in *Combating Terrorism: Strategies of Ten Countries*, ed., Yonah Alexander (New Delhi: Manas Publications), pp. 301-336.

Secularism

Ashutosh Varshney has divided the ideological concept of nationalism into three broad categories – secular nationalism, religious nationalism and a third one focusing on our caste system – and calls them the three 'master narratives in Indian politics in the twentieth century'.[1] He goes on to explain that by master narrative he means 'the major organizing devices for mass politics, or the leading political idioms that mobilize large numbers of people. Master narratives tell stories that make the critical issues in politics intelligible to the masses. They are ways of putting together popular social coalitions so that politics can be altered and political power won'. Varshney also describes these master narratives as 'competing national imaginations'. It is evident that throughout recent history, all these three narratives have consistently generated remarkable passion in politics.

Caste, being confined to the Hindu community, plays no part in the greater context of Hindu-Muslim riots and as such falls outside the scope of this subject. As communal riots are often seen as a fallout of the clash between the ideologies of secular nationalism and religious nationalism, we will deal only with these two competing national imaginations.

SECULARISM IN INDIA AND THE WEST

Writers and commentators with a Western-centric bias usually maintain that the concepts of democracy, human rights, liberalism and secularism have emerged in the Western world through an evolutionary process; and are, therefore, alien to civilizations in other parts of the world. The contention is that it is difficult to superimpose these values on the socio-political systems of nations whose civilizational ethos is different from that of the West.

This argument has one major flaw. In our perception, secularism in India is not an alien concept; it has its roots in ancient India, and since it has followed its own evolutionary path it differs significantly from the Western concept.

In Western societies, beginning in the middle ages, a conflict between religious faith and human reason, which was primarily scientific in its basis, took place. This conflict led to the struggle for supremacy between the ecclesiastical and political authorities; and eventually resulted in the segregation of the state and the church. Therefore, the Western notion of 'secularism' emphasizes prohibition of religious association in state activities, whereas in India the emphasis is on neutrality among the different religions, which does not preclude the state from participating in activities of certain religious institutions, provided that equidistance from all religions is maintained.

Amartya Sen in his illuminating work, *The Argumentative Indian*, has traced the evolution of secularism over millennia in our country.[2] Sen has argued that the long history of heterodoxy in India has had a bearing not only on the development and survival of democracy, it has also richly contributed to the emergence of secularism that is unique to India. In history, the tolerance of religious diversity is reflected in India being a shared home for Hindus, Buddhists, Jains, Jews, Christians, Muslims, Parsis, Sikhs, Bahais, and others.

The Vedas dating back to the second millennium BC paved the way for Hinduism. Buddhism and Jainism emerged in the sixth century BC; the Jews came to India in waves, after the fall of Jerusalem. Christians too came early and settled in the areas now known as Kerala. Later, Parsis and Bahais, persecuted in their homeland, came and settled here. Muslim Arab traders came and settled in India not long after Islam came into being, followed by the Muslim invaders who conquered territories and settled down in this land.

The long process by which people of different origins and faiths migrated to this land, made it their home and became part and parcel of mainstream Indian culture (while retaining their distinct ethnic and religious affiliations) is well encapsulated by the eminent Urdu poet, Raghupati Sahai Firaq: '*Sar Zamin e Hind par Aqwam e Alam ke Firaq Qafile baste gayey,* Hindustan *banta gaya.*' (Caravans from all over the world settled in this land and contributed towards the shaping of Hindustan.)[3] All such peoples, through a process of acculturation and assimilation, assumed the Indian identity. It is for this reason that Rabindranath Tagore's 'idea of India' itself militates 'against the intense consciousness of the separateness of one's own people from others'.[4]

In one of his edicts, Emperor Ashoka, who later converted to Buddhism, specifically enjoined that 'a person must not do reverence to his own sect or disparage the beliefs of another without reason'. Many centuries later, Emperor Akbar laid the formal foundations of the secular legal structure and the religious neutrality of the state. Although a faithful Muslim himself, Akbar ensured that all religions are equal under his regime. He made a well-meaning attempt to launch Din-i-Ilahi based on the best features of different religions. It is a different matter that the concept did not take root and ceased to exist after the demise of the emperor.

Amartya Sen has also referred to the tolerance of variation in different walks of life from the beginning of Indian history, evident from Sanskrit dramas like *Sudraka's Mricchakatikam* and *Mudraraksasam*.[5] The same commitment to diversity continued in the medieval period with its rich culture of non-sectarian religious poetry, particularly drawing upon the Hindu Bhakti and Muslim Sufi traditions. Interreligious tolerance is a persistent theme in the poetry of Kabir, Dadu, Amir Khusrau, Ravi Das, Sena and others.

Secularism in India, thus, is based on the pluralistic and syncretic character of society. Through pluralism we celebrate diversity. Followers of all faiths and denominations are free to pursue their religious or cultural practices and the state would not discriminate against or in favour of any of them. '*Sarva Dharma Sambhava*', that is, equal respect for all religions is the guiding principle of our country's secular ethos. For instance, the Sufis emerged from Islamic tradition but threw their *ibadatgahs* (places of worship) open to devotional music and dance, and strove to establish man's communion with God, very much linked to the ancient Indian tradition of *bhajan* and *kirtan*. This was indeed a significant marker of India's composite culture.

SECULARISM AS A GANDHI-NEHRU CONSTRUCT

While secularism is an integral part of our heritage, its present-day avatar is a Gandhi-Nehru construct. It was due to them that secularism was formally adopted as an organizing principle of Indian society. As Mani Shankar Aiyar puts it:

> ... the Gandhi-Nehru tradition exults in our composite culture. It not merely accepts but celebrates the immense variety of India. It does not just come to terms with diversity; it treats diversity as the cornerstone of our unity. It is a tradition that holds that if India is not a palimpsest of every

> major – and several minor – religions of the world, it would not be the Bharatvarsha we have known for 5000 years and more.[6]

India's freedom movement was led by the most charismatic and saintly figure of the modern era, Mahatma Gandhi. Some see a contradiction in the Mahatma being a devout Hindu and yet secular in his outlook. It is interesting to note how the Mahatma is viewed in a scholarly work from a Pakistani Muslim perspective. In the book *The British Raj in India – An Historical Review*, S.M. Burke and Salim Al-Din Quraishi have given a detailed, and to an extent, unbiased account of Mahatma Gandhi's enormous contribution and stellar role in leading the freedom movement against the Raj.[7] They have also lavished fulsome praise on Mahatma Gandhi for the sacrifices he made, his asceticism and the magical hold he had over the Congress party and over the masses. On the question of his religiosity, Burke and Quraishi have this to say:

> Gandhi never made any secret of the fact that he was a devout Hindu nor that he believed religion was inseparable from politics. 'Every fibre of my being is Hindu,' he affirmed. That he respected other religions as much as his own did not make him less of a Hindu, for Hinduism is defined by its followers as a perpetual search for truth. Followers of other religions stoutly maintain that their own particular religion is the only true one, though they may be tolerant of the other faiths.[8]

However, Burke and Quraishi have also observed this from a Pakistani perspective:

> But the Mahatma's leadership suffered from one major shortcoming. It was Hindu in character and unsuited to cure the Hindu-Muslim discord which was India's most serious political malady. Even his most notable endeavour – to unite Hindus and Muslims by championing the cause of the Khilafat – served, in the long run, to drive the two communities further apart.[9]

Mahatma Gandhi believed that there was no contradiction at all between his personal religiosity and an eclectic view about all religions. He had once said:

> If the Hindus believe that India should be peopled only by Hindus, they are living in a dreamland. The Hindus, the Muslims, the Parsis and the Christians who have made India their country are fellow countrymen. ... Should we not remember that many Hindus and Muslims own the same ancestors and the same blood runs through their veins? Do people become enemies because they change their religion? Moreover, there are deadly proverbs as between the followers of Siva and those of Vishnu, yet nobody suggests that these two do not belong to the same nation. It is said that the Vedic religion is different from Jainism, but the followers of the respective faiths are not different nations.

Jawaharlal Nehru, often referred to as the architect of modern India, was Gandhi's principal acolyte and disciple; yet in many ways they were studies in contrast. Although the Harrow-Cambridge-educated Nehru made tremendous personal sacrifices in the cause of India's freedom and remained incarcerated in British prisons for long periods, he was no ascetic and had a taste for the good things of life. Nehru did not share Gandhi's romantic view of village life. He was pro-industrialization and, as a Fabian Socialist, for compulsory redistribution of wealth.

Unlike Gandhi, Nehru had no time or patience for religious rituals. Some writers seek to distinguish Gandhi's commitment to secularism, which was based on his religiosity, from Nehru's, who was an agnostic. But Nehru's belief in secularism was derived from his sense of history and our civilizational ethos. However different, both were great leaders and firm believers in the imperative of giving equal treatment to the followers of all religions. It is irrelevant to draw a distinction in their conception of secularism on the basis of their personal beliefs.

After Independence, Nehru had to fight hard for secularism to be made a cornerstone in the architecture of state policy. In a nutshell, this is how he viewed secularism:

> The word 'secular' perhaps is not a very happy one. And yet, for want of a better, we have used it. What exactly does it mean? It does not obviously mean a state where religion as such is discouraged. It means freedom of religion and conscience, including freedom for those who may have no

> religion. It means free play for all religions, subject only to their not interfering with each other or with the basic conceptions of our state. It means that the minority communities, from the religious point of view, should accept this position. It means, even more, that the majority community, from this point of view, should fully realize it. For, by virtue of numbers as well as in other ways, it is the dominant community and it is its responsibility not to use its position in any way which might prejudice our secular ideal.[10]

Before we recount certain historical events pertaining to the evolution of the concept of secularism in the post-Independence period, it would be appropriate to spell out the nature and depth of Nehru's commitment to the secular ideology. His writings and speeches are peppered with references to India's secular destiny, the imperative of giving equal treatment to followers of all religions and the need to protect the rights of minorities.

While Nehru was not a religious person, he was deeply attached to certain symbols that were venerated by the masses, such as the river Ganga. For the agnostic Nehru such symbols had an emotional appeal not because of any religious significance, but as a part of our great civilizational heritage. In this context, the following words quoted from his will are emblematic of his thinking:

> Ganga has been to me a symbol and a memory of the past of India, running into the present, and flowing on to the great ocean of the future. ... And though I have discarded much of past tradition and custom, and am anxious that India should rid herself of all shackles that bind and constrain her and divide her people, and suppress vast numbers of them, and prevent the free development of the body and the spirit; though I seek all this, yet I do not wish to cut myself off from that past completely. I am proud of that great inheritance that has been, and is, ours and I am conscious that I too, like all of us, am a link in that unbroken chain which goes back to the dawn of history in the immemorial past of India; that chain I would not break, for I treasure it and seek inspiration from it. And, as witness of this desire of mine and as my last homage to India's cultural inheritance, I am making this request that a handful of my ashes be thrown into the Ganga at Allahabad to be carried to the great ocean that washes India's shores.[11]

CERTAIN HISTORICAL DEVELOPMENTS IN THE POST-INDEPENDENCE PERIOD

The creation of Pakistan was the culmination of the two-nation theory and, in due course, Pakistan was declared an Islamic republic. The Congress had always opposed the two-nation theory and since Independence was won under its aegis, India opted to become a secular state. However, within the Congress party, an influential section was not fully in sync with the secular ideology. In the early years of Independence, Nehru had to really exert pressure to ensure that India remained firmly committed to secularism and avoided any actions smacking of obscurantism or a pro-Hindu bias.

Although Nehru wanted C. Rajagopalachari, the interim governor-general, to become the first president of the Republic of India, Sardar Vallabh Bhai Patel, with his stranglehold in the Congress Parliamentary Party, made sure that Dr Rajendra Prasad became the president.

As soon as he came into office, President Rajendra Prasad wanted to change the date fixed for Republic Day from 26th January since his astrologers had told him it was not auspicious.[12] It was the very day, two decades earlier, on which the Congress had formally given the call for Purna Swaraj (complete self-governance). Nehru made it clear to Rajendra Prasad that astrologers could not be allowed to have a say in such a matter and India was thus declared a republic on 26 January 1950.

For election to the office of the Congress president in 1950, Nehru supported Acharya J.B. Kripalani against Purushottam Das Tandon as the latter was strongly under the influence of the Hindu right wing. But Tandon was elected with the backing of Sardar Patel and some powerful chief ministers of the time. Soon afterwards, Nehru came into conflict with Tandon on issues of economic policy and communalism. Eventually, Tandon had to resign and Prime Minister Nehru himself assumed the office of Congress president.

The rebuilding of the Somnath Temple, which had been vandalized and demolished by Mahmud of Ghazni centuries ago, was an emotive issue for Hindus. President Rajendra Prasad wished to be present at the inaugural function of the temple. Nehru tried to dissuade him from doing so.[13] When Rajendra Prasad insisted, he was told that he could be present at the event only in his personal capacity and not as the president of India because a religious function of this nature could not be treated as an official one. In his communication to the chief ministers on 2 May 1951, Nehru made his stand clear:

> You must have read about the coming ceremonies at the Somnath Temple ... It should be clearly understood that this function is not governmental and the Government of India as such has nothing to do with it ... We must not do anything which comes in the way of our state being secular. That is the basis of our Constitution and governments, therefore, should refrain from associating themselves with anything which tends to affect the secular character of our State.[14]

With the passing away of Sardar Patel and the waning influence of his erstwhile lieutenants, the pro-Hindu forces in the Congress party lost out, at least for some time. Nehru was able to make secularism one of the basic issues of the election campaign for the first general election held in 1952. He personally campaigned across the length and breadth of the country and won a famous victory for the Congress party. The communalist forces, represented by the Jan Sangh and the Hindu Mahasabha, were decimated at the polls, getting only two seats and less than 2 per cent of the votes. The election victory was a blow in favour of secularism in our polity from the very beginning of the country as an independent republic.

Politics and Secularism

With the passage of time, the policies of the state – be they of the central government or state governments – have not consistently adhered to the Gandhi-Nehru model, which has been written into the Constitution of India. Although, through an amendment of the Constitution in 1976, India was formally declared a 'secular' republic, even the Congress party has at times been accused of playing 'vote bank politics' either by pampering the minorities (as in the law enacted after the *Shah Bano* case) or, at the other extreme, by adopting a soft-Hindutva approach. However, Prime Minister Narasimha Rao has been rightly criticized for not intervening effectively to prevent the demolition of the Babri Masjid in 1992.

The BJP-led NDA government, on the other hand, paid only lip service to the secular ideals enshrined in the Constitution. When it came to the crunch, it did not come forward to protect the minorities or their rights. The most glaring instance was its non-intervention during the riots in Gujarat in 2002, when thousands of Muslims were butchered, as the state government remained a mute spectator in utter disregard of its duty to protect the lives and property of the minority community.

SECULARISM AND THE INDIAN CONSTITUTION

The debate of 'secularism' versus 'pseudo-secularism' was begun by the collective of the Hindu right wing, also known as the Sangh Parivar. The Parivar has consistently accused the Congress and the Left parties of being 'pseudo-secular'. According to these right-wing organizations, any differential treatment given to the minorities goes against the grain of secularism. This debate is part of the current political dialectic and will continue to be so in the foreseeable future.

It would be apposite to state the Constitutional position regarding secularism in our country with respect to the commitment made by the founding fathers of the Constitution, which was subsequently reaffirmed and even strengthened by certain amendments. The Constitutional position has been brought out succinctly in an article by Mathew John, the relevant excerpt of which is given below:

> Unlike the very general and almost vague clauses granting religious freedom and preventing the establishment of religion in the US Constitution, the Indian Constitution is considerably more detailed in the manner in which it organizes itself in relation to religion. Subject to express restraint in the interests of public order, health and morality, the Indian Constitution also provides for grant of religious liberty to individuals to practice, profess and propagate religion. Further, the constitution also provides for corporate freedom to all religious denominations, permitting them to maintain their affairs in matters of religion, to own and acquire property and to administer properly in accordance with law. The Indian Constitution however, sets itself apart from the standard liberal (American and possibly European) constitutional models by the manner in which it qualifies its grant of religious freedom. Beyond normal liberal qualifications to freedom in the interests of public order, Article 25(2) (a) and (b) of the Indian Constitution stipulates that the state can make laws to regulate economic, financial, political or other secular activity associated with religious

> practice. It also allows the state to make laws providing social welfare and reform or the throwing open of Hindu religious institutions of a public character to all classes and sections of Hindus. Further Article 27 seems to indicate that taxes could be levied for religious purposes as long as it is not specifically appropriated for the payment of expenses of any particular religion. Lastly and probably a little less controversially Article 28 of the constitution provides that religious instruction could be provided even in educational institutions partly funded by the state provided that the institution had been established under an endowment or trust, which required that religious education be imparted. In such institutions however no one can be required to attend religious instruction without their consent. The Indian Constitution therefore seems far less troubled by the liberal preoccupation with liberty and seems to allow a wide mandate for the interventionist state presence in 'secular' religious affairs.[15]

Through its judgements in a number of cases, the Supreme Court has interpreted the Constitution in a way that enables the state to intervene in religious matters of a 'secular' nature. We may touch upon the implications of a few of the important ones here.

The apex court first declared secularism to be part of the un-amendable basic structure of the Indian Constitution in the *Keshavananda Bharati* case of 1973. This case was decided by a bench of thirteen judges of the Supreme Court. It held by a majority of seven to six that 'although no part of the Constitution, including fundamental rights, was beyond the amending power of the Parliament (thus overruling the 1967 case), the "basic structure of the Constitution could not be abrogated even by a Constitutional amendment"'.[16] The judges then indicated the elements of the basic structure of the Constitution which included its secular character.

In the *S.R. Bommai vs Union of India* judgement delivered in 1994, the Supreme Court clearly spelt out the place of secularism in the Constitution. The court asserted, firstly, that secularism was crucial to ensure the right to freedom of religion and the concomitant right to be treated equally by the state irrespective of religious affiliation. It was held that the concept of a secular state is, therefore, essential for the successful working of the democratic form of government. Secondly, it was affirmed that secularism derives from the Indian civilizational or cultural ethos of tolerance and communal harmony. Thirdly, flowing from its understanding of secularism as part of the Indian civilizational ethos, the court enunciated a positive secularism, asserting for itself a reformist role to decisively intervene in situations where such secular civilizational values appear under threat. Thus, as a definitive judicial position on the matter, the *Bommai* judgment elaborates the interventionist structure of the Indian Constitution in allowing the court to deal with situations where communal harmony and tolerance are under imminent threat.

Certain famous one-liners cited by Dhananjay Mahapatra from the judgements in the *Bommai* and *Ismail Faruqi vs Union of India* (1994) cases, which bring out, in essence, the secular features of our Constitution, are worthy of note:[17]

- 'Secularism in the Constitution is not anti-God.'
- 'Matters which are purely religious are left personal to the individual and the secular part is taken charge [of] by the state on grounds of public interest, order and general welfare.'
- 'The secular government should negate attempts to divide people on religious lines and bring order in society.'
- 'Any step taken to arrest escalation of communal tension and to achieve communal accord and harmony cannot be termed non-secular or against secularism.'

SECULARISM AND DISPLAY OF RELIGIOUS SYMBOLS

It is worthy of note that in some Western democratic countries, like France and Britain, the government, from time to time, prohibits women from wearing headscarves or veils and men from wearing turbans in schools or workplaces and imposes other such prohibitions on public dress codes. Such bans have evoked protests from Muslims or Sikhs as the case may be. Bans imposed on wearing such items, which are treated as religious symbols, stem from the prohibitory nature of secularism in the West.

President Sarkozy's inveighing against the wearing of the burqa, during his recent address to the French parliament, has kept alive the controversy surrounding Muslim women's attire in the West. Its repercussions are being felt even in India. However, in India, such issues do not usually arise, so long as a symmetrical approach is adopted by the state towards the use of such religious symbols by the followers of different religions or denominations.

....

However, the issue of whether it should be mandatory for women to wear helmets when riding on the pillion of a two-wheeler came into the public domain a few years ago due to religious reasons. According to Sikh belief, Sikh men and women are allowed to wear only turbans over their heads and to make it mandatory for Sikh women to wear a helmet was unacceptable to some of them. The Punjab and Haryana High Court had made it mandatory but the decision was reversed by the Supreme Court in a ruling given in October 2004. In this ruling, all women, irrespective of religion, were exempt from wearing a helmet when riding on the pillion. The controversy surrounding this matter has since subsided.

ACADEMIC DEBATES ON THE SECULAR-COMMUNAL QUESTION

Beyond the polemics of who is 'secular' and who is 'non-secular', the secular-communal question is a persistent theme of debate among scholars in Indian academia. Some scholars generally lay emphasis on the exploitative aspects of the socio-economic structure of society, which result in exacerbating the communal divide. On the other hand, certain academics have been described as 'anti-secularist' (though they may not themselves accept this label). These scholars tend to argue in favour of sustenance of religious traditions since these actually promote harmony among communities and not discord. In this sense, they derive from India's enduring civilizational ethos of tolerance.

In her work, *Beyond Secularism – The Rights of Religious Minorities*, Neera Chandhoke cogently argues in favour of the Nehruvian concept of secularism but laments how political developments since Independence have consistently undermined it.[18] To substantiate this point, she cites the acts of 'later prime ministers such as Indira Gandhi who overtly adopted religious symbols and practices as legitimizing devices, and who was to play the Hindu card in the late seventies and the early eighties'. The adoption of these legitimizing devices created a feeling among minority groups that they were being marginalized in the country. She also considers the opening of the gates of the Babri Masjid for worship by Hindus as a reason for the alienation of Muslims.

In his essay 'Secularism and its Discontents',[19] Amartya Sen has critically examined the various arguments advanced by the critics of Indian secularism and found them to be untenable. Sen has dealt with six distinct lines of arguments put forward by anti-secularists and given his counterarguments to show how the same are flawed. These are: a) the 'non-existence' critique; b) the 'favouritism' critique; c) the 'prior identity' critique; d) the 'Muslim sectarianism' critique; e) the 'anti-modernist' critique; and f) the 'cultural' critique. The one line of argument out of these six which I would like to briefly discuss pertains to communal violence and its causation. This relates to the anti-modernist critique of secularism by Sen.[20]

Anti-modernist Critique of Secularism and How it is Flawed

Ashish Nandy has argued that 'it is not modern India which has tolerated Judaism in India for nearly 2,000 years, Christianity from before the time it went to Europe, and Zoroastrianism for more than 1,200 years; it is traditional India which has shown such tolerance ... As India gets modernized, religious violence is increasing'.

This approach towards secularism posits that it is a Western concept with foundations in the Enlightenment and Reformation. The rise of Protestantism led to the separation of the church and the state. It is in this backdrop that secularism became embedded in Western culture. According to the 'anti-secularists' there is no such civilizational niche for secularism in India. It is also argued that communal riots did not take place in traditional India for traditional religiosity led to principles of religious tolerance and coexistence.

Nandy has also said, 'To accept the ideology of secularism is to accept the ideologies of progress and modernity as the new justification of domination, and the use of violence to achieve and sustain ideologies as the new opiates of the masses.' Amartya Sen does not accept this characterization of secularism. The Indian conception of secularism demands that there should be symmetrical treatment of different religious communities in politics and in the affairs of the state. It is difficult to comprehend how such treatment could induce inescapable 'violence' to achieve and sustain this ideology.

As Ashutosh Varshney has pointed out, the anti-secularist scholars have not distinguished between different types of traditions since all of these are not of the tolerant kind.[21] The Mughal ruler Akbar built bridges across communities and represents the spread of tolerance in medieval India. But Aurangzeb did the opposite. He followed a policy of repression of non-Muslims. The differing approach of these two Mughal rulers towards followers of other religions shows how tradition can veer from tolerance to intolerance and thereby, is not an absolute category to uphold against modernism.

Varshney has also argued that as in the case of tradition, modernity and secularism can come in various forms. Thus he characterizes Nehru's ideology as 'secular tolerance' which implies that even though Nehru had reservations about religion, he did not allow it to be translated 'into an arrogant abuse of religion or into an opportunistic acceptance of religion in public life'.[22] On the other hand, Indira Gandhi exemplified 'secular arrogance'. According to Varshney, this is 'the idea that political power may be used either to co-opt the believer or to subdue him'.[23] He cites how armed forces were used to neutralize Sikh separatists – who had occupied the Golden Temple at Amritsar – as an instance of secular arrogance.

For Varshney, Rajiv Gandhi represented 'secular innocence'. The way Rajiv Gandhi handled the *Shah Bano* judgement is a case in point. Moreover, his government took the initiative to get legislation passed which made the Shariat take precedence over civil law in matters concerning marriage, divorce, etc., for Muslim women (this subject has been dealt with in the chapter on the Uniform Civil Code) that betrayed his 'secular innocence'.

THE LAST WORD

We may or may not agree with Varshney's typology of secularism. It is possible that considerations of realpolitik may have led governments of the day to deviate from the Gandhi-Nehru construct of secularism in implementing certain policies. But such deviations have to be treated as transient aberrations because it is that template of secularism, written into the Constitution of India, which is to be followed. That alone can promote harmony and tolerance. Upholding secularism should, therefore, not lead us into violence but away from it.

The results of the general elections of May 2009 may have dealt a body blow to the proponents of Hindutva, who keep harping on 'policies of appeasement' and 'minorityism' coming in the way of creating a truly secularist state. In an attempt to woo Hindu voters, the right wing once again raised issues like the building of a Ram temple at Ayodhya and bringing a Uniform Civil Code into force, which fell flat. The majority of voters decided in the favour of the Congress party and the right-wing alliance got much lower votes than last time. It appears that our electorate is now matured enough to rebuff politicos wishing to milk their divisive agenda and recognizes their values as antithetical to the essential secular ethos of India.

Notes

1 Varshney, *Ethnic Conflict and Civic Life*, p. 55.
2 Sen, *Argumentative Indian*, pp. 16-18.
3 Saeed Naqvi, 'The Parade of Paranoia', *The New Indian Express*, 29 January 1999.
4 Sen, *Argumentative Indian*, p. 72.
5 Ibid., p. 19.
6 Aiyar, *Confessions of a Secular Fundamentalist*, p. 34.
7 Burke and Quraishi, The British Raj in India, pp. 181-201.
8 Ibid., p. 195.
9 Ibid., pp. 194-195.
10 Mushirul Hasan, *Moderate or Militant: Images of India's Muslims* (New Delhi: Oxford, 2008), p. 7.
11 M.J. Akbar, *Nehru: The Making of India* (New Delhi: Roli Books, 2003), pp. 583-584.
12 Ibid., p. 459.
13 Ibid., p. 462.
14 Aiyar, *Confessions of a Secular Fundamentalist*, p. 134.
15 Mathew John, 'Decoding Secularism – Comparative Study of Legal Decisions in India and US', *Economic and Political Weekly*, 30 April 2005, pp. 1901-1906.
16 'Basic Structure', http://en.wikipedia.org/wiki/Basic_Structure.
17 Dhananjay Mahapatra, 'In a Week, Two Assaults on Secularism', *The Times of India*, 17 September 2007.
18 Neera Chandhoke, *Beyond Secularism – The Rights of Religious Minorities* (New Delhi: Oxford, 2002), pp. 43-74.
19 Sen, *Argumentative Indian*, pp. 294-316.
20 Ibid., p. 229.
21 Varshney, *Ethnic Conflict and Civic Life*, p. 78.
22 Ibid., p 79.
23 Ibid.

Religious Nationalism: The Muslim Version

The ideological opposition to secular nationalism originates from religious nationalism. Throughout the independence movement, seen as a struggle by the nationalists against British rule, there existed a substratum of conflict between the forces of secular and religious nationalism.

Secular nationalism was represented by the Congress, which claimed to speak and act for all Indians, irrespective of their religious affiliation; Muslim nationalism was represented by the Muslim League and its tallest leader, Mohammad Ali Jinnah espoused the two-nation theory, believing that Hindus and Muslims should constitute separate nations; and the Akhil Bharatiya Hindu Mahasabha (All-India Hindu Assembly) was the foil to the Muslim League and also believed in the two-nation theory, albeit from a perspective that India should not be partitioned and the minorities would have to accept the primacy of mainstream Hindu culture. In this view, the religious identity of individuals in a nation was considered to be the overarching one, subsuming all other identities within it. Ironically enough, both Hindu and Muslim nationalists shared their ideological principles but from opposite directions. In this respect Jinnah's views found an echo in those of V.D. Savarkar, who was the loudest voice among Hindu nationalists.

In the earlier phase of the independence movement, till the First World War and in its immediate aftermath, the focus remained on independence from British Raj. The demand of a separate homeland for Muslims was not articulated till then. And if at all it was, it lacked any degree of seriousness or conviction.

MUSLIM NATIONALISM IN A HISTORICAL PERSPECTIVE

We need to briefly recount the history of the rise of Muslim nationalism (that may as well be labelled Muslim communalism), which became virtually extinct after losing its raison d'être once the country had been partitioned, and the demand for creation of Pakistan was met. Yet Muslim communalism does survive, though only as a pale shadow of its earlier version, inasmuch as certain elements in the community sometimes agitate over sectarian issues in a manner which is inconsistent with the secular ethos of the country.

Much before the idea of a separate homeland for Muslims had been conceived or articulated, the idea of Muslims as a '*qaum*' (meaning people, community or nation) had taken hold among certain Muslim intellectuals. Sir Sayyid Ahmed Khan believed that the interest of the *qaum* lay in reconciliation with the British. In 1866, Sayyid Ahmed launched the British India Association in Aligarh. This was not an association exclusively for Muslims. However, Sayyid Ahmed gradually became alienated from Hindus because some Hindus in Banaras started campaigning for substitution of Hindi for Urdu in the judicial courts. Sayyid Ahmed believed that Urdu was a 'memento of Muslim rule in the country' and at the heart of any common Hindu-Muslim culture.

Founding of Aligarh Muslim University

In the aftermath of the revolt of 1857, Muslims were more alienated from the British than the Hindus. In this situation the British found in Sir Sayyid Ahmed a valuable ally. Sayyid Ahmed wished to set up a college for extending benefits of modern education to Muslims. This was facilitated by the Raj which allotted seventy-five acres of land in Aligarh on which the Mohammedan Anglo-Oriental (MAO) College, offering arts, science and law courses in English, was founded. This was to later become the Aligarh Muslim University (AMU). In course of time, the AMU came to represent the educational and political aspirations of the Muslim masses in India. It emerged as the intellectual centre for a movement which eventually led to the partition of India and the creation of Pakistan in 1947.

Muslims who believed that the community had special interests which needed to be addressed – as distinct from the pan-Indian struggle against the British rule – got together in 1906 to establish the Muslim League. Their first key objective was to obtain separate electorates for Muslims. This was achieved, as far as the imperial council and legislative councils were concerned, through the passing of the Indian Councils Act of 1909, based on the Morley-Minto Reforms. Those regulations laid down the procedures for election and nomination of members to the different councils and also stipulated the requisite qualifications of persons who could be elected or nominated to these. Representation in these councils was determined to be on the basis of reservations for different kinds of communities and groups. Thus, these constituencies were not supposed to be 'general' constituencies.

The Muslim League

In a resolution passed at the Lahore Congress on 27 December 1909, these regulations were condemned because of: '(a) the excessive and unfairly preponderant share of representation given to the followers of one particular religion; (b) the unjust, invidious, and humiliating distinctions made between Muslim and non-Muslim subjects of His Majesty in the matter of electorates, the franchise and the qualifications of the candidates ...'[1]

Lucknow Pact

While for most of its history the Congress remained opposed to separate electorates because it claimed to represent all communities and denominations, there was a phase when, in the interest of obtaining cooperation from all Muslims, it tempered down its stand on the issue. With the demand for separate electorates conceded by the British, there was a stage when a rapprochement of sorts took place between the Congress and the Muslim League. Both the Congress and the League held their sessions at the same place and at the same time in Lucknow in December 1916. Both parties agreed to a scheme that came to be known as the 'Lucknow Pact' and laid down that Muslims would be elected to the imperial legislative council and the provincial legislative councils by separate electorates. Under this pact it was also agreed that no bill, in any of the councils, affecting one or the other community, would be passed if three-fourth of the members of that community opposed it. Further, Muslims were given a third of the seats in the imperial legislature although their population in British India was not more than one-fourth.[2]

Khilafat Movement

There was another issue on which the Congress, led by Mahatma Gandhi, extended support to Muslims. This was the Khilafat question. After the defeat of Turkey in World War I, Indian Muslims wished that the Ottoman Sultan should retain his territories in order to be able to command resources to maintain his status as the *khalifa* (or caliphate) of the Muslim world and the keeper of the holy places of Islam. An organization for his support, the Khilafat Conference, came into being in 1919 and held a public session in Delhi on 23rd and 24th November.

Mahatma Gandhi made common cause and showed his solidarity with the Muslims by attending the conference in Delhi and, on 24th November, by presiding over it. The Congress also passed a resolution urging the British government to settle the Turkish question in accordance with the sentiments of Indian Muslims. Gandhi's decision to support the Khilafat Movement was criticized later because the issue of the caliphate was a purely Muslim question which had no link with the movement for self-governance. At the time, however, Mahatma Gandhi justified his approach by writing in *Young India* that 'We talk of Hindu-Mohammedan unity. It would be an empty phrase if the Hindus held aloof from the Mohammedans when their vital interests are at stake'.

It is not necessary to trace the history of the Khilafat Movement which died a natural death when, on 29 October 1923, Turkey formally became a republic with Kemal Ataturk as its president and on 3 March 1924 the institution of the caliphate was abolished. The reforms ushered in Turkey, at the instance of Kemal Ataturk, exposed the obscurantism inherent in the Khilafat Movement.

The support extended by Mahatma Gandhi to the Khilafat Movement, however, proved counterproductive in the long run. The Muslim cause of preserving the temporal and spiritual status of the Sultan of Turkey was not an Indian issue. It was a pan-Islamic movement. It, therefore, did not serve the purpose of consolidating Muslim sentiment in favour of the united national movement against British rule in India. Actually, it had the opposite effect of further enhancing the feelings of religious nationalism among Indian Muslims, which in time developed into the demand for Pakistan.

Other Issues

Another issue on which the Muslim League and the Congress made common cause was the massacre of an unarmed gathering at Jallianwala Bagh in Amritsar on 13 April 1919. Under Brigadier-General Dyer's orders British troops opened fire, killing some 379 persons and wounding many more. This was the official statistic given out by the Hunter Commission but it is believed the actual number of victims was much larger.

Both the Congress and the Muslim League were also opposed to certain other measures sponsored by the Raj such as the Rowlatt Bill that was enacted into law in the teeth of a strong, united opposition.

Rift between the Congress and the League

The détente between the Congress and Muslim League was fragile and did not last long. The support temporarily extended by Congress to separate electorates, under the Lucknow Pact, went against the essential ethos of the Congress. Consequently, it was only a matter of time before the party reverted to its earlier stand of opposing separate electorates.

Moplah Rebellion

At this time, the Moplah Rebellion also dealt a grievous blow to the Hindu-Muslim alliance. Moplahs were poor peasants and fishermen and were descendants of Arab settlers living on the Malabar Coast of South India. There had been a history of clashes between the Moplahs and the authorities as well as the prosperous Hindu landlords and moneylenders. They arose in revolt in August 1921. They killed a few Europeans. But their wrath was mainly focused on the Hindus, many of whom were forcibly converted to Islam, their women raped, temples desecrated and properties looted. The rebellion was brought under control by military action but not before it had adversely impacted the relations between Hindus and Muslims.

Non-Cooperation Movement and Mahatma Gandhi

The non-cooperation movement was launched by the Khilafatists under Mahatma Gandhi's leadership in 1920. Initially, it was embraced by the Muslims, although a section of the leadership of the Congress including veterans such as C.R. Das, Bipin Chandra Pal, Annie Besant, Madan Mohan Malaviya and Jinnah opposed it. Nevertheless, Gandhi's word carried the day and it was adopted by the Congress which met in a special session at Calcutta on 4 September 1920. The adoption of the resolution supporting the non-cooperation movement by the Congress was finally confirmed in the annual session at Nagpur in December 1920.

Another important resolution passed at the Nagpur session called for the establishment of Swaraj within one year. Inter alia, it also called for the advancement of Hindu-Muslim unity, abolition of untouchability and reform of Hinduism regarding its treatment of the suppressed classes.

Jinnah, now the president of the Muslim League, started distancing himself from the non-cooperation movement. He was critical of various aspects of the movement such as the boycott of foreign goods, boycott of the councils and also the measures outlined by Gandhi to paralyze the foreign government. When the non-cooperation resolution of the Calcutta special session was confirmed at the Nagpur session, Jinnah spoke out against it. He was heckled and he left the meeting in protest.

Interestingly, however, a Muslim League session convened immediately after the Congress session, and presided over by the veteran Congress leader M.A. Ansari, passed a resolution supporting non-cooperation which echoed the Nagpur Congress resolution in several respects. At this time Jinnah seemed to be isolated as neither the Congress nor the Muslim League appeared to go along with his views. Prominent Muslim nationalists such as the Ali brothers, Abul Kalam Azad, M.A. Ansari, Kichlew and Hasrat Mohani, all came out in support of Mahatma Gandhi and against the British Raj.

Civil Disobedience

The non-cooperation movement was further intensified when Mahatma Gandhi decided to embark upon civil disobedience, unless certain demands, including the freeing of all the non-cooperating prisoners, were met. The viceroy rejected these demands and Mahatma Gandhi left for Bardoli in Gujarat to personally lead the movement. On 4 February 1922, however, the Chauri Chaura tragedy occurred, in which a few policemen were killed by angry protestors, among whom a few people had been killed by the police during the protest. Mahatma Gandhi immediately suspended the civil disobedience movement. This decision left the followers of Gandhi, both Hindus and Muslims, bewildered and eroded the Hindu-Muslim unity that had been forged during the Khilafat and non-cooperation movements.

MOHAMMAD ALI JINNAH

Disillusioned with politics, for some time Jinnah removed himself from the centre of politics and settled in the UK to practise law. After a few years he was persuaded to return, primarily at the instance of Liaqat Ali Khan. After Jinnah returned to India in April 1934, the Muslim League unanimously made him its permanent president. In October 1934, while he was in London, Jinnah was elected to the central assembly (in New Delhi) by the Muslims of Bombay. He attended the assembly session in February 1935. Jinnah now transformed himself from being the 'ambassador of Hindu-Muslim unity' to a hardliner who would have no truck with the Congress. In time, rather than separate electorates, he began to stridently demand a separate homeland for the Muslims and a partition of the country.

Jinnah became the unquestioned leader of Muslims in their quest for Pakistan, an Islamic country exclusively for Muslims. His persona had undergone a transformation and the ambassador of Hindu-Muslim unity had reinvented himself as a defender of Islam and of Muslim interests. It is ironical that a person who was not a practising Muslim and enjoyed his peg of whisky donned the mantle of a defender of the faith.

Incidentally, it was the earlier persona of Jinnah, when he had broadly supported the Congress ideology, that had impelled L.K. Advani to controversially certify Jinnah's secular credentials, when he visited Jinnah's mausoleum in Pakistan. Jinnah, however, did not remain 'secular' for long and later in his political career, transformed himself into a champion of Muslim separatism.

That the ideological evolution of Jinnah from a secular nationalist to an Islamic fundamentalist runs almost parallel to the course of our independence movement, and that he shifted his focus from participating in a united struggle against the British Raj to the partition of India, is one of the quirks of our modern history.

In the 1930s, certain actions of the Congress were also responsible for a majority of Muslims drifting away from it and from the mainstream nationalist movement against British rule. Through the elections held in 1937, Congress came to power in the provinces. Unfortunately, it was short-sighted enough not to give Muslims a visible share in the ministries. As a result, Congress rule came to be regarded as a Hindu rule by a majority of the Muslims. To quote Rajmohan Gandhi:

> Congress's inability to speak in an Indian rather than a Hindu idiom gave a fillip to separatism. Most members elected in the elections of 1937 belonged to Congress; most Congress ministers were Hindus; deliberately or unconsciously, they presented their Hindu face. The fasts of their guide, the Mahatma, his use of the term Ram Rajya for the ideal society of the future, the description by some ministers of schools as temples of learning, the singing, at government functions, of songs that were patriotic to the Hindus but sounded Hindu to the *qaum's* ear, and the use by ministers of Sanskritized Hindi – these were part of a Hindu idiom that lent some credibility to the League's cry of Hindu rule.[3]

ABUL KALAM AZAD

Islam in India evolved in two forms: syncretic and exclusivist. Syncretic Islam merged itself with existing Indian culture and contributed to it. Although in his personal life and beliefs Jinnah always remained ambivalent, in the run-up to the Partition he became a standard-bearer of exclusivist Islam. Congress, on the other hand, continued to claim the loyalty of many Muslim stalwarts who believed in the syncretic version of Islam. No one exemplifies this facet better than Abul Kalam Azad.

Azad was a Qur'anic scholar, well-versed in the scriptures and a powerful orator. He started the paper *Al Hilal* that commanded a wide readership and influence. The paper preached pure Islam and Indian independence simultaneously. Azad's magnum opus, *Tarjuman*, was a translation of and commentary on eighteen of the Qur'an's thirty chapters. He found the Qur'anic concept comprehensive enough to include all forms of monotheism and Hindus too had a place in his interpretation of Qur'anic injunctions.

Al Hilal, a medium through which Azad gave expression to his beliefs carried this significant passage on 1 January 1913:

> Islam does not command narrow-mindedness and racial and religious prejudice. It does not make the recognition of merit and virtue, of human benevolence, mercy and love dependent upon and subject to distinctions of religion and race. It teaches us to respect every man who is good, whatever his religion.[4]

No one can doubt Azad's commitment to Hindu-Muslim unity which is reflected in the following words:

> If an angel descends from the heavens today and proclaims from the Qutb Minar that India can attain Swaraj within 24 hours provided I relinquish my demand for Hindu-Muslim unity, I shall retort to it: No my friend, I shall give up Swaraj, but not Hindu-Muslim unity, for if Swaraj is delayed, it will be a loss for India, but if Hindu-Muslim unity is lost, it will be a loss for the whole of mankind.[5]

The following stirring passage from Abul Kalam Azad's speech, as the president of the Indian National Congress in 1940, is worth quoting:

> I am a Muslim and proud of that fact, Islam's splendid traditions of thirteen hundred years are my inheritance ... In addition, I am proud of being an Indian. I am part of the indivisible unity that is Indian nationality. ... It was India's historic destiny that many human races and cultures and religious faiths should flow to her, and that many a caravan should find rest here ... One of the last of these caravans was that of the followers of Islam ... We brought our treasures with us, and India too was full of the riches of her own precious heritage ... Full eleven centuries have passed by since then. Islam has now as great a claim on the soil of India as Hinduism. If Hinduism has been the religion of the people here for several thousand years, Islam has also been their religion for a thousand years. Just as a Hindu can say with pride that he is an Indian and follows Hinduism, so also we can say with equal pride that we are Indians and follow Islam. I shall enlarge this orbit still further. The Indian Christian is equally entitled to say with pride that he is an Indian and is following a religion of India, namely Christianity.
>
> Eleven hundred years of common history have enriched India with our common achievement. Our languages, our poetry, our literature, our culture, our art, our dress, our manners and customs, the innumerable happenings of our daily life, everything bears the stamp of our joint endeavour. There is indeed no aspect of our life which has escaped this stamp ...
>
> The joint wealth is the heritage of common nationality and we do not want to leave it and go back to the times when this joint life had not begun.[6]

The personalities of Jinnah and Azad present interesting studies in contrast. The former, epicurean in his personal tastes, became the undisputed leader of Muslims pressing for vivisection of the country. Azad, religious in his personal life, closely following the tenets of Islam, was a truly secular nationalist with an abiding commitment to Hindu-Muslim unity.

Despite all the efforts of Azad and like-minded Muslims, the onward march of exclusivist Islamic forces could not be halted and inexorably led to the partition of India. No doubt, as we have seen, short-sighted actions of the Congress leadership were also responsible for a majority of the Muslims leaning in favour of dividing the country.

OUTCOME OF THE RIFT

Early in 1946, elections were held to the various provincial assemblies. In the campaign leading to the elections the Congress asked for votes for its programme promising land reforms, workers' rights, etc. But the Muslim League made it a referendum on the question of Pakistan. The results of the elections showed how the majority of the Muslims had veered round to the separatist idea. While the Congress did very well in the seats in the general category, the Muslim seats were swept by the League. In Bengal, the League won 114 out of 119 seats reserved for Muslims. In the United Province the League won 54 of the 66 Muslim seats. In the province of Madras the League won all 29 seats reserved for Muslims. Overall in the general constituencies the Congress won 80.9 per cent of the votes, whereas in the seats reserved for Muslims the League secured 74.7 per cent.[7]

COMMUNAL RIOTS

Going back in time, we have seen how the Moplah Rebellion of 1921 triggered the disaffection between the Hindu and Muslim communities. This was followed by Hindu-Muslim riots erupting at several places. In 1923, severe rioting took place in Bengal and Punjab. At this juncture two Hindu and two Muslim communal movements also came into being. The Hindu movements were designated as *sangathan* (or simply, organization), which promoted a physical culture so that the community could come together and fight effectively during communal trouble, and *shuddhi* (or purification), which was a plan to re-convert Muslims into Hinduism. The corresponding Muslim movements were known as *tanzim* (organization) and *tabligh* (missionary effort).

These developments ran counter to the efforts of secular nationalists, although many Hindus and Muslims forged and retained the unity in the struggle against British rule. The year 1924 also witnessed communal riots breaking out in several places including Delhi, Gulbarga, Lucknow, Shahjahanpur, Jabalpur and Kohat. The following year of 1925 witnessed sixteen communal riots at various places, once again including Delhi, Aligarh and Calcutta. Large number of persons, both Hindus and Muslims, were killed in these riots. Communal riots continued on a fairly substantial scale in the following years up to 1929. In fact, there were hundreds of such riots during these years and they became an endemic feature in pre-independent India at the time of the freedom struggle.

The most violent and large-scale of such Hindu-Muslim riots of course took place immediately before and after Partition, when hundreds of thousands were killed on both sides of the newly demarcated border. The administration was often a helpless spectator to the ongoing carnage, and Mahatma Gandhi undertook fasts, on more than one occasion, to restore sanity, albeit without complete success.

The proximate cause of these riots, again, was usually an offence caused by one community towards the other while celebrating some festival, but they were representative of a deeper malaise that had begun to affect harmonious relations between the two major communities nearly three decades before.

COMMUNALISM VIS-À-VIS FUNDAMENTALISM

Muslim communalism in India virtually became extinct after the partition of the country. This can possibly be countered by citing the numerous Hindu-Muslim riots that have taken place since Independence and particularly since 1961, which was the year of the resurgence of communal outbreaks in India, subsequent to the pre- and post-Partition violence. I will, however, argue that the riots in the post-Independence period cannot be ascribed to any rise of Muslim communalism. In fact, in most such riots, Muslims were the victims and the disturbances have at times even been classified as 'pogroms' against them, rather than as riots. The Gujarat riots of 2002 are a case in point.

Muslim communalism is not to be confused with or equated to Islamic fundamentalism that has its fallout in terms of terrorist and militant activities. The rise of Islamic fundamentalism, especially in the aftermath of the events of 9/11, and the Afghanistan and Iraq wars, is the focus of worldwide attention and India too, has been subjected to acts of terror. This has been dealt with in an earlier chapter but the point to be made here is that Islamic fundamentalism, related to pan-Islamic causes, is a phenomenon which is quite distinct from Muslim communalism as a competing ideology to Hindutva within the territory of India.

Muslim communalism, as it existed before Independence in India, does not exist any more. Still, some elements who constitute a very small minority among Muslims do take up sectarian issues and, therefore, can be labelled communal. But their impact on the public discourse is negligible. However, its counterpart, Hindu nationalism, or Hindutva, does exist in full force and is worth examining in detail.

NOTES

1 Burke and Quraishi, *The British Raj in India*, pp. 126-127.
2 Ibid., p. 164.
3 Rajmohan Gandhi, *Understanding the Muslim Mind* (New Delhi: Oxford, 2000), p. 313.
4 Ibid., p. 223.
5 Ibid., p.230.
6 Varshney, *Ethnic Conflict and Civic Life*, p. 67.
7 Ramachandra Guha, *India After Gandhi: The History of the World's Largest Democracy* (New Delhi: Picador, 2007), p. 29.

Religious Nationalism and Hindutva

In the pre-Independence period there was tough contestation between secular nationalism, represented in the political arena by the Indian National Congress and Muslim nationalism represented by the Muslim League. Hindu nationalism, on the other hand, given the name 'Hindutva' by V.D. Savarkar, did not gain much political salience in the pre-Independence period. Although the Akhil Bharatiya Hindu Mahasabha had come into existence, it had minimal following. The Hindu nationalists did not play any significant role in the freedom movement against the British. In fact, they have sometimes been accused of collaborating with the British rulers.

Hindu nationalists believe that being in the majority, Hindus must have primacy in the cultural and political life of India. Their culture should be treated as the mainstream culture of the nation. After Independence, although the votaries of Hindutva cast themselves in an ideologically adversarial role to secular nationalists, it took them forty years to carve out any significant space in the political consciousness of most Indians. In the first few decades after India became independent, the Congress, which had led the freedom movement and was committed to secularism, remained the dominant force in our polity. Hindu nationalism really gained salience when the movement around the building of the Ram temple at Ayodhya, described later in this chapter, gathered momentum in the 1980s.

Since the ideologies of secular nationalism and Hindutva have been competing to garner political space, this has come in the way of establishment of harmonious relations between Hindu and Muslim communities in India. Tensions between the two communities have been kept alive, particularly in the northern and western parts of the country, resulting in outbreaks of communal violence from time to time. This context makes it relevant to trace the evolution of Hindu nationalism in the country, both as an ideology and as a vehicle for gaining political salience.

EVOLUTION OF HINDU NATIONALISM AS AN IDEOLOGY

The term 'Hindu' is derived from the name of river Indus or Sindhu and was used successively by the Greeks and the Muslims to refer to the people living beyond the river Indus. The people, however, did not refer to themselves as Hindus till the medieval period.

Invaders who came to India before the Muslims were assimilated into its indigenous culture. An example is that of the Huns, who are now known as Kshatriyas. They adopted caste-related practices and recognized the authority of the Brahmins. The believers of Islam, however, resisted such assimilation. They were unwilling to modify their religious practices and were prepared to clash with the indigenous people on these issues. This antagonism contributed to the emergence of Hindu consciousness.

Hinduism is not a revealed religion and does not have any Book, like the Bible or the Qur'an, as a common reference point. What is called Hindu philosophy is not just one school of thought, it is a compendium of many systems of thought, recognizing and advocating divergent images of society and many different schemes of values.[1]

For the first time in history, an ecclesiastical structure was provided to Hinduism by the philosopher Adi Shankara in the eighth century AD. Prior to his emergence, Hindus were divided into many sects which were antagonistic to each other. There were atheists who followed the Mimamsa and Sankhya philosophies. There were numerous theistic sects and even those who rejected the Vedas such as the Charvakas. Shankara unified the theistic sects into a common framework. He stressed on the importance of the Vedas and his teachings had a unifying influence on Hindus.

It was in response to the spread of Buddhism that Shankara set up monasteries in four corners of India – Shringeri in the South, Dwarka in the West, Badri in the North and Puri in the East – headed by *shankaracharyas*, who were ordained to exercise spiritual authority over the followers of what came to be known as Hindu religion.

Inherent to the great tradition of Hinduism is a '... belief in a privileged connection between India and Dharma that underlies the logic of the social system of the *varnas*, which consists of Brahmins (priests and men of learning), Kshatriyas (warriors), Vaishyas (merchants and artisans) and Shudras (the servile castes). In a foundation myth of the Vedas – the basis of the Brahminical Great Tradition – these *varnas* are described as owing their origin to the sacrificial dismemberment of the cosmic Primeval Man, the Virat Purusha, when the Brahmin proceeded from his mouth, the Kshatriya from his arms, the Vaishya from his thighs, and the Shudra from his feet. This division of the social structure into four parts reflects the belief in a correspondence between Hindu society and the totality of the cosmic order'.[2]

With the advent of Muslim rule, Hindu religion and the indigenous culture had to cope with the challenge posed by a proselytizing religion with an egalitarian ethos. British rule brought in its wake Christian missionaries and their growing influence had to be countered as well. Hinduism, with its polytheism and caste system, was denigrated both by the preachers of Islam and Christianity. In this milieu, certain thinkers and reformers emerged who re-interpreted Hindu beliefs and practices so that a reformed version of Hinduism would be fashioned to withstand the challenge posed by the advent of Islam and Christianity.

The first such thinker was the famous Bengali novelist, Bankim Chandra Chattopadhyay, whose writings emphasized that national glory could be regained through the regeneration of culture, a strong nationally organized religion, comprehensive and popular education of the masses and an enlightened readership provided by his own class, the Bengali *bhadrolok* (upper class gentlemen). Bankim's vision aimed at promoting Hindu consciousness and had an anti-Muslim bias.

To meet the challenge of Western influence, the spiritual content of Indians' way of life was posited against the materialism of the West. Foremost among the reformers and thinkers who led the way in promoting Hindu identity in the service of Indian nationalism were Vivekananda, Dayananda, Aurobindo and Savarkar. The historical construct they relied upon depicted that before India was subjugated and enslaved through foreign conquest – first Islamic then Christian – there was a 'golden age' that belonged to the Aryan race.

As per this historical interpretation, the Aryans were the chosen people to whom the formless God revealed the perfect knowledge of the Vedas. In course of time, as a result of the rise of the priestly class, the emergence of Buddhism and Jainism, and the *varna* system degenerating into a pernicious caste system, the essence of the Vedas got diluted and the society moved away from a state of harmony to disarray.

According to Western scholars, the aim of these reformers was both the stigmatization and the emulation of those who threatened Hindu society. Their endeavour was to preserve the basic elements and traditions of Hindu society while adapting the tradition to the modernizing ethos of the West.

Arya Samaj and Swami Dayananda

The Arya Samaj, founded in 1875 in Punjab by Dayananda Saraswati, proved to be the most influential movement that aimed to reform Hindu practices. Born in 1824, Dayananda was a sannyasi from his boyhood days. He was a scholar and translated the Vedas from Sanskrit to Hindi so that common men could read them. He was also a champion of equal rights for women.

The Arya Samaj aimed at doing away with the polytheistic practices, certain aspects of the caste system and many of the popular rituals that had debilitated Hindu religion. The movement simultaneously opposed the activities of Christian missionaries and the spread of Muslim influence in education, language and social life.

Dayananda believed in the divine origin of the Vedas. He described his faith in the Vedas in the following words:

> We believe that the Vedas alone are the supreme authority in the ascertainment of true religion – the true conduct of life. Whatever is enjoined by the Vedas we hold to be right; whilst whatever is condemned by them we believe to be wrong. Therefore, we say that our religion is Vedic. All men, especially the Aryas, should believe in the Vedas and thereby cultivate unity in religion.[3]

Dayananda preferred to call Hinduism the 'Vedic religion'. Dayananda's adherence to the Vedas was absolute and he was opposed to sects and religions such as Jains, Buddhists, Saivites and Vaishnavites, who in his view, perverted the Vedic idea of an abstract omniscient, omnipotent and all-merciful God.

Dayananda also initiated the *shuddhi* (purification) movement that aimed to halt the conversion of Hindus to Islam and Christianity and worked towards reconverting the converts back to Hinduism. Thus, for the first time, Dayananda introduced a proselytizing element into Hinduism.

The programme of the Arya Samaj encompassed the promotion of modern education and the Samaj, in pursuance of this objective, established a system of educational institutions all over North India named the Dayananda Anglo-Vedic (DAV) Colleges. To strengthen cultural nationalism the Arya Samaj also promoted the learning and spread of Sanskrit and Sanskritized Hindi through its publications.

Overall, Dayananda and the Arya Samaj made a significant contribution in promoting Hindu consciousness and cultural nationalism.

Swami Vivekananda

Perhaps the most charismatic figure among the proponents of Hinduism in the early twentieth century was Vivekananda. Swami Vivekananda, as he later came to be known, was born as Narendra Datta on 12 January 1863 in Calcutta. At a young age he came under the influence of Sri Ramakrishna, a mystic who was a priest in the temple of Goddess Kali. In time, he became Sri Ramakrishna's favourite disciple. He travelled throughout the country to preach the message of Vedanta.

His eloquent address at the World Parliament of Religions in Chicago on 11 September 1893 created a 'timeless mystique' around him. Relevant excerpts on the subject of Hinduism are reproduced below:

> I am proud to belong to a religion which has taught the world both tolerance and universal acceptance. We believe not only in universal toleration, but we accept all religions as true. I am proud to belong to a nation which has sheltered the persecuted and the refugees of all religions and all nations of the earth. I am proud to tell you that we have gathered in our bosom the purest remnant of the Israelites, who came to Southern India and took refuge with us in the very year in which their holy temple was shattered to pieces by Roman tyranny. I am proud to belong to the religion which has sheltered and is still fostering the remnant of the grand Zoroastrian nation. ...
>
> The present convention, which is one of the most august assemblies ever held, is in itself a vindication, a declaration to the world of the wonderful doctrine preached in the *Gita*: 'Whosoever comes to Me, through whatsoever form, I reach him; all men are struggling through paths which in the end lead to me.' Sectarianism, bigotry, and its horrible descendant, fanaticism, have long possessed this beautiful earth. They have filled the earth with violence, drenched it often and often with human blood, destroyed civilization

> and sent whole nations to despair. Had it not been for these horrible demons, human society would be far more advanced than it is now. But their time is come; and I fervently hope that the bell that tolled this morning in honour of this convention may be the death-knell of all fanaticism, of all persecutions with the sword or with the pen, and of all uncharitable feelings between persons wending their way to the same goal.

It is an irony of history that this unique message of universal peace and tolerance was delivered exactly, to the day, 108 years before 11 September 2001 (also referred to as 9/11), when world peace was rudely shattered by the brutal *fidayeen* attacks on the twin towers of the World Trade Centre at New York.

Vivekananda had also presented a paper on Hinduism at the Parliament of Religions. His words and persona captured the imagination of not only the gathering present but, by extension, of the entire Western civilized world. Sister Nivedita was moved enough to describe the general import of his address at the Parliament in these words: 'when he began to speak, it was of the religious ideas of the Hindus; but when he ended, Hinduism had been created. …'[4]

Vivekananda emphasized the spiritual superiority of Hinduism over other philosophical systems. He believed that the Vedas were the only force that had the capacity to unify all sects within Hinduism. He called them the scriptures of the Hindus. He rejected the Puranas because he believed that they were produced by men of limited intelligence, full of errors, fallacies and feelings of class and malaise.

Although Vivekananda had reservations about the doctrinaire nature of Islam he also recognized that it had shown the way towards a practical ideal of brotherhood and equality. In his words:

> For our own motherland a junction of the two great systems, Hinduism and Islam – Vedanta brain and Islam body – is the only hope. I see in my mind's eye the future perfect India rising out of this chaos and strife, glorious and invincible, with Vedanta brain and Islam body.[5]

It must be noted that while Vivekananda emphasized toleration he believed in the inherent superiority of the Vedic system of belief that for him was the 'mother of all religions'.

Dayananda and Vivekananda were men of religion who sought to reform Hindu society and reinstate the true traditions of Hinduism, which had been defiled, to some extent, by practices and rituals that were later accretions. They represent a broad capacious view of Hinduism which eschews bigotry.

Vinayak Damodar Savarkar

V.D. Savarkar, born on 26 May 1883, was the progenitor of the nationalist political ideology of Hindutva. He was commonly addressed as 'Veer' (meaning 'brave') Savarkar by his followers. He believed in gaining independence from the British through revolutionary means. In 1910, he was arrested for being associated with violent revolutionary groups and was imprisoned in the Cellular Jail in the Andaman and Nicobar Islands.

Although Savarkar was not a practising Hindu – he did not observe religious rituals in his personal life – more than any other person, he politicized religion and pursued the objective of establishing India as a Hindu nation with single-minded determination. While he was part of the nationalist movement, he gave priority to the creation of a 'Hindu *rashtra*' (Hindu nation) which was more important to him than independence from the British Raj.

Savarkar was greatly influenced by the writings of Giuseppe Mazzini, the Italian patriot and revolutionary. 'In Mazzini, Savarkar found an ideological framework and a political philosophy that combined cultural pride and national self-assertion with a modernist outlook and a vision of a strong, culturally homogenous nation embodied by a unitary state'.[6]

Savarkar's antagonism towards Islam and Muslims is evident from his writings. He articulated his views on Hindu nationalism in his work *Hindutva*. Central to his beliefs is the averment, 'Every person is a Hindu who regards and owns this Bharat Bhoomi – this land from the Indus to the seas as his Fatherland (*pitrabhu*) and Holy land (*punyabhu*) – the land of origin of his religion and cradle of his faith'.[7]

It is clear from this formulation that while Sikhs and Jains were to be treated as Hindus, Christians, Muslims or for that matter, even Parsis and Jews could not be a part of Hinduism since their 'holy land' was situated outside the territory of India.

That Savarkar could not accept Muslims as a part of the indigenous mainstream culture is clear from the following view: '...

their holy land is far off in Arabia or Palestine. Their mythology and godmen, ideas and heroes are not the children of this soil. Consequently their names and their outlook smack of foreign origin'.[8] Savarkar also emphasized the ethnic and racial substance of the Hindu nation thus:

> The Hindus are not merely the citizens of the Indian state because they are united not only by the bonds of the love they bear to a common motherland but also by the bonds of a common blood. They are not only a nation but race-*jati*. The word *jati*, derived from the root *jan*, to produce, means a brotherhood, a race determined by a common origin, possessing a common blood. All Hindus claim to have in their veins the blood of the mighty race incorporated with and descended from the Vedic fathers.[9]

Savarkar was the president of the Hindu Mahasabha from 1937 to 1942. His tenure in this office was largely coterminous with the period of the Second World War. In this period he seems to have been influenced, to a considerable extent, by the Nazi ideology, particularly with regard to dealing with Muslims in India. He drew parallels between the status of Jews in Germany with that of Muslims in India. In his speech, in the 21st session of the Hindu Mahasabha in 1939, he made an explicit comparison between the Muslim question in India and the Jewish 'problem' in Germany in the following words:

> ... the Indian Muslims are on the whole more inclined to identify themselves and their interests with Muslims outside India than Hindus who live next door, like Jews in Germany.[10]

Adapting the classical tenets of cultural nationalism, Savarkar focused on four of these to define the boundaries of Hindu nationalism. The first was the primacy of territory, which in this case was the civilization developed through millennia on the eastern side of the river Indus. This covered the entire Indian subcontinent. The second element was the notion of antiquity and emotional attachment to the name of the nation known as 'Hindustan'. The third element was the unity of language as the central carrier of cultural essence and feeling that for Savarkar was Sanskrit in earlier times and Hindi in modern times. The fourth element was that of shared blood and race.

For Bankim Chandra Chattopadhyay, Vivekananda, Dayananda, etc., Hindu nationalism was confined to the spiritual and cultural domains. With Savarkar, Hindu nationalism took on a more strident anti-Muslim posture and was also transferred to the political domain. But the Hindu Mahasabha remained only a fringe player in the run-up to Indian independence. Whatever prominence it gained in the political arena is attributable, to a large extent, to the efforts of Savarkar and his acolytes.

It would be apposite to look into the historical evolution of some of the national-level Hindutva organizations in India.

The Hindu Mahasabha

The Akhil Bharatiya Hindu Mahasabha (or All-India Hindu Assembly) was founded in 1915 and was set up as a counterpoise to the Muslim League and the secular INC. V.D. Savarkar was its founding president.

A Hindu nationalist organization, it espoused the cause of Hindu nationalists who believed that India should be a Hindu *rashtra*. Shortly after Independence, and subsequent to the assassination of Mahatma Gandhi, the organization was weakened because many of its members joined the Bharatiya Jan Sangh under the leadership of Shyama Prasad Mukherjee.

The Rashtriya Swayamsevak Sangh

The RSS (or National Volunteers Union) was founded in 1925 by Keshav Baliram Hedgewar to promote Hindu nationalist ideology. The purpose was to develop an organization at the grass roots to spread the message. Hedgewar was influenced by Savarkar's conception of the nation. His mentor was B.S. Moonje who was greatly impressed by Mussolini and the Italian version of fascism. It is no surprise that Hedgewar was among the promoters of a campaign in favour of militarization of society according to the fascist model.

In organizing the RSS, he placed emphasis on training and discipline. Akin to terrorist societies, the RSS adopted the military style of training recruits while at the same time emphasizing religiosity. The basic unit of the RSS, the *shakha* (or branch), also had a close affinity with the older institutions such as *akharas* (wrestling arenas). An *akhara* is a place where the young men of a locality gather for doing bodybuilding exercises and sports, such as wrestling and weightlifting. Generally, there is a temple of Lord Hanuman attached to an *akhara* that gives it a spiritual dimension. The RSS *shakha* in certain ways was modelled on the age-old *akharas*.

The core of the RSS comprised *swayamsevaks* (volunteers or those who believe in self-service), who were selected from the youths attending training at the *shakhas*. These *swayamsevaks* 'pledge[d] to consecrate themselves to the RSS with [their] whole body, heart and money, for in it lies the betterment of Hindus and the country'.[11] The religious element was always present inasmuch as the pledge had to be taken before an image of Hanuman.

While Hedgewar was the founder, his successor Madhav Sadashiv Golwalkar was unquestionably the spiritual guru of the RSS. Golwalkar translated a monograph by G.D. Savarkar (elder brother of V.D. Savarkar), 'We or Our Nationhood Defined' into English. He also authored a work called *A Bunch of Thoughts*. The ideological predilections of Golwalkar come through clearly in these two works.

The following two passages from 'We or Our Nationhood Defined' bring out his antipathy towards Muslims and the racist overtones in the conception of Hindu nationhood and nationalism:

> Ever since the evil day when Muslims first landed in Hindustan ... the Hindu Nation has been gallantly fighting on to shake off the despoilers. The Race Spirit has been awakening ... National consciousness blazes forth and we Hindus rally to the Hindu standard, the Bhagwa Dhwaja [which the RSS still raises in preference to the national flag], set our teeth in grim determination to wipe out the opposing forces. We Hindus are at war with the Muslims, on the one hand, and with the British, on the other.
>
> ... as far as the Nation is concerned, all those who fall outside the five-fold limits (earlier defined as geographical, racial, religious, cultural and linguistic) can have no place in the National life unless they abandon their differences and adopt the religion, culture and language of the Nation and completely merge themselves in the National Race ... There are only two courses open to the foreign elements, either to merge themselves in the National Race and adopt its culture, or to live at its mercy so long as the National Race may allow them to do so, and to quit the country at the sweet will of the National Race ... the foreign races in

> Hindustan must either adopt the Hindu culture and language, must learn to respect and hold to reverence (the) Hindu religion, must entertain no idea but those of (the) glorification of the Hindu race and culture, that is, of the Hindu Nation, and must lose their separate existence to merge in the Hindu race; or may stay in the country wholly subordinated to the Hindu Nation, claiming nothing, deserving no privileges, far less any preferential treatment, not even citizens' rights.

In his work, *A Bunch of Thoughts*, Golwalkar targeted and denigrated other religions too, including Buddhism, Judaism and Christianity.

In his conception of a Hindu Rashtra there was no place for the pluralistic and syncretic culture of India. All those who did not belong to the Hindu race, religion, culture and language were out of the pale of national life according to him.

Objectives and Organization of the RSS

Thinkers and reformers like Dayananda and Vivekananda sought to reinvigorate Hinduism by harking back to its glorious past, so that it could hold its own in the face of the challenge posed by the proselytization done by Islam and Christianity. Vivekananda, in particular, emphasized the holistic nature of Hinduism and his attitude towards other religions was not confrontational because, in his conception, there was space for all in Hinduism and in the Indian cultural milieu.

Savarkar and Golwalkar too were revivalists who sought restoration of the values of the 'golden age' of the Vedic civilization. Their conception of Hindu nationalism was, however, much more aggressive and intolerant. It would be fair to describe their view of the status of Hinduism in relation to other religions as hegemonic.

Since the RSS was conceived as the instrument that would translate into reality the Savarkar-Golwalkar conception of the Hindu Rashtra, its objectives had to be defined accordingly and the organization structured suitably to achieve those goals.

The ideals of the RSS have been summed up in its formal constitution thus: 'To eradicate differences among Hindus; to make them realize the greatness of their past; to inculcate in them a spirit of self-sacrifice and self-devotion to Hindu society as a whole; to build up an organized and well-disciplined corporate life; and to bring about the regeneration of Hindu society.'[12]

Generally, the stand taken by the RSS leadership has been that it is not a political or religious body, but a cultural organization. At the same time, the RSS rejects the tenet of secularism embodied in the Indian Constitution that religion is a private matter. It believes that 'we make war or peace, engage in arts and crafts, amass wealth and give it away – indeed we are born and die – all in accord with religious injunctions'.[13]

The task of the RSS is to defend the Hindu nation, the *rashtra* which is distinct from the *raj* or state. The function of the *raj* is to enforce law and order but the *rashtra* encompasses all aspects of culture, viz., language, literature, religion, the arts, territory and race. The word 'Hindu' is used as an *adjective* for culture and not only for religion, which is one of the components of culture.

To elaborate further, the basic task of the RSS is to transform Hinduism that had become degraded and weak. According to certain Western scholars, even as the Hindu nationalists demonized Islam and Christianity as threatening and alien, they sought to emulate these 'muscular' religions to bring greater cohesion and strength to Hinduism. This is the reason why the RSS places great stress on discipline, cultural pride and religiosity.

It has also been said that the mimetic dimension of the RSS is easily identified since one feature of its volunteers' uniform, the khaki shorts, has been borrowed from the British police. Such borrowed features of the RSS coexist with authentic Hindu elements. The RSS aims to spread the network of its *shakhas* throughout India although so far their coverage has been limited to northern and western regions. From small beginnings, the number of *shakhas* has now reached about 25,000 and 31,000 *up-shakhas* (sub-branches). The current membership of the RSS is around two million.[14]

Since the RSS professes to be essentially a cultural organization, in order to reach out to all segments of society, it has spawned other organizations that can be described as its affiliates. These outfits together are often referred to as the Sangh Parivar or the 'family of the Sangh', which is the RSS.

Bharatiya Janata Party

The RSS ostensibly stayed away from politics, that is, from taking part in the democratic process after Independence. Nevertheless, through its cadres, it extended support to like-minded or allied political parties. Before Independence, and for a short span of time afterwards, the Hindu Mahasabha received tacit support from the

RSS. Thereafter, the Jan Sangh (or People's Union), founded by Dr Shyama Prasad Mukherjee in 1951, commanded the loyalty and support of Hindu nationalists. Neither the Hindu Mahasabha nor the Jan Sangh, however, was able to make much of an impact in electoral terms. The number of their members who got elected to state legislatures or to the Lok Sabha were too few to be able to create anything more than a ripple in these legislative bodies.

The political party, with its core ideology of Hindu nationalism, which was finally successful in occupying substantial political space, was the Bharatiya Janata Party (BJP or Indian People's Party), the successor of the erstwhile Jan Sangh. Although it has emerged as a national-level political party, the BJP retains its links with the RSS.

Akhil Bharatiya Vidyarthi Parishad

In 1948, Delhi-based RSS functionaries set up the Akhil Bharatiya Vidyarthi Parishad (ABVP or All-India Students Council). Its objective was to counter the communist influence on university campuses and promote a religious nationalistic outlook among students. With the politicization of student unions, this organization virtually acts as the student wing of the BJP.

Bharatiya Mazdoor Sangh

In 1955, the RSS set up a trade union, the Bharatiya Mazdoor Sangh (Indian Workers' Union). This organization aims to oppose the communist unions and spread the Hindu nationalist ideology among organized workers in the country. It has expanded considerably and is India's largest trade union today.

Vanavasi Kalyan Ashram

In 1952, the RSS founded a tribal welfare movement, the Vanavasi Kalyan Ashram (VKA or Centre for Tribal Welfare). This organization works primarily to counter the influence of Christian missionaries among tribals of Central India, where many conversions have taken place due to the evangelical activities of the missionaries. The VKA has been organizing re-conversions of the tribals to Hinduism.

Vishwa Hindu Parishad

In 1964, the RSS along with some prominent religious figures launched the Vishwa Hindu Parishad (VHP or International Hindu Council). It was founded in the ashram of Swami Chinmayananda. The VHP has been gaining prominence and, unlike the RSS, it has been using all the instruments of modern media to publicize its aims and activities, which are focused on organizing all sects of Hindus to unite against the forces that are perceived as a threat to Hinduism. These are identified as Christianity, Islam and Communism. However, Communism is no longer seen as a threat to the unity and integrity of India; so VHP has been concentrating its attention on the other two religions.

To consolidate its position and expand its activities, the VHP has been making use of three constituencies. Firstly, it has involved the leaders of various Hindu sects and monastic orders, including the widely respected *shankaracharyas* and other religious gurus. The involvement of such religious figures has helped the VHP gain ground as an organization that promotes religious learning and piety in public life. The second constituency of the VHP is the business community and large business houses that have long been patrons of Hindu causes.

The third constituency the VHP has cultivated are the Indian emigrants, particularly in North America and Europe. There has been a campaign to encourage non-resident Indian Hindus to identify themselves not primarily as Indians, but specifically as Hindus. As a result, the largely successful Indian (Hindu) diaspora abroad has come forward generously to finance the activities of the Sangh Parivar, particularly those of the VHP. The India Development and Relief Fund (IDRF), a Maryland-based charity organization established in 1989, has been a key fundraiser for the Sangh Parivar in the US. The IDRF has been accused by groups in the US and India of financing the RSS and the VHP to support the violence against Muslims in Gujarat, especially during the Gujarat riots in 2002.[15]

Bajrang Dal

An offshoot of the VHP, the Bajrang Dal (or Hanuman's Army) was founded in 1984 by an RSS *pracharak* (campaigner), V. Katiyar. It comprises youthful militants, who are believed to have taken an active part in the demolition of the Babri Masjid in 1992. The Bajrang Dal represents an aggressive and militant brand of Hindutva and is alleged to be behind numerous incidents of outbreak of communal violence.

The Sangh Parivar's conception of Hindutva is well summed up in D.R. Goyal's authoritative history of the RSS:[16]

> Hindus have lived in India since times immemorial; Hindus are the nation because all culture, civilization and life is

contributed by them alone; non-Hindus are invaders or guests and cannot be treated as equal unless they adopt Hindu traditions, culture etc.; the non-Hindus, particularly Muslims and Christians, have been enemies of everything Hindu and are, therefore, to be treated as threats; the freedom and progress of this country is the freedom and progress of Hindus; the history of India is the history of the struggle of the Hindus for protection and preservation of their religion and culture against the onslaught of these aliens; the threat continues because the power is in the hands of those who do not believe in this nation as a Hindu Nation; those who talk of national unity as the unity of all those who live in this country are motivated by the selfish desire of cornering minority votes and are therefore traitors; the unity and consolidation of the Hindus is the dire need of the hour because the Hindu people are surrounded on all sides by enemies; the Hindus must develop the capacity for massive retaliation and offence is the best defence; lack of unity is the root cause of all the troubles of the Hindus and the Sangh is born with the divine mission to bring about that unity.

HINDUISM – THE ECLECTIC VIEW

The early reformer, Vivekananda represented, quintessentially, the eclectic view of Hinduism. As one who believes in this approach I too take pride in the fact that Hinduism is unique in that it is the only major religion in the world that does not claim to be the only true religion. It is also the one religion with the self-confidence to know that 'Truth is not revealed in an instant or in a flash but evolves through a long process of absorption, assimilation and synthesis'.[17]

The essence of this vision is encompassed in the Sanskrit credo '*Sarva Dharma Sambhava*', that is, all religions are worthy of respect. The liberal broad-minded Hindu cannot be a 'fundamentalist' because there are no 'fundamentals' in his religion. He willingly accepts the tenets and practices of other religions that are part of India's civilizational heritage through the ages, be it Buddhism, Jainism, Judaism, Zoroastrianism, Christianity, Islam or the youngest of them all, Sikhism.

This capacious view of Hinduism is well-contrasted with the narrow sectarianism of the protagonists of Hindutva, which began to be formulated by the likes of V.D. Savarkar and was followed up by K.B. Hedgewar and M.S. Golwalkar. It is summed up in the following words of Amartya Sen:

> Not for them the sophistication of the Upanishads or *Gita*, or of Brahmagupta or Sankara, or of Kalidasa or Sudraka; they prefer the adoration of Ram's idol and Hanuman's image. Their nationalism also ignores the rationalist traditions of India, a country in which some of the earliest steps in algebra, geometry, and astronomy were taken, where the decimal system emerged, where early philosophy – secular as well as religious – achieved exceptional sophistication, where people invented games like chess, pioneered sex education, and began the first systematic study of political economy. The Hindu militant chooses instead to present India – explicitly or implicitly – as a country of unquestioning idolaters, delirious fanatics, belligerent devotees, and religious murderers.[18]

EVOLUTION OF HINDU NATIONALISM AS A POLITICAL FORCE

The rise of the BJP to political prominence has been remarkable. In the Lok Sabha in 1984 it had just two seats. In 1989 it increased its tally to eighty-five seats and in 1991 to 119 seats. In the 1998 and 1999 elections it garnered 182 seats and assumed power at the centre along with its allies that formed the National Democratic Alliance or the NDA. After completing a full term in office, it lost to the United Progressive Alliance (UPA), headed by the Congress, successively in the 2004 and then in the 2009 general elections.

However, the BJP continues to be the principal Opposition party in Parliament and rules in several states, including Gujarat and Himachal Pradesh, where it won the assembly elections in 2007 with comfortable majorities. While the BJP claims its successes to be the result of its developmental agenda, there is little doubt that its ascent to prominence in the political domain is due considerably to the communalization of politics and the consequential polarization, from time to time, of the Hindu vote in its favour.

The BJP has been the beneficiary of systematic political mobilization around certain sensitive issues that were initiated and sustained over a period of time by the Sangh Parivar. We shall now trace the course of these developments that have been responsible for the political ethos of the country having shifted from the broad secular consensus, which prevailed in the political sphere for about two decades after Independence, to the changed scenario of contention for political space between parties professing secular and Hindu nationalist ideologies.

Hindutva and History

When the BJP-led coalitions came to power after the 1998 and 1999 elections, the National Council of Educational Research and Training (NCERT) was given the task of producing new textbooks for Indian schools that would not carry certain sections in the existing books which had been written by reputed historians. It appears that the objective was to make schoolchildren learn history from a Hindu nationalist perspective. Amartya Sen in his book, *The Argumentative Indian*, has recounted in detail how two scholars even resorted to subterfuge to distort historical facts in their publication. Below is a synoptic version of Sen's account of the episode.[19]

In order to show that Hindus alone had a right to India's civilizational heritage, it became necessary for the Hindu nationalists to claim greater antiquity for the Sanskritic culture of India than was warranted by an objective evaluation of historical facts and events. The Indus Valley Civilization, dating from the third millennium BC, was in existence well before the time of the earliest Hindu literature, the Vedas, which are dated at the second millennium BC. The civilization flourished in a large part of the area covered under the north-west of the undivided subcontinent. This was around the same time when the Egyptian and Mesopotamian civilizations were reaching their apogee in another part of the world.

The undoubted antiquity of the Indus Valley Civilization is a matter of national pride for Indians. But the fact that Indo-Europeans (Aryans) had arrived (migrated) from the West to India, riding on horses, speaking in what is now called Vedic Sanskrit, did not suit the Hindu nationalists. The imaginative creators of the Hindutva version of history wished to trace the origin of Indian civilization to the Vedas. They were confronted with two problems: the first of having to accept that the foundational basis of Hindu culture came originally from outside India; and, second, in not being able to place Hinduism at the very beginning of India's cultural history and its urban heritage.

The relics of the Indus Valley Civilization show the presence of bulls but not horses. The Vedas, on the other hand, carry numerous references to horses. As the creed of Hindutva has considerable following in the Indian diaspora, two non-resident Indian (NRI) historians, Natwar Jha and N.S. Rajaram published a book titled *The Deciphered Indus Script* (New Delhi: Aditya Prakashan, 2000), in which they produced a picture of a terracotta seal with a horse on it. This was presented as a proof of the Vedic identity of the Indus Civilization, which was labelled the 'Indus-Saraswati' civilization.

This claim led to vigorous debate both within and outside the academia. Eventually, it was demonstrated that the picture of the horse seal was the result of a simple fraud based on a computerized distortion of the image of a broken seal of a unicorn bull. The definitive demonstration of the fraud (perpetrated as late as at the end of the twentieth century!) came from Michael Witzel, professor of Sanskrit at Harvard University, in a joint essay with Steve Farmer: 'Horseplay in Harappa'. The two NRI historians were thus ridiculed and disregarded in the mainstream arena of historical debate.

Communalization of Festivals

Certain sectarian activities are considered legitimate so long as those exposed to such activities belong exclusively to the concerned community. These activities can become exceptionable once they cross the thin dividing line and enter into the arena of public discourse. In the words of a social scientist:

> ... a cultural organization may in principle hold any sectarian view as long as it only claims to be true for its own limited constituency and community. However, if it ventures to move into the realm of public politics, where the nation must be represented within the parameters of the authorized discourse of a single composite culture, sectarian utterances will appear as communal. Obvious examples are religious processions and festivals that celebrate a particular god, mythology, or religious ritual without being perceived as communal. The moment a song, symbol, or imagery employed on such an occasion comments upon political events, or recommends that the particular values of the community be the basis of political decisions, or a religious symbol is displayed and invoked at a political rally, the thin line separating secular and communal politics may be crossed. So what signifies communalism in the political part of the public realm may well pass for culture in another part of the public realm ...[20]

The public celebration of festivals, both by Hindus and Muslims, has long been creating tension and rift between the two communities. When religious processions are directed through a certain route in a town or city – usually in a locality with a sizeable population of the other community – they often lead to communal flare-ups. These are not merely celebrations but are done with a view to antagonize the other community and engender hostility.

Much before Independence, political leaders had envisioned the benefits to be gained from mobilization by displaying religious symbols at public places or functions. Way back in 1893, Bal Gangadhar Tilak gave a nationalist flavour to an old religious event, the Ganesh Chaturthi (or Ganpati festival), by reorganizing and celebrating it as a popular *mela* (fair) with processions, lectures and songs. Regarding the celebration of this festival, the following observation was made in the 1918 report of the Sedition Committee presided over by Justice Rowlatt:

> Public Ganpati festivals appear to have arisen out of an anti-Mohammadan movement after which riots broke out in the city of Bombay in 1893 between Hindus and Mohammadans. Agitators who were interested in widening the breach between these two communities encouraged the holding of public celebrations in honour of Ganpati, the elephant-headed god of wisdom and success, on a much larger scale than in previous years. The idea appears to have been to make the procession in which the god is carried to his final resting-place in the water as offensive as possible to Mohammadans. During the ten days' celebrations of the festival, bands of young men paraded the streets of Poona, singing verses calculated to intensify the feeling against Mohammadans and Government.[21]

Similarly, in 1895, a Shivaji festival was celebrated with great pomp at Raigarh which has been Shivaji's capital. The public processions featured volunteers displaying their skill in fencing and nationalist sentiments were roused through religious and patriotic songs.[22]

In later chapters on certain incidents of communal riots, I have demonstrated how religious processions lead to tension between Hindus and Muslims. Some of these processions are indeed taken out with the malicious intent of creating trouble. The Hindu right wing has benefited politically from such events by strengthening its Hindu vote bank.

Cow-protection Movement

The cow has always been treated as a sacred animal in Hindu religion and mythology, therefore the demand for a ban on cow slaughter has often been a rallying cry for Hindus to unite. In searching for an issue to urge the Hindu youth to sacrifice their all, M.S. Golwalkar declared, 'Such a point of honour in our national life is none else but MOTHER COW, the living symbol of the Mother Earth – that deserves to be the sole object of devotion and worship. To stop forthwith any onslaught on this particular point of our national honour, and to foster the spirit of devotion to the motherland, [a] ban on cow-slaughter should find topmost priority in our programme of national renaissance in Swaraj.'[23] In the cow, Golwalkar found a symbol to unite Hindus who were otherwise divided by caste, sect, language and region.

Cows are revered by most Hindus, especially in North India, but Christians and Muslims cook them for food. The RSS, therefore, conceived a nationwide campaign to unite the Hindus and simultaneously target Muslims and Christians by demanding a ban on cow slaughter. Fourteen years after Golwalkar wrote the article in 1952, from which his words have been quoted, a large crowd marched to the Parliament in Delhi demanding ban on cow slaughter and creating considerable mayhem.

Cow slaughter is indeed banned in certain states and the demand is raised, from time to time, for purposes of political mobilization of Hindus, to impose a total ban throughout the country. However, the movement has met only with limited success in terms of the political mileage it gained for Hindu nationalists.

Ekatmata Yatra/Yajna

We have seen that processions have since long been used as an organizing device for promoting Hindu consciousness. In November-December 1983 the VHP, with its RSS cadres, took a major initiative in organizing a month-long Ekatmata Yatra/Yajna (journey/religious sacrifice for national unity). It had two objectives: firstly, to give a dramatic demonstration of all-India Hindu solidarity with the message that *Bharatiya* (endemic Indian) culture was the key to India's national integration; and secondly, to raise funds for missionary work among tribals and to 'win back' those who had been converted to Islam or Christianity.

The event comprised three main *yatras* (journeys). Two crossed India from North to South connecting certain sacred spots such as the river Ganga at Haridwar, Kanyakumari and Rameshwaram. The third crossed India from East to West from Gangasagar on the Bay of Bengal to the temple at Somnath on the coast of the Arabian Sea. En route these *yatras* were joined by numerous local processions – an estimated 2,000 in all.

The activities during the *yatras* relied heavily on religious symbolism, such as collecting water from all the sacred rivers, lakes, tanks and wells and distributing the Ganga water the processionists were carrying at the stoppage points on the route. The slogans the processionists shouted were full of religious significance for Hindus, exhorting them to be united, thereby excluding the non-Hindus from their project of national integration.

Shah Bano Controversy

A broad outline of the controversy relating to the *Shah Bano* case has been covered in the chapter on Uniform Civil Code. The negation of the judgement of the Supreme Court in this case through the enactment of the Muslim Women (Protection of Rights on Divorce) Bill in Parliament in May 1986, was interpreted as an act of 'appeasement' of Muslims by the Hindu right.

The controversy was exploited by the RSP-VHP-BJP combine that criticized the ruling party of playing 'vote bank' politics. It also gave fresh impetus to the call of Hindu nationalists for a Uniform Civil Code, especially for imposing on Muslims, which now found greater resonance among the people because of the manner in which the controversy had been handled.

The Legend of Ram and the Ayodhya Movement

The centrepiece around which the Ayodhya movement has been built is the legend of Ram, who is the protagonist of Valmiki's epic, *Ramayana*. There are many versions of the Ram legend and in not all of them has Ram been deified. The historicity of Ram has been a subject of persistent, though not always well-informed, debate.

Hindu nationalists who have thrust the issue into the public domain and made it a subject of agitational politics, would have it that Ram is an incarnation of Lord Vishnu who was born at a well-identified spot, 900 millennia ago, exactly where the Babri Masjid (now demolished) stands in Ayodhya in UP. Hence, the avowed aim of the Hindu nationalists is to build a magnificent temple of Ram at this spot, where it is claimed the original temple stood that was demolished by Babar to build the mosque.

The issue whether a temple did indeed exist at the site that was demolished has not been settled. The matter has even been referred to the judiciary, though such a question of historical authentication, involving history, archaeology and mythology, can hardly be decided through a judicial pronouncement.

On the subject of the historicity of Ram, Rabindranath Tagore had said that the story of the *Ramayana* is not to be interpreted as a matter of historical fact, but in the plane of ideas as a marvellous parable of reconciliation.[24] And the following tribute to Ram was paid by Dr Allama Iqbal:

> *Hai Ram ke wajood pe Hindustan ko naaz*
> *Ahl-e-nazar samajhte hain usko Imame-Hind;*
> *Ezaaz ous chiraag-e-hidaayet kaa hai yaha hee*
> *Ranshantar azsaher hai zamane mein sham-e-Hind.*
> (India is rightfully proud of the existence of Ram. The farsighted see him as the spiritual leader of India. The miracle of the Guiding Star is to be seen in the fact that brighter are Indian evenings than mornings elsewhere).[25]

Thus, two of undivided India's greatest poets in the twentieth century, one of them a Muslim, underlined that Ram is unquestionably a part of our common civilizational heritage. It is indeed a travesty that around this nationally revered figure a movement has been built to further sectarian ends, which have served only to exacerbate the differences between the two major communities in the country.

The first episode marking the commencement of the present-day agitational politics around the building of the Ram temple at Ayodhya occurred on 22-23 December 1949. Hype was created by certain interested elements who gave publicity to the allegedly miraculous appearance of the idols of Ram and Sita inside the premises of Babri Masjid, the spot where devotees believed that Ram was born. The factual position reported by the then DM, K.K. Nair to the chief minister of UP, G.B. Pant, the chief secretary and the home secretary was that a few Hindus had entered the Babri Masjid at night, when the *masjid* was deserted, and installed the idols there.

This incident was seized upon by some leaders of the Hindu right to demand that Hindus be allowed to worship the deities within the premises of the mosque. The Muslims were of course against any such move. At the intervention of Prime Minister Nehru the premises were locked up to prevent Hindus from performing worship. Nehru wanted the idols to be removed, but the state government and the DM did not do so for fear of repercussions.

Justice Srikrishna, who enquired into the Bombay riots of 1992-1993, which occurred in the aftermath of the demolition of Babri Masjid, observed that the vacillating attitude of the central government at the time had emboldened the sudden installation of the idols of Ram Lalla in the disputed structure and spawned the demand for permission to carry out a *puja* (worship) therein. This resulted in the Babri Masjid becoming a rallying point for the Muslims too and they formed a Babri Masjid Protection Committee (later known as Babri Masjid Action Committee or BMAC).

While Hindu nationalists pressed from time to time for the unlocking of the Babri Masjid to allow Hindus to worship the deities, the demand did not gain momentum till the VHP took it up aggressively in the 1980s. In September 1984, a Sri Ram-Janki Rath Yatra (chariot procession with idols of Ram and Janki – another name for his wife, Sita) was started from Sitamarhi in Bihar for purposes of 'awakening the nation'. This was followed, in October 1984, by a gathering of numerous sadhus and Ram *bhaktas* (devotees of Ram), who took a vow on the bank of river Sarayu in Ayodhya and undertook a *pada yatra* (journey by foot) to Lucknow. At the conclusion of the march, a *dharmasabha* (religious meeting) was organized to demand the unlocking of the Babri Masjid. Within the same month, several such *yatras*, religious discourses, demonstrations and public meetings were organized by the VHP and the Bajrang Dal to arouse the people, so that they come out in support of the demand to allow Hindu worship inside Babri Masjid.

Activists of the VHP, the Bajrang Dal and some local leaders tried to keep the issue alive throughout the remainder of 1984 and 1985 till, on the orders of the Faizabad district court, the premises were unlocked and thrown open to Hindus for worship in February 1986. Though this was done under a court order, the media and some writers alleged that the motivation of the ruling dispensation was to give a sop to Hindus, who were incensed by the concessions given to Muslims, especially the enactment of the Muslim Women (Protection of Rights on Divorce) Bill in the same year.

After the premises were opened to Hindus, the BMAC, headed by Syed Shahabuddin, became active in voicing protests on behalf of Muslims. A call was also given to Muslims to boycott the Republic Day celebrations in 1987, though this call was subsequently withdrawn. A rally was held on the Boat Club lawns of Delhi by the

BMAC that attracted media attention and was attended by a large crowd of Muslims. Provocative speeches were made at this rally. These developments contributed to the build-up of communal tensions and the outbreak of communal violence in Meerut from 18 to 23 May 1987 was a fallout of these preceding events.

Between 1987 till the Lok Sabha elections in 1989 the VHP, the BJP and the Shiv Sena kept up the tempo of the movement by organizing *yatras*, *dharmasabhas* and other events that received considerable media coverage.

That the Ayodhya movement had started yielding political dividends is evident from the fact that the BJP succeeded in increasing its tally of seats in the Lok Sabha to 85 in the 1989 elections from only two in the elections of 1984.

At this time, the VHP initiated a programme for consecrating bricks in villages, in all parts of India, to be brought to Ayodhya by *kar sevaks* (volunteers) for constructing the Ram temple. Consecration of these bricks was done ceremoniously though Ram *shila pujans* at various locations. Thereafter, the bricks were to be brought in processions to Ayodhya. These processions began to be taken out in October 1989, shortly before the November 1989 general elections.

During the passage of the processions, communal feelings were inflamed through provocative sloganeering. These activities had very unfortunate fallouts in terms of communal riots erupting at a number of places including Indore, Mhow, Ratlam, Kota, Jaipur and Bhagalpur. The rioting at Bhagalpur, which has been covered in this book, was particularly severe and one in which many lives were lost and properties damaged, mostly of Muslims.

The foundation stone (*shilanyas*) of the Ram temple was laid on 9 November 1989 at a site very close to the Babri Masjid. There is little doubt this was done with the tacit support of the state and central governments.

While the Ram Janmabhoomi (place of birth) Movement was organized and spearheaded by the VHP-BJP-Shiv Sena combine, analysts believe that the Congress was also complicit, since the *shilanyas* ceremony could not have been otherwise performed at a spot duly approved by the local DM.

After the elections of 1989, a National Front government, headed by V.P. Singh, was formed with outside support of the BJP.

Mandal Commission and Advani's Rath Yatra

Some months later, in August 1990, the government announced the decision to implement the report of the Mandal Commission, whereby it was decided to implement reservations for backward castes – in education and public sector employment – through affirmative action. This prompted the BJP to withdraw support from the government as it did not want the political debate to focus on the empowerment of the backward classes. It thus took steps to shift the debate towards religion and the *mandir-masjid* question. The party announced a *yatra* to be led by L.K. Advani from the ancient temple of Somnath in Gujarat to Ayodhya in UP.

The Rath Yatra that commenced on 25 September 1990 was planned to reach Ayodhya five weeks later, after traversing over 6,000 miles, through eight states. A historian has describes the progress of the Rath Yatra thus:

> Militants of the Vishwa Hindu Parishad (VHP) flanked the van, flagging it off from one town and welcoming it at the next. At public meetings they were complemented by saffron-robed sadhus, whose 'necklaces of prayer beads, long beards and ash-marked foreheads provided a strong visual counterpoint' to these armed young men. The march's imagery was 'religious, allusive, militant, masculine, and anti-Muslim'. This was reinforced by the speeches made by Advani, which accused the government of 'appeasing' the Muslim minority and of practising 'pseudo-secularism' which denied the legitimate interests and aspirations of the Hindu majority. The building of a Ram temple in Ayodhya was presented as the symbolic fulfilment of these interests and aspirations.[26]

The event succeeded in rousing passions among the people who participated in it at many stages. The main *yatra* was halted with the arrest of L.K. Advani in Bihar at the instance of the then Chief Minister Lalu Prasad Yadav. But thousands of *kar sevaks* continued to converge, from all parts of the country, journeying towards Ayodhya. The state government in UP as well, headed by Mulayam Singh Yadav, dealt with the aggravating situation firmly.

Thousands of *kar sevaks* were detained. Large contingents of police and paramilitary forces were deployed to prevent the *kar sevaks* from reaching the Babri Masjid. Nevertheless, thousands of these *kar sevaks* surged towards Babri Masjid and the police had to use force to prevent them from destroying the structure. At least twenty of the *kar sevaks* died in the clash between the security forces and the volunteers.

VHP activists declared these *kar sevaks* to be 'martyrs' and carried their ashes in urns in large tracts of North India giving calls for revenge. A series of religious riots, in various towns of UP, ensued, in which mainly Muslims suffered. The towns and cities affected by such riots were Aligarh, Agra, Khurja and Bulandshahar. The Provincial Arms Constabulary (PAC) played a very partisan role and was complicit at several places in the killing of Muslims and in damaging their properties.

It has been aptly said that L.K. Advani's Rath Yatra became a 'Rakt Yatra', a journey of blood.

Halfway through the general elections in 1991, Rajiv Gandhi was assassinated. The Congress derived some benefit and as a result of a sympathy wave it won 244 seats in the Lok Sabha. It then formed the government, headed by Narasimha Rao, with some outside support. But the BJP too improved its position in these elections, securing 120 seats, thirty-five more than in the 1989 elections.

Destruction of Babri Masjid and its Aftermath

The VHP and the RSS continued to keep the spotlight on the Ayodhya temple issue. While the central government temporized and initiated moves to have a dialogue to resolve the issue, the VHP announced that 6th December had been chosen as the auspicious day for commencement of work to build the temple.

Hundreds of thousands of *kar sevaks* reached the temple town with *trishuls* (tridents that are associated with Lord Shiva and have now been co-opted as an identifying symbol of the Hindu right in India), bows and arrows and other weaponry, even as large contingents of police and paramilitary forces were stationed in the vicinity. Yet, the ceremonies commenced on the morning of 6 December 1992 without any interference from the police forces.

The proceedings that began with speeches and prayers soon became unruly and in no time the *kar sevaks* surged towards the monument. The police at the spot fled and the well-armed *kar sevaks* took over and swarmed the building. They started using hammers and axes to break the structures; and one by one the domes collapsed, until, by late afternoon, the building that had survived the onslaughts of nature for many centuries, was reduced to rubble.

While leaders such as L.K. Advani termed the destruction of the structure as 'unfortunate', the rank and file of the VHP and RSS welcomed it with glee. There were reports of triumphant celebrations in various parts of the country. The state government of UP was then being led by the BJP, with Kalyan Singh as chief minister. It clearly acquiesced to the demolition of the disputed structure. The central government played a passive role and intervened to dismiss the state government only after the Babri Masjid had been demolished.

Once more, communal riots engulfed the country. These were sparked either by the celebrations by triumphant right-wing Hindus or by protests and demonstrations by Muslims. These riots covered large areas in northern and western India. As many as 246 persons died in Gujarat, 120 in Madhya Pradesh (MP), 100 in Assam, 201 in UP and 60 in Karnataka.[27]

The worst hit was Bombay, the commercial capital of India. The riots that occurred in Bombay have been covered in detail later in the book. After the Bombay riots, the series of bomb blasts that shook the city sounded the death knell for communal harmony in India. It transpired that these blasts were organized by Muslim dons of the Bombay underworld, who wanted to take revenge for the killings and displacement of their brethren in the preceding riots. Apart from the bloodletting and the human toll, these riots had very adverse repercussions for the economy and businesses.

The VHP, which was at the vanguard of the Ayodhya movement, was evidently filled with a sense of accomplishment. Its leader, Ashok Singhal, commenting on the destruction of the Babri Masjid stated that it was 'a catalyst for the ideological polarization which is nearly complete'.[28] The BJP did benefit from this polarization by winning 161 seats in the general elections of 1996 and 182 seats each time in the subsequent mid-term elections of 1998 as well as 1999.

IMPACT ON HINDU-MUSLIM RELATIONS

Aside from the medium-term impact of this polarization in changing the grammar of electoral politics, it had deleterious consequences for relations between Hindus and Muslims in the cities, towns and villages, wherever they lived side by side. It altered, almost irrevocably, the chemistry and nature of civic engagement between the two communities. An atmosphere of mutual suspicion and hostility between members of the two communities was created. It also engendered feelings of insecurity among Muslims. It will take long for this damage done to the psyche of Indians to be healed.

While the question of building a Ram temple at Ayodhya has been in the works over decades, other emotive issues have been played up in recent times by Hindutva activists to keep the tensions between the two major communities alive. The controversies over the Ram Setu (ancient bridge in Rameshwaram Island in Tamil Nadu that may be in danger due to the proposed construction of a navigational sea route) and the one relating to the transfer of land to the Amarnath shrine board (in the state of J&K, which has become split along communal lines) are cases in point. Till a societal consensus emerges, not to exploit such issues for political gains, the re-establishment of harmonious relations between Hindus and Muslims will remain a distant dream.

Notes

1 Christophe Jaffrelot, *The Hindu Nationalist Movement and Indian Politics: 1925 to the 1990s with a new afterword* (New Delhi: Penguin Books, 1999), p. 1.
2 Ibid., pp. 3-4.
3 Jyotirmaya Sharma, *Hindutva: Exploring the Idea of Hindu Nationalism* (New Delhi: Penguin Books, 2003), p. 22.
4 Swami Vivekananda, *Life of Swami Vivekananda* (Calcutta: Advaita Ashram, 1960), p. 308.
5 Sharma, *Hindutva*, p. 113.
6 Hansen, *The Saffron Wave*, p. 77.
7 Aiyar, *Confessions of a Secular Fundamentalist*, pp. 17-18.
8 Marzia Casolari, 'Hindutva's Foreign Tie-up in the 1930s Archival Evidence', *Economic and Political Weekly*, 22 January 2000, pp. 224.
9 Jaffrelot, *Hindu Nationalist Movement and Indian Politics*, p. 28.
10 Casolari, *op. cit.*
11 Jaffrelot, *Hindu Nationalist Movement and Indian Politics*, p. 37.
12 Rafiq Dossani and Henry S. Rowen, *Prospects for Peace in South Asia* (California: Stanford University Press, 2005), p. 121.
13 Ibid.
14 Christophe Jaffrelot, 'Hindus and Muslims in the Communal Era' (International South Asian Forum Conference, Vancouver, 10-12 August 2001).
15 Naunidhi Kaur, 'The Foreign Hand', *Frontline* 19 (25), 7–20 December 2002.
16 D.R. Goyal, *Rashtriya Swayamsevak Sangh* (New Delhi: Radhakrishna Prakashan, 2000), pp. 17-18.
17 Aiyar, *Confessions of a Secular Fundamentalist*, p. 33.
18 Shashi Tharoor, *The Elephant, the Tiger and the Cellphone: Reflections on India in the Twenty-first Century* (New Delhi: Penguin Books, 2007), p. 72.
19 Sen, *Argumentative Indian*, pp .65-69.
20 Hansen, *The Saffron Wave*, p. 56.
21 Burke and Quraishi, *The British Raj in India*, p. 85.
22 Ibid., p. 68.
23 Guha, *India after Gandhi*, p. 633.
24 Sen, *Argumentative Indian*, p. 48.
25 Guha, *India after Gandhi*, p. 635.
26 Ibid., p. 635.
27 Ibid., p. 641.
28 Ibid., p. 643.

The Clash of Civilizations

The hypothesis put forward by Samuel P. Huntington, in a paper titled 'The Clash of Civilizations?'[1] that the fundamental source of conflict in the post-Cold War era will not be primarily ideological or economic but cultural, created quite a stir in intellectual circles. This view attracted a plethora of responses from international political theorists, both in agreement and in criticism and the Harvard University professor expanded his thesis into what turned out to be an influential and oft-quoted book, assertively titled *The Clash of Civilizations and the Remaking of the World Order.*[2] He argued that while ideology alone would no longer suffice to bring about a major war, the division along cultural and religious lines would 'dominate global politics'.

The reason we need to consider the propositions put forward by Huntington is that they have provided an intellectual prop for many in equating and identifying terrorism with Islam. At one remove, the idea that conflict among cultures is the order of the day in the new globalized world has been extended by Huntington to explain the phenomenon of religious revivalist movements. A discussion about these ideas, therefore, becomes relevant and germane to the theme of this book.

HUNTINGTON'S HYPOTHESIS – ITS BROAD CONTOURS

Prior to the French Revolution, according to Huntington, the conflicts in the Western world were largely among princes, emperors and monarchs attempting to extend their influence, strength and territories. In the process they created nation states; consequently, the principal lines of conflict after the French Revolution came to be drawn among nations rather than among monarchs. This pattern lasted till the First World War.

Then, as a result of the Russian Revolution, and the reaction against it, the conflict of nations yielded to the conflict of ideologies.

First among communism, fascism and liberal democracy, and then between communism and liberal democracy. During the Cold War, this conflict was embodied in the struggle between the two superpowers, that is, the United States of America and the Soviet Union. With the end of the Cold War, international politics moved out of its Western phase. Its centrepiece became the interaction between Western and non-Western civilizations. Thus, we have now entered an era of conflict of civilizations, as per Huntington's hypothesis.

In his conception, a civilization represents the highest cultural grouping of people. It is defined both by common objective elements and by the subjective self-identification of people as that civilization. In defining the elements that constitute a civilization, Huntington mentions language, history, religion, customs, institutions, etc., but when it comes to the issue of conflict, he seems to assign religion supervening importance.

The seven major civilizations in the modern world are claimed to be Western, Confucian, Japanese, Islamic, Hindu, Slavic-Orthodox, Latin American and possibly African. He has identified the key fault lines among these civilizations which will determine the battle lines of the future. The conflicts are inevitable because of their differing value systems, especially in the modern era.

Huntington says that cultural characteristics and differences are less mutable and hence less easily compromised and resolved than political and economic ones. This implies that conflicts between civilizations will be much more difficult to resolve than ideological conflicts or conflicts between nation states that had occurred in the past.

The processes of economic modernization and social change throughout the world separated people from their long-standing local identities. They also weakened nation states as a source of identity. Thus, in many parts of the world, religion moved in to fill this gap in the form of movements that are known as 'fundamentalist'. The rise of fundamentalism has, therefore, taken place in Western Christianity, Judaism, Buddhism, Hinduism and Islam. Huntington has referred to the 'Hinduization' of India with the end of the legacy of Nehru and 're-Islamization' of the Middle East, due to the rejection of Western assertions of its supremacy regarding values and political systems.

Thus, his contention is that as people define their identity in ethnic and religious terms, they are likely to see an 'us versus them' relation between themselves and the people of some other ethnicity or religion. In a book published later,[3] Huntington observed that 'America was created as a Protestant society just as and for some of the reasons Pakistan and Israel were created as Muslim and Jewish societies in the twentieth century'. While earlier immigrants to America merged themselves with the dominant culture, newer groups have tended to maintain their distinct identities. He fears that if communities do not adopt the dominant culture and values, the country would be divided into a 'bilingual, bicultural society'.

This view is shared by some influential people in Australia, where the earlier immigration was mainly from the European nations but later, on a large scale, supplemented by the arrival of people from the Asian subcontinent. This prompted the former prime minister of Australia, John Howard, to emphasize the need for a 'dominant culture'.[4] He said that the Australian culture, its language, its literature and its institutions were Anglo-Saxon. The former prime minister of Singapore, Lee Kuan Yew controversially ascribed the success of the Singapore state to the dominance of Chinese culture in the country.

In India, we are familiar with the ideologues of the Hindu right, like M.S. Golwalkar, who have argued that India should have a dominant culture, that is, Hindu culture. This view did not, of course, find favour with those who framed the Indian Constitution. And just as well because, arguably, India has survived and flourished as a multicultural, pluralist society.

The 'clash of civilizations', therefore, occurs at two levels. At the micro level, groups along the fault lines between civilizations' struggle, often violently, over the control of each other's territory, like in the case of India and Pakistan. At the macro level, states from different civilizations compete for relative military and economic power, the control of international institutions and competitively promote their particular political and religious values, as in the case of Israel and the Palestine.

'Muslims Vs Non-Muslims'

Huntington strikes a chord with the current major concerns that have emerged in the Western world post 9/11, by emphasizing the conflicts along the fault lines between Western and Islamic civilizations, which have been going on for 1,300 years. He prognosticates that the centuries-old hostile interaction between the West and Islam is unlikely to decline. It could only become more virulent. In this context, he has approvingly cited M.J. Akbar's assertion that the West's 'next confrontation is definitely going to come from the Muslim world. It is in the sweep of the Islamic nations from the Maghreb to Pakistan that the struggle for a new world order will begin'.

However, the interactions between civilizations vary greatly inasmuch as they are likely to be characterized by violence. The following observation by Huntington reveals the extent to which he is fixated on the nexus between Islam and violence:

> In Eurasia the great historic fault lines between civilizations are once more aflame. This is particularly true along the boundaries of the crescent-shaped Islamic bloc of nations from the bulge of Africa to central Asia. Violence also occurs between Muslims, on the one hand, and Orthodox Serbs in the Balkans, Jews in Israel, Hindus in India, Buddhists in Burma and Catholics in the Philippines. Islam has bloody borders.[5]

Huntington's main focus is on the cleavage between the Islamic and the Western world. A passage that quintessentially reflects his perception of Islam is excerpted below:

> The underlying problem for the West is not Islamic fundamentalism. It is Islam, a different civilization whose people are convinced of the superiority of their culture and are obsessed with the inferiority of their power. The problem for Islam is not the CIA or the US Department of Defence. It is the West, a different civilization whose people are convinced of the universality of their culture and believe that their superior, if declining, power imposes on them the obligation to extend that culture throughout the world. These are the basic ingredients that fuel conflict between Islam and the West.[6]

It is more than a decade since these words appeared in print. Since then, the world has moved on. The tensions between the Islamic and the Western world have been further exacerbated. India too has suffered from what is euphemistically referred to as 'cross-border terrorism'. As noted in the chapter on terrorism and the Indian Muslim, perpetrators of the regular terrorist attacks in India are

Muslim militant organizations based in Pakistan, albeit abetted by agents belonging to 'sleeper cells' set up in India. But the vast majority of Muslims in India are well-integrated in society and are strongly opposed to the Islamic fundamentalists whose numbers are minuscule and who belong to the fringe. It is indeed ironical that Indian Muslims have to bear the cross for the actions of a few misguided militant elements. Therefore, Huntington's myopic view of Islam and its variant cultures bears no weight even in these times of global threat posed by fundamentalist elements.

Religious Revivalism

Of particular interest to us are Huntington's observations about the nature of religious revivalism that has been taking place in recent times. Participants in religious resurgence come from all walks of life but overwhelmingly from two constituencies, both urban and both mobile. One constituency comprises the recent migrants to the cities who need emotional, social and material guidance which religious groups provide in another way. The second constituency is the new middle class among all religions. Religious revivalism is therefore an urban phenomenon that appeals to people who are modern-oriented, well-educated and are pursuing professional careers in various fields.

Within India, the leaders of Hindu revivalist movements come from the indigenized second generation and are often successful businessmen and administrators labelled informally in the Indian press as 'scuppies' – saffron-clad yuppies – a term coined in the early '90s. Supporters of the revivalist movement in India mostly come from India's solid middle-class Hindus, its merchants and engineers, senior civil servants, intellectuals and journalists.

The current Asian economic boom is also leading to a shift in power among civilizations. The likely emergence of China as a superpower will have a deeply destabilizing effect on the West-dominated global economic order. Similarly, India could also emerge as the major contender for influence in world affairs as a result of rapid economic development. The Islamic resurgence that is taking place will leave important legacies. Muslims will have much greater awareness of what they have in common and what distinguishes them from non-Muslims. This could result in even more intense anti-Western nationalism among Islamic countries than at present.

Since these observations were made by Huntington some years before 9/11 and the military action against Afghanistan and Iraq by the USA, it is to be granted that they were prescient inasmuch as we have witnessed a hardening of stance among Islamic fundamentalist groups against the West, particularly the USA. There has also been an increase since then in terrorist groups and terror-related incidents affecting many countries across the globe.

In some ways, however, Huntington's prognosis has become dated. In India, the political party (BJP) that provides muscle to Hindu revivalist movements has, since 2004, suffered an erosion of its support base. There appears to be widespread disenchantment with the Hindutva ideology among the middle classes or at least it does not seem to enthuse them any longer. This is even more true of the younger generation. Having shed their saffron robes, they are no longer 'scuppies'; not even 'yuppies', because such terms have lost their relevance in the twenty-first century.

Clearly, over time, Huntington's views about the 'Hinduization' of India are losing validity. But we cannot, for this reason, reject outright all the elements of his vision of the future. We have, to some extent, the benefit of hindsight in seeing how events are shaping up rather differently vis-à-vis Huntington's Cassandra-like predictions.

Huntington's Prophecy

Huntington predicts that a global war involving the core states of the world's major civilizations is highly improbable but not impossible. If it does come about it would be the result of the escalation of a fault line war among groups from different civilizations, most likely involving Muslims on the one side and non-Muslims on the other. If indeed a global war occurs, it is interesting to note that Huntington foresees an alliance between the United States, Europe, Russia and India against China, Japan and most Islamic countries.

However, Huntington also points out that to whatever degree they may divide humankind, world's major religions do share key values in common. If humans are to develop a universal civilization, it will emerge gradually through the exploration and expansion of these commonalities.

EMPIRICAL CRITIQUE OF HUNTINGTON'S HYPOTHESIS

Huntington's paradigm of clash of civilizations, which appears grand and visionary, got worldwide attention and even high acclaim. But it has also been subject to close scrutiny, examination and criticism. We can consider the critiques at two levels, that is, the empirical and the analytical. A few of these are discussed here.

Contrary to Huntington's divide between 'the West and the rest', particularly between Islam and the West, a study by Jonathan Fox proves that after the Cold War only a small number of ethnic conflicts (6.7 per cent) occurred between Islamic and Western civilizations. Studies by Andrej Tusicisny that appeared in the *Journal of Peace Research* in 2004 and those by Philip Roeder that appeared in *Comparative Political Studies*, based on detailed statistical data, reached similar conclusions.[7]

Contrary to the hypothesis that the Cold War suppressed conflicts and that these increased in the post Cold War period, Andrej Tusicisny's 'Civilizational Conflicts' observes that during the Cold War, a clash of civilizations occurred in 43.9 per cent of the conflict years, while it went down to 33.1 per cent after the Cold War. In a paper named 'Clear and Present Strangers', Henderson and Tucker studied the incidence of inter-civilizational conflict in three periods – pre Cold War, Cold War and post Cold War. The statistical analysis revealed that the Cold War did not suppress inter-civilizational conflicts. In fact, they found that Huntington's study, 'Clash of Civilizations?', on the basis of figures from the Correlates of War (COW) project, shows that the opposite is true – the Cold War did not suppress but exacerbate regional conflicts.[8]

These are a few illustrative examples of the empirical studies which show that Huntington's hypotheses are not substantiated, when put under the lens of verifiable data of the events that occurred after the Cold War. However, the visionary and persuasive scenario envisaged by Huntington cannot be debunked merely by citing certain studies based on data that could be selective. It is necessary to analyze Huntington's hypothesis at the logical level, on the basis of which his assumptions and conclusions can be scrutinized and questioned.

COUNTERPOINTS AT THE LOGICAL LEVEL

Amartya Sen in his seminal work, *Identity and Violence: The Illusion of Destiny*, has provided certain new perspectives from which the key elements of Huntington's hypothesis can be reviewed. A host of deficiencies, shortcomings and contradictions in the assumptions and conclusions made by Huntington can be pointed out through Sen's analyses.

First of all, the categorization of civilizations made by Huntington closely follows broad religious divisions. Thus Huntington contrasts Western Christian civilization with Islamic civilization, Hindu civilization, Buddhist civilization and so on. In fact, people of the world can be classified according to many systems of demarcation such as class, occupation, social status, language, politics, etc. Categorization exclusively on the basis of religion is inappropriate and incomplete.

Amartya Sen rightly points out that the type of classification made by Huntington betrays a rather foggy perception of world history because it overlooks the extent of internal diversity within these civilizational categories; the reach and influence of interactions of the intellectual as well as the material go right across the regional and religious borders of so-called civilizations.

The Issue of 'Identity'

A person's religion need not be his or her all-encompassing and exclusive identity. Sen provides, by way of illustrations, the following description of his own identity:

> I can be, at the same time, an Asian, an Indian citizen, a Bengali with Bangladeshi ancestry, an American or British resident, an economist, a dabbler in philosophy, an author, a Sanskritist, a strong believer in secularism and democracy, a man, a feminist, a heterosexual, a defender of gay and lesbian rights, with a nonreligious lifestyle, from a Hindu background, a non-Brahmin, and a non-believer in an afterlife (and also, in case the question is asked, a non-believer in a 'before-life' as well).[9]

Since Huntington's focus has been on Islam and the danger posed by Islam to non-Islamic civilizations, it needs to be stated that Muslims also see themselves in different ways. For instance, a Bangladeshi Muslim is not only a Muslim but also a Bengali and a Bangladeshi, typically quite proud of the Bangladeshi language, literature and music. He or she may also have numerous other identities connected with class, gender, occupation, political affiliation, etc. It is significant that the Bangladeshis in their struggle to break away from Pakistan (in 1971) were inspired by their Bengali identity rather than their religious identity which they shared with the Pakistanis. This is a clear instance of a Muslim-majority country subordinating its religious identity to that of language and cultural inheritance when it came to a do-or-die struggle for political independence from another country – in which the levers of power were controlled by their non-Bengali co-religionists.

Staying with the issue of identity, we are all individually involved in identities of various kinds for disparate contexts in our respective lives, arising from our background associations or social activities. For example, we can think of a person born in Orissa, whose mother tongue is Oriya, who is a professor of philosophy in a college, whose hobbies include photography and instrumental music, who is a member of a musical society, who is president of the resident welfare society of his housing colony, a non-vegetarian by preference, a Hindu and an Indian citizen.

It must be recognized that identities of individuals are plural and one identity need not obliterate all others. The person has to make a choice among identities based on their relative importance and in a particular context, among divergent loyalties and priorities that may compete for precedence. It is evident that the importance of a particular identity of an individual will depend on the social context. For an Oriya-speaking individual, his identity as a non-vegetarian may become more crucial when going to a dinner rather than his proficiency in photography.

The centrepiece of the argument is that the plural affiliations of an individual are important rather than singular affiliations, even if they relate to his or her religious identity. A person is free to choose an identity depending on the context and his or her multiple identities cannot be subsumed by a singular overarching identity. Naturally, zealots wishing to exploit the religious identity of an individual, for political or other reasons, would strenuously oppose this view as it does not subserve their designs. A VHP activist or a Muslim cleric would inevitably stress on the primacy of religious identity so that they can mobilize their brethren as and when required.

Internal Variations among Cultures

When Huntington adumbrates on clashes arising out of different cultures and value systems, he seems to overlook the fact that many of these cultures contain internal variations. 'For example, Indian traditions are often taken to be intimately associated with religion, and indeed in many ways they are, and yet Sanskrit and Pali have a larger atheistic and agnostic literature than any other classical language: Greek or Roman or Hebrew or Arabic. When a doctrinal anthology such as the fourteenth-century Sanskrit book *Sarvadarshanasamgraha* (literally translated as "collection of all philosophies") presents sixteen chapters respectively sympathetic to sixteen different positions on religious issues (beginning with atheism), the aim is to cater to informed and discerning choice, rather than to indicate incomprehension of each other's positions.'[10]

In contemporary India too, diversity is in evidence everywhere. Among Muslims there are those who follow the liberal Sufi ways, whereas others believe in orthodox practices. Among Hindus, traditions vary between the North and the South; even in the South we have the Vaishnavites and the Shaivites following divergent religious traditions and practices. There is much substance in the clichéd phrase of there being 'unity in diversity' in the case of India.

Unidimensional View

Huntington's categorization of people as members of the 'Western World', 'Islamic World', 'Hindu World' or the 'Buddhist World' reduces people to one dimension. This is a deficiency that has to be addressed even before considering the hypothesis that people belonging to such worlds would 'clash'.

This is an important issue because when it is argued that people belonging to the Islamic world, Hindu world, or Christendom are peace-loving and prefer to have harmonious relations with others, it is implicitly accepted that human beings around the world can be understood and pre-eminently characterized in terms of the distinct civilizations to which they belong. For instance, when in rebuttal of the generalization that followers of Islam have a belligerent cultural ethos, it is argued that their culture actually emphasizes peace and goodwill, it is implicitly accepted that Muslims would be basically similar to each other in most ways. Thinkers like Amartya Sen question this assumption because people across the world cannot be classified on the basis of a singular affiliation even if it is religion.

IS INDIA A 'HINDU' CIVILIZATION?

It is in this backdrop that the classification of India as a Hindu civilization can be questioned. Even for argument's sake, if we consider the singular affiliation model of a people, it has to be noted that India is home to the second largest number of Muslims in the world after Indonesia. They comprise approximately 14 per cent of the population. Besides, there are many other minorities including Christians, Sikhs, Parsis, Jains, Buddhists, et al., who are citizens of this country. Muslims in the past and in contemporary India have contributed immensely to the enrichment of Indian arts, literature, music, films and the range of contributions in these fields have come from them and others in a thoroughly intermingled way.

The characterization of India as a Hindu civilization is also politically combustible. As perceptively pointed out by Amartya Sen, 'it tends to add some highly deceptive credibility to the extraordinary distortion of history and manipulation of the present realities that Hindu sectarian politicians have tried to champion in trying to promote a "Hindu civilization" view of India. Huntington is indeed frequently quoted by many leaders of the politically active "Hindutva" movement, and this is hardly surprising given the similarity between his seeing India as a "Hindu civilization" and the promotion of a "Hindu view" of India that is so dear to the political gurus of Hindutva'.[11]

Sen has also made the point that though political parties committed to a Hindu view of India had mixed fortunes in the electoral arena, political attempts at seeing India as a Hindu civilization will not easily die away. A simplistic characterization of India along an artificially singular religious line remains politically explosive, in addition to being descriptively flawed.

ARE WESTERN VALUES UNIQUE?

The great political ideologies of the twentieth century include liberalism, socialism, anarchism, corporatism, Marxism, communism, social democracy, conservatism, nationalism, fascism and Christian democracy. According to Huntington, all these share one thing in common: they are products of Western civilization and no other civilization has generated a significant political ideology. The following excerpt reveals the hubris in the way Huntington views Western civilization vis-à-vis other civilizations and the USA's role in the world:

> The West differs from other civilizations not in the way it has developed but in the distinctive character of its values and institutions. These include most notably its Christianity, pluralism, individualism, and rule of law, which made it possible for the West to invent modernity, expand throughout the world, and become the envy of other societies. In their ensemble these characteristics are peculiar to the West. Europe, as Arthur M. Schlesinger, Jr., has said, is 'the source – the unique source' of the 'ideas of individual liberty, political democracy, the rule of law, human rights, and cultural freedom ... These are European ideas, not Asian, nor African, nor Middle Eastern ideas, except by

> adoption'. They make Western civilization unique, and Western civilization is valuable not because it is universal but because it is unique. The principal responsibility of Western leaders, consequently, is not to attempt to reshape other civilizations in the image of the West, which is beyond their declining power, but to preserve, protect, and renew the unique qualities of Western civilization. Because it is the most powerful Western country, that responsibility falls overwhelmingly on the United States of America.[12]

It may appear to be a digression from the main theme of the book, but as the dichotomy between Western and Eastern values is identified as a cause of divide among nations, states and their peoples – especially by anti-secularists and the right wing – the claim of the 'uniqueness' of Western values deserves to be examined critically. Amartya Sen, in his books, *The Argumentative Indian* and *Identity and Violence*, has given examples to show how this claim is untenable. It is pertinent to mention here some of his observations regarding the flaws in Huntington's arguments.

The championing of political liberty and religious tolerance in their full contemporary forms is not an old historical feature of any country or civilization in the Western world. The edicts issued by Emperor Ashoka in third century BC show that he was a champion of religious and other kinds of tolerance. His ideas on secularism and tolerance 2,300 years ago are indeed of relevance even today. Similarly, in the sixteenth century, Emperor Akbar made similar pronouncements on religious tolerance. In contemporary Europe at the time, religious inquisitions were extensive and perceived heretics of Christianity were being burnt at the stake.

Similarly, it is an incorrect contention that democracy is essentially a Western idea, alien to the non-Western world. Amartya Sen cites examples from Iran, Bactria and India, that had incorporated elements of democracy in municipal government in the centuries following the flowering of Athenian democracy and much before such practices had emerged in European countries.

It may also be mentioned that democracy is not just about ballots and votes. The practice of 'government by discussion', which is a hallmark of democracy, was prevalent in India at the same time as it was in Greece, when open general meetings, aimed specifically at settling disputes between different points of view, took place in Buddhist councils. Emperor Ashoka hosted the third and the largest

Buddhist council in third century BC in the then capital of India, Patliputra. Ashoka also tried to codify and propagate the earliest formulation of rules for public discussion in India.

There are other examples of democratic institutions and values that were established in non-Western parts of the world very early in the world's history. In seventh-century Japan, a ruling prince promulgated a constitution of seventeen articles which, inter alia, decreed that 'Decisions on important matters should not be made by one person alone. They should be discussed with many'. This was 600 years before the Magna Carta was signed in the thirteenth century in England. The seventh-century constitution of Japan has been seen by scholars as the first step towards democracy.

Middle Eastern history and the history of Muslim people also have a great many accounts of public discussion and political participation through dialogue. Thus, contrary to Huntington's assertion, the Western world has no proprietary right over democratic ideas. While modern institutional forms of democracy are relatively new everywhere, the history of democracy in the form of public participation and reasoning was spread across the world from early on. And in the contemporary world, the largest thriving democracy is situated in a region geographically quite a distance away from the 'West'!

Since Islam has been targeted for its alleged bellicose propensities, the point needs to be made that history is replete with examples of Muslim tolerance and diversity. For instance, Dara Shikoh, the eldest son (and legitimate heir) of Emperor Shah Jahan, who was killed by his younger brother Aurangzeb, was a student of Sanskrit and a serious scholar of Hinduism. His translation of the Upanishads from Sanskrit into Persian was, for a period, one of the main foundations of European interest in Hindu religious philosophy.

CONCLUSION

We have gone into the dialectics concerning Huntington's hypotheses relating to the 'clash of civilizations' as his categorization of people, countries and civilizations has influenced profiling and stereotyping of certain people in an adverse way. This is especially true with respect to the adherents of Islam. What emerges from the analysis is that it is futile and counterproductive to place civilizations, countries and peoples in certain straitjackets and then ascribe to them certain immutable characteristics. It is best to avoid such generalizations that create prejudice and in turn lead to strife and violence.

Notions such as 'ideology being the basis of conflicts in the world before the Cold War and a clash of cultures since then' appear very attractive when mooted and can be made to look persuasive and even conclusive, by citing selective data. But these are really a priori conjectures. In reality, if we consider the myriad conflicts taking place in the world, the reasons would be varying and multitudinous. These reasons cannot rightly be classified under a singular label of being 'ideological' or 'cultural' in nature. Quite possibly, the underlying causes could be the clash of economic interests or just a matter of settling old scores. We may perhaps leave it at that.

✪

NOTES

1 Samuel P. Huntington, 'The Clash of Civilizations', *Foreign Affairs*, 1993, p. 1.
2 Samuel P. Huntington, *The Clash of Civilizations and The Remaking Of World Order* (New Delhi: Penguin, 1997).
3 Samuel P. Huntington, *Who Are We: The Challenges to America's National Identity* (New York: Simon & Schuster, 2005).
4 Guha, *India after Gandhi*, p. 769.
5 Huntington, 'The Clash of Civilizations', *op. cit.*, p. 9.
6 Huntington, *Clash of Civilizations*, *op. cit.*, pp. 217-218.
7 Radhieka Mittal, 'Islam Wants Democracy, Liberal Ethos', *The Hindustan Times*, 2 October 2006.
8 Ibid.
9 Amartya Sen, *Identity and Violence: The Illusion of Destiny* (London: Penguin, 2006), p. 19.
10 Ibid., p. 35.
11 Ibid., p. 48.
12 Ibid., p. 311.

IN RETROSPECT: A FEW CASE STUDIES

Jabalpur, Madhya Pradesh, 1961

After the trauma of Partition with large-scale communal riots and massacres preceding it and also occurring in its immediate aftermath, communal violence in the country abated. The decade of the 1950s witnessed very few incidents of such violence. During this period other issues and agitations were in the fore, such as the demand for reorganization of states on a linguistic basis. It was widely believed, rather naïvely perhaps, that with the division of the country and the creation of Pakistan, communal tensions had eased and widespread communal disturbances would be a thing of the past. In this backdrop the communal rioting that occurred on 4 February 1961 and the following days in Jabalpur, and the nearby areas, marks a watershed. This really was the first major communal flare-up after the relatively peaceful decade of the 1950s, and the first one of many that occurred in the following decades.

One reason I have taken up this particular riot for analysis is that it marks the recrudescence of Hindu-Muslim riots after an interregnum, when relative harmony prevailed in the relations between the two major communities. Moreover, being fortuitously posted as the assistant collector and magistrate in Jabalpur at the time, I had first-hand experience of watching the riots unfold. I was assigned magesterial duties in one of the sectors of Jabalpur city and was a part of the administrative machinery dealing with the situation. The then district magistrate (DM) R.C. Srivastava, who was responsible for my training, took me under his wing and I spent much time with him during the riots, learning the ropes in the process.

The state government of Madhya Pradesh (MP) later appointed a sitting judge of the MP High Court, Justice Shiv Dayal Srivastava, to enquire into the disturbances and the report of the enquiry commission was published in 1962.[1] In describing the causes, the events and various related issues relating to the disturbances, I have relied upon the report of the Justice Shiv Dayal Commission and on my personal recall.

The precipitating incident that sparked off the riots was the suicide of a Hindu unmarried girl, Usha Bhargava, around twenty years of age, who studied at a local college in Jabalpur. On 3 February 1961 she attempted to commit suicide by pouring kerosene oil over her body and setting herself on fire. She was rushed to a local hospital where, according to the doctors who attended on her and tendered evidence before the Commission, she had 90 per cent burns of the third degree. She could not be saved and succumbed to her burns. But before that her dying declaration was recorded by the doctor on duty, since no magistrate could be contacted in time and brought to the hospital for the purpose.

It has been mentioned in the Commission's report that apparently all the magistrates and even senior police officers were occupied at the residence of the divisional commissioner, C.L. Gupta, in connection with his daughter's wedding. The Commission commented that there was no serious effort made to get a magistrate to record the dying declaration – there is no evidence to show that any magistrate was contacted, who avoided coming to the hospital. There is no explanation, however, why no police officer, in the absence of a magistrate, could record the dying declaration. I remember attending the gala wedding reception on the sprawling lawns of the commissioner's residence, oblivious to events unfolding elsewhere in the town that would lead to the worst communal violence since the post-Partition riots.

It was alleged that Usha Bhargava committed suicide since she was raped by two Muslim boys, Latif and Maqsood. Maqsood was the son of a prominent *beedi* (Indian cigarette) merchant of the city. Both Latif and Maqsood were arrested by the police on the night of 3 February 1961.

Rumours regarding the incident spread in the town and the *Yug Dharma*, a local Hindi daily, known to have links with the Rashtriya Swayamsevak Sangh (RSS) and Jan Sangh establishments, published the news of the rape incident using inflammatory language with the following banner headlines (translated):

'HINDU GIRL RAPED BY MUSLIM SCOUNDREL ON POINT OF DAGGER'

'HELPLESS STUDENT POURED KEROSENE OIL AND BURNT HERSELF'

....

'ACCUSED SON OF INDUSTRIALIST'
'SENSATION AND TENSE ATMOSPHERE IN THE WHOLE CITY'

It may be mentioned that the other local dailies that published the news did not sensationalize the event. They avoided indicating that the girl was a Hindu while the alleged molesters were Muslims. It is pertinent to mention that newspapers play an important role in either containing or exacerbating communal flare-ups, depending on their predilections.

On 4 February the trouble began with a procession being taken out in the morning, at around 9 a.m., by students of local colleges shouting agitated and instigative slogans. The police tried to control the situation and persuaded them to disperse, informing them that their main demand of arresting the alleged culprits had already been met. The procession, however, did not disperse and reached the Anjuman Islamia School. Since the students of this school, mostly Muslims, were unwilling to join the procession, the school was attacked and pelted with stones. The incident thus sparked off a communal clash. More mobs from different localities also joined the procession and swelled its number. There were several incidents en route and clashes began to occur with local residents. At a location known as Omti Crossing, a Muslim mob collected and clashed with the procession. The police force led by the city superintendent of police (CSP) resorted to the use of teargas to disperse the mobs.

An order under Section 144 of the Code of Criminal Procedure (CrPC) was promulgated by the DM in the afternoon, banning processions, assemblies of five or more persons, etc. It was early in the afternoon of 4 February that I was summoned to the police control room in the central *kotwali* (police station) by the DM. Along with other magistrates and police officers, the DM and the SP, Jabalpur, briefed us about the developments and our duties. I was assigned to the Omti police station area, along with a senior police officer, to ensure that the locality remained peaceful.

The trouble, however, had already spread to other areas of the town and there were cases of arson involving residential and commercial properties of Muslims. Certain well-known establishments such as Sulemanji Ganibhai's shop of paints, varnishes, etc., a big concern, were set on fire. Some mosques were attacked, including one at Andherdeo where the *pesh imam* (priest) was belaboured with *lathis*. The DM felt that the situation was grave and would not come under control easily. Hence he requisitioned the military from the local cantonment to come and assist the civil administration. An army detail under Major D.B. Lahiri patrolled the city and I accompanied him when he was in the Omti area. It was a revelation for me to witness the sobering effect on the local populace on seeing an army column on the move – patrolling by the police had had no such impact.

At about 5 p.m. the *beedi* merchant Anwar Khan's (father of Maqsood) house was attacked by a Hindu mob of 600-800 people. A column of the army was dispatched to the spot along with a magistrate, who handed over the situation to the commanding officer of the army unit. The situation was brought under control without the army having to use force.

It was also reported to the control room that Muslim mobs had attacked the Khermai Temple. A magistrate with a police party went to the spot. Hindu mobs had also collected at the spot and there was a clash between the two groups. The police had to eventually resort to firing to control the situation.

There was also an unfortunate incident of rape of a Muslim girl (Khairunnisan). The police arrested thirteen persons in connection with this incident. In the incidents of 4 February, several persons died and were injured. Properties of sixty-four Muslims and six Hindus were also damaged.

With additional police force coming in from neighbouring districts the situation was gradually brought under control on 5-6 February, though there were a few stray incidents of clashes between individual Hindus and Muslims or small groups of them.

On 7 February the situation appeared to have been brought to near normalcy. I went back to my regular duties, the magistrates having been withdrawn from their assigned areas. However, late in the evening after 9 p.m., the control room received information that a 200-strong Muslim mob had collected and was attacking Hindus in certain localities adjoining Hanumantal police station. A police party was dispatched to deal with the situation and it was reported that the mob was shouting religious slogans. Since information had spread about the attack on Hindu houses by a Muslim mob, a Hindu mob also collected and stones and other missiles were exchanged between the two groups. The police party resorted to *lathi* charge to control the crowd; and subsequently also resorted to tear-gassing and firing at the mobs.

....

According to the evidence tendered to the Commission, several other groups of people also collected in the neighbouring localities and police parties had to be dispatched to control them, which they did using differing degrees of force. It was reported that most of these mobs comprised Muslims and they were very aggressive, even shouting slogans like 'Pakistan *Zindabad*'. I recall being summoned again in the early hours of the morning and directed to take up my post at the Omti police station. On reaching there, I, with my police counterparts and escort, patrolled the area in a jeep. At several places we found mobs collecting with intent to loot or riot. But on being warned by us they dispersed.

On the early morning of 8 February, there was a meeting of senior officials in the control room, where I was present. The DM and the senior superintendent (SSP) were of the view that curfew should be imposed in the town. However, they were dissuaded from doing so by the divisional commissioner. In its report, the Commission commented adversely on the intervention of divisional commissioner who, strictly speaking, does not have a role in dealing with law and order situations. Thereafter, on 8 February, stray incidents continued to take place in which people mostly from the Muslim community suffered injuries to person and property. These could perhaps have been obviated had curfew been imposed and enforced.

With the arrival of additional police force, and the patrolling of affected areas, the situation gradually came under control, though minor incidents continued to take place till 12 February.

While observing that, on the whole, the action taken by the administration and police to control the situation could not be criticized, certain adverse comments were made by the Commission regarding the delay in imposing an order under Section 144 CrPC on 3 February and not imposing curfew on 8 February.

The failure of intelligence was also commented upon since the administration was caught off-guard when violent Muslim mobs collected late in the evening of 7 February, and rioting in the city reccurred. At the instance of the district authorities, certain peace committees had been formed in the localities affected by the riots, comprising representatives of the Hindu and Muslim communities. The objective of such committees is to work for restoration of harmonious relations between the two communities in the *mohallas* or colonies. However, citing the evidence of the SSP, the Commission observed that the committees were not effective.

As regards the causes of the riots in Jabalpur, the 'immediate' one was the alleged rape of a Hindu girl by two Muslim boys. This incident was played up by the press, particularly one Hindi newspaper, which resulted in inflaming the passions of the Hindus, who took to the streets to avenge the crime. A vicious cycle of attacks by mobs and counterattacks by the two communities ensued, which is a common phenomenon in such episodes. The disturbances spread to the adjacent rural areas of Jabalpur district and the neighbouring districts of Sagar, Damoh and Narsimhapur, where, however, the scale and magnitude of the problem was lesser in comparison to Jabalpur and the situation could be controlled with minimum use of force. It may be noted that police had to resort to firing on nine separate occasions in Jabalpur in the course of bringing the disturbances under control.

There were some other versions relating to the rape and suicide of the Hindu girl which had been perceived to be the precipitating incident for the riots. S.B. Kolpe, who covered the communal violence at Jabalpur for the *Free Press Journal*, reported[2] that according to police sources, the girl was freely going out with one of the Muslim boys arrested for the alleged rape. She had been having an affair with him and may have committed suicide as marriage was ruled out due to the prevailing orthodoxy.

Asghar Ali Engineer[3] has opined that the real cause of the riots was that the Muslim *beedi* magnate, whose son was one of the alleged rapists, had succeeded in establishing control over the local *beedi* industry. His Hindu competitors were very sore over this development and as a consequence of the riots the *beedi* industry belonging to the Muslims suffered heavily. Clearly, the implication is that the riots were engineered by the business rivals of the Muslim *beedi* magnate consequent to the suicide of the girl.

According to the statistics given in the appendices of the Commission's report, the riots in Jabalpur (urban) caused the death of twenty-two persons, of whom twenty-one were Muslims. In Jabalpur (rural), nineteen persons were killed of whom eighteen were Muslims. As regards injury of persons and damage to property, the ratio was similarly skewed against the Muslims.

Both in terms of loss of life and damage to property, the Muslims suffered much more than the Hindus, but it has been made out that in the incident which precipitated the riots the offenders were Muslims and when rioting broke out again after a lull, the aggressors were from the Muslim community. A feature common to most

Hindu-Muslim riots is that a particular incident is played up by interested parties – including some sections of the news media – in a way that it results in arousing communal passions and leads to the outbreak of violence. Thus, in the case of a so-called 'precipitating incident' of a communal riot, Muslims are generally portrayed as the aggressors with the Hindus being presented as the victims. Common sense indicates that since Muslims are finally the worst sufferers in the riots, why would they provoke them?

ISSUES ARISING OUT OF THE JABALPUR RIOTS

There are certain features of the Jabalpur riots that are common to many such incidents which occur all over the country:

(i) The 'precipitating' incident, where a Hindu girl had allegedly been assaulted by Muslim youths, may or may not have been verifiable; it was probable that it was seized upon and deliberately played up by vested interests to create disaffection among the communities.

(ii) A section of the vernacular press incited the sentiments of the Hindu community by giving it an overtly communal colour and the reportage was directly responsible for the outbreak of the riots.

(iii) There was failure of intelligence in anticipating further rioting, especially on 7 February. The district administration got into a self-congratulatory mode a little too soon, for having brought the situation under control.

(iv) There was ineffective enforcement of the prohibitory orders under Section 144 of CrPC. There was also a failure to impose curfew after the flare-up on 7 February that was to prove a costly error.

(v) Given the seriousness of the situation, there was delay in calling the army in aid of the civil authorities.

NOTES

1 Justice Shiv Dayal Srivastava, 'A Report of the Commission of Enquiry on Jabalpur Riots 1961' (MP: Bhopal Government Central Press, 1962).

2 S.B. Kolpe, 'Caste and Communal Violence and the Role of the Press', in *Communal Riots in Post-Independence India*, ed., Asghar Ali Engineer (Mumbai: Sangam, 1997), pp. 340-341.

3 Asghar Ali Engineer, *Communal Riots After Independence: A Comprehensive Account* (Delhi: Shipra, 2004), p. 32.

Indore, Madhya Pradesh, 1969

Indore is the most populous city in Madhya Pradesh and also its commercial capital. Although a few communal clashes had occurred in the city in the distant past, generally speaking it did not have a history of communal discord.

In the period preceding 2 June 1969 there had been a few times when communal tensions had surfaced without breach of peace having occurred. One such instance involved the murder of a person called Avanti Sonkar, allegedly by some persons of the Muslim community. On 1 January 1969, Hindus took out a procession in the city with the body of the deceased woman. Some anti-Muslim slogans were shouted by the processionists and the procession also deviated from the designated route on its way to the cremation ground. However, the police party accompanying the procession made sure that no untoward incident occurred. At the cremation ground inflammatory speeches were made that could have provoked Hindus into committing violence against Muslims.

Tension prevailed in some areas of the city in the following days. I was then posted as DM at Indore, and one C.S. Kadam was the SP. We took precautionary steps to diffuse the tension. A peace committee comprising respected Hindu and Muslim citizens was formed and they assisted the administration in keeping surveillance in the sensitive localities. In March, during Holi, special precautions were taken to ensure that the festival passed off peacefully. As a result of these efforts there was no breach of peace; I recall I received a letter of commendation from the state government for having successfully handled a tense and delicate situation.

Later in the month, on the occasion of Mahavir Jayanti, processions were taken out in the city and some tension was reported but again with adequate precautions, the event passed off peacefully. Similarly, on 29 May 1969 Muslims took out a procession on the occasion of Barawafat. It was reported that some of the slogans could have raised the ire of the majority community, but again no untoward incident took place.

I have mentioned these matters because notwithstanding the amicable relations prevailing between the two major communities in Indore in the past, there was some evidence of tension in the city preceding the events in June. The city was then engulfed in communal violence on 2 June 1969 and in the subsequent days, till the situation was brought under control. As DM, I had to deal with the situation, take all necessary measures to quell the violence and restore normalcy in Indore.

THE OUTBREAK OF VIOLENCE

An organization known as the Dugdha Vikreta Sangh had arranged to fète the well-known wrestler, Master Chandgi Ram, who had been crowned 'Bharat Kesri' (Lion of India) after defeating another wrestler, Meher Deen. The reception for Chandgi Ram had assumed communal overtones but the administration was not cognizant of it. A procession with Chandgi Ram was taken out from the railway station, where he was received, through a designated route. CSP S.P. Shukla along with around sixty policemen accompanied the procession, for which permission had been given under Section 30 of the Police Act prescribing the route and under certain conditions.

On the same evening a freestyle wrestling show was organized at the Nehru Stadium, in which some well-known wrestlers, such as King Kong and Randhawa, were taking part. Adequate police arrangements had been made to ensure that the event went off peacefully.

The route of Chandgi Ram's procession traversed through an area known as Bombay Bazaar, predominantly a Muslim residential and business locality. It seems a crowd had collected at the Bombay Bazaar crossing and there was an altercation when the procession reached this point. The procession was obstructed, resulting in a clash between the processionists and the crowd. Soon mobs of both communities gathered on either side of Jawahar Marg, near Bombay Bazaar crossing, and soda water bottles, iron bars, etc., were used in the ensuing fracas. CSP Shukla and some other policemen also suffered injuries. The police had to open fire to control the situation.

Around 9.30 p.m. I received a call from CSP Shukla when I had just reached my residence back from office. He informed me about the serious nature of the trouble and expressed the apprehension that it could escalate to other areas too, though the crowd had been dispersed. I immediately rushed to Nehru Stadium where some magistrates and police parties still happened to be present, though the wrestling show had got over and most of the spectators had left. I personally dispatched a police party with a town inspector to the Bombay Bazaar area and advised the other CSP Bhatnagar and the magistrates present to proceed to the control room, so that the situation could be monitored from there and necessary measures taken to prevent further violence. I too reached the control room at around 10 p.m. to take charge of the situation. SP C.S. Kadam was away on leave and a relatively inexperienced Addl SP was in charge of the police force at the time.

Before police forces could be deployed in different areas of the city, trouble spread in the entire Bombay Bazaar area and the adjacent localities. The city of Indore is densely populated and its streets are narrow. Mobs had collected at various places and were throwing stones. CSP Bhatnagar reached some of the trouble spots and had to open fire on a few occasions to disperse the rioting crowds. After organizing the control room, I proceeded with police force to Bombay Bazaar and other areas where arson and acts of hooliganism were being committed by the mobs. The fire brigade had been called in and the personnel were trying to control the fire from spreading further and dousing the same wherever possible.

Returning to the control room I contacted authorities at the state headquarters and also the divisional commissioner at his residence in Indore and requested for police reinforcement. A senior police officer, S.P. Mishra, who had earlier been the SP, and was still posted in Indore as a commandant of the Special Armed Force (SAF) was asked to come over and take charge of the police forces in the absence of SP Kadam.

While the situation was soon brought under control in the Bombay Bazaar area, the violence was refusing to abate in other areas like Juni Indore, Malharganj, etc. The mayor of Indore and other politicians also came to the *kotwali* informing us of the developments in various parts of the city and gave their views regarding the action to be taken. I again visited some of the trouble spots and gave overall directions for crowd control and speedily attending to arson cases.

By 3 a.m. on 3 June, the control room at the *kotwali* was abuzz with activity and we put the internal security scheme into operation for Indore city. The station officers were accordingly directed to commence preventive arrests of the listed antisocial elements (*goondas*) who were likely to indulge in rioting and arson. The city was divided into five sectors with a police officer made in charge of each along with a magistrate.

Curfew

An order under Section 144 CrPC imposing curfew in designated areas of the city was promulgated. Police pickets were positioned at strategic locations and patrolling by mobile vans was started. It must be stated here that the imposition of curfew through a magisterial order is one thing, but its effective enforcement is another, and depends on the adequacy of police personnel available for the purpose. At the time we were indeed handicapped because a comprehensive police deployment was not possible for enforcing the curfew orders properly. Consequently, sporadic cases of arson and mob violence continued through the night and during the day on 3 June. S.P. Mishra and I took rounds of the city and went to some of the trouble spots. Mostly, the mobs fled on our approach with the police contingent.

As we were sitting in the control room, the mayor rushed in and told us that a fully-armed crowd of Muslims had gathered inside Hammalon Ki Masjid with the intention of attacking Hindus. On reaching there we found that a Hindu mob had collected outside the *masjid* and was pelting it with stones. Some of these persons reiterated what the mayor had told us – that a large number of Muslims had armed themselves in the premises of the mosque and were planning to come out and launch attacks on Hindu localities in the city.

We persuaded the crowd to disperse and thereafter got the gates of the mosque opened. We found around twelve persons, including women and children, huddling inside the mosque. They were in a state of abject fear and panic. There was no collection of lethal weapons or ammunition of any kind. We were able to evacuate the persons to safety under a police escort. This is only one small instance of how false information is spread during such riots, targeting the minority community.

At the time Indore had six large-sized textile mills employing about 22,000 workers of whom around 500 were Mulims and the remaining Hindus. With the start of the communal rioting in Indore the Muslim workers were not allowed to report for work at the mills. These workers feared for their lives if they did not submit to the pressure. It was an unfortunate development since the industrial area had earlier been free from the virus of communalism.

We took the trade unions into confidence and sought their help in sorting out the matter so that the Muslim workers could go back to work. This was an economic boycott of Muslims which, if allowed to continue, would have set a very unhealthy trend. Fortunately, after ten days, with the help of the trade unions, we could get the Muslim workers to resume their duties in the textile mills and the problem blew over.

Military Called In

On the afternoon of 3 June, seeing that the situation was grave and may not necessarily be brought under control by use of police force alone, I alerted the station commander of the army at Mhow to be ready to move in to assist the civil administration and requested for the posting of a military liaison officer at Indore. Liaison Officer Captain Raghubir Singh accordingly reported to me at the control room soon afterwards. Meanwhile, police forces from the neighbouring districts also started arriving to supplement the forces available in Indore.

I would like to iterate that I had to take the decision to call in the military on my own, based on my assessment and also suggestions from the mayor and other local leaders, though the senior police officers were ambivalent about it. I believe that this is the normal reaction of the police in such situations, since they often feel that requisitioning the army casts an unfavourable shadow on their ability to bring the situation under control.

The internal security column arrived from the Mhow cantonment in the evening and, as advised by the district authorities, conducted a flag march through a designated route in the city the next day, mainly with a view to announce their presence. The arrival of the armed forces and the flag march had a very salutary effect on the public at large, and was instrumental, to a considerable extent, in restoring order. The arrival of additional police forces, intensive patrolling and effective imposition of the curfew orders also contributed significantly to expediting peace. However, on 5 and 6 June stray cases of stabbing and arson continued in different localities of the town; at some places mobs also collected and police had to open fire to disperse them when *lathi* charge and use of teargas shells did not prove effective.

As the situation improved from 6 June onwards, the hours of curfew were relaxed and on 7 June the internal security column of the army returned to Mhow. Normalcy in the city was restored and thereafter with police vigilance further untoward incidents were prevented.

By the end of the violence in the city, twelve persons had been killed, of whom ten were Muslims. There was considerable damage to residential and commercial properties and the majority of the sufferers were again Muslims. The state government sanctioned compensation for the victims and their families, both for loss of lives and property. Through the revenue department in the district we organized relief and rehabilitation measures that were effective and appreciated by all the stakeholders, like local leaders and organizations.

Long after the violence had subsided, on 26 June 1969 an injured cow was spotted somewhere in the city. Rumours spread that the injury had been caused by gun pellets and its tongue had been sliced by a sharp instrument. The cow was examined by a veterinarian and it was found that the wounds were due to natural causes. A press release was issued to set the record straight to prevent a recrudescence of trouble due to false rumours on this score.

ROLE OF THE PRESS

During the entire period, particularly from 3 June till around 14 June, we issued daily press notes about the situation in Indore and held press briefings at the *kotwali* every evening. The press generally remained supportive of the role of the administration. However, one Hindi daily, *Swadesh*, known for its close connections with the Jan Sangh and RSS establishments, published several news items containing material designed to incite hatred between the communities. Since the paper could not be persuaded to desist from publishing false and inflammatory news, I reported the matter to the state government with a request for action under Section 12 of the Public Security Act. A formal warning was issued to the publisher of *Swadesh* but it did not have any effect.

Finally, somewhat belatedly, the state government issued a notification stopping the publication of this newspaper for one month on 9 July 1969. Action was also taken by the police to prosecute the newspaper under Section 153-A of the Indian Penal Code (IPC). Similarly, action was taken by the police under the said section against publication of *Saptahik Matribhoomi*; the declaration of *Dainik Kiran* being published from the *Swadesh* press was also cancelled by the sub-divisional magistrate.

The role of the press in such situations becomes very important and a responsible press can help diffuse the situation and bring about peace and normalcy at the earliest. On the other hand, publishing news items about incidents that are either false or exaggerated leads to fuelling of rumours and inevitably results in increasing tension and violent reactions by the communities concerned. It has been seen, time and again, that sections of the vernacular press often act irresponsibly in such situations. While freedom of the press is guaranteed by our Constitution, it is necessary to have some strict curbs on irresponsible reporting which may result in communal violence.

JUDICIAL ENQUIRY

The state government set up a judicial enquiry commission to enquire into the disturbances and Justice T.C. Srivastava, a retired judge of the MP High Court was appointed as the one-man Commission. The Commission invited statements from the administration, representative bodies in the public, and others; held oral hearings and recorded the evidence of hundreds of witnesses. As DM I filed a statement and was also verbally examined and cross-examined over two days. The unedited version of the statement submitted by me forms part of an annexure to this book. It has important additional information and will give the reader a glimpse into the times in which the incident occurred.

The report of the Commission was submitted to the state government; though it was not published, I was able to peruse it at a later date. On the whole the Commission found that the situation was handled very well by the local administration and it vindicated our actions.

ISSUES ARISING OUT OF THE DISTURBANCES AT INDORE

The issues that surfaced are not so different from other Hindu-Muslim riots:

(i) There was failure of specific intelligence inasmuch as the district administration could not anticipate that allowing two events – the freestyle wrestling bouts and the reception for Master Chandgi Ram – to happen simultaneously would severely hamstrung the police in controlling any possible outbreak of violence. As the DM I own responsibility for this lack of foresight.

In extenuation it may be said that the judicial enquiry commission, taking into account the totality of circumstances, did not fault us on this score.

(ii) The question of calling in the army is debatable because the local police usually feel slighted when this is done.

(iii) The economic and social boycott of Muslims in the textile mills area was unfortunate and at that time considered to be an unusual fallout of a communal conflict. It was indeed a portent for the future. Something similar, on a much larger scale, was to be witnessed in the case of the Bombay riots of 1992-93.

(iv) The role of the press came into focus since at least one newspaper contributed to aggravating the situation and was consistently tendentious in its reportage.

(v) Political leaders often act irresponsibly and contribute to spreading false rumours, in such situations, which result in inflaming passions that lead to violence. As in the Hammalon Ki Masjid incident mentioned earlier, the mayor was responsible for giving us wrong and biased information, which on verification turned out to be totally false. Though this is an instance of an occurrence which happened nearly forty years ago, some things have not changed – in fact, only worsened. Political leaders at the grass-roots level are wont to act as 'conversion specialists' a la Paul Brass,[1] a term discussed in the chapter on causal factors and dynamics of Hindu-Muslim riots earlier in the book.

Notes

1 Brass, *Production of Hindu-Muslim Violence.*

Bhagalpur, Bihar, 1989

Bhagalpur in Bihar has been a communally sensitive town with a history of Hindu-Muslim discord. It has a fairly large Muslim population and harbours both Hindu and Muslim criminals in substantial numbers.

At the time the riots occurred in Bhagalpur in 1989, there were two notorious criminal gangs: one headed by the 'Sallan group' patronized by Bhagwat Jha Azad and the other the 'Ansari group' of which Shiv Chandra Jha was the patron. Both Bhagwat Jha Azad and Shiv Chandra Jha were former chief ministers of Bihar.[1] These gangs were at war with each other but also ready to seize any opportunity to create mayhem. They got such opportunities galore once the riots broke out on 24 October and afterwards.

As a part of the political mobilization by the forces of Hindutva around the issue of building a Ram temple at Ayodhya, Ram *shila pujan* processions were being taken out at various places in the country. One such procession was to be taken out in Bhagalpur on 24 October, which was to pass through Tatarpur, a Muslim-dominated locality in the town. The Muslims objected to the route of the procession; the DM and SP nevertheless allowed it and themselves accompanied the procession.

The processionists reportedly shouted objectionable anti-Muslim slogans. Many Muslims had collected near Tatarpur opposing the entry of the procession into their *mohalla* (locality). Some bombs were thrown at the procession perhaps by the Ansari gang standing nearby.[2] The procession broke up and mobs were let loose in the town indulging in killings, looting and arson. The DM and SP narrowly escaped. The DM was not willing to give permission for firing on the crowd but the SP, without such permission, fired on the mob reportedly killing four persons.[3] Muslim antisocial elements also launched counterattacks and killed Hindus and destroyed their properties.

A false rumour was spread that hundreds of Hindu students had been killed by Muslims and their bodies were thrown into the nearby wells. The spreading of this rumour resulted in inciting Hindus further who launched attacks on Muslims in their neighbourhoods. In different localities of the town, Hindu mobs indulged in killing and destruction of Muslim property. Many Muslim shops were looted. A large number of mosques and *mazars* were also destroyed.

On 26 October a gruesome massacre took place at the Min locality in which eighteen persons – five men, two women and eleven children – were brutally murdered.[4]

The riots spread to the villages on the outskirts of Bhagalpur. Asghar Ali Engineer has given detailed descriptions of some of the atrocities perpetrated by the rioters in these villages.[5] In Chanderi village, members of several families were murdered. The lone survivor of the massacre, Malika Begum, in a statement before the Patna High Court, recalled how her father, mother and maternal uncle were killed in her presence, by certain persons who she named. On 26 October, the entire Timoni village was wiped out. All the 125 Muslim households tell the tale of horror which befell them that morning. Every house was burnt and looted by a mob reportedly 10,000 strong. Even wooden doors and frames were extracted. Fortunately, the death toll here was low. According to the Nathnagar circle officer, Mohammed Rahmatullah, eleven persons lost their lives at the hands of the marauding mob. The reason for the relatively low toll was that most old men, women and children were evacuated from Timoni on the night of 25 October.

Not only did the killings occur in the town and neighbouring villages – in an incident at Murapur station near Bhagalpur, about 100 armed persons pulled out four persons from the 115-Up Tinsukia Express and killed them. At this station, five passengers travelling in the Azamganj Passenger train were also slaughtered.[6]

On 27 October, a brutal massacre of 116 Muslims took place at Logain village, under Jagdishpur police station of Bhagalpur district. The victims were buried in a mass grave, which was camouflaged with a cauliflower plantation to escape detection. In this case justice was done when, eighteen years later, fourteen of the accused persons were convicted. They were awarded life imprisonment. To begin with, twenty-four persons had been named as accused, six died during the trial, while four were proclaimed as absconders by the court and their properties were ordered to be attached.[7]

This was the solitary case where justice was done, even if many years later, since, in our judicial system, the wheels of justice indeed grind very slowly. Barring this one case where the culprits were at least apprehended, prosecuted and convicted, there are so many others where the culprits literally get away with murder.

It has been reported that the toll of the riots was as follows:

Villages affected	206
Houses burnt to ashes	3,932
Shops looted and burnt	891
Powerlooms looted and burnt	3,000
Muslims killed	876
Hindus killed	150
Missing persons	106
Hindus arrested	1,100
Muslims arrested	900
Persons who lost their means of livelihood	50,000 to 60,000

Also, thirty-seven mosques, seven madrasas, eight tombs and five Shiva temples were destroyed. The exact number of Hindu houses gutted completely is not known but the figure is more than 300.[8]

SOME SALIENT ASPECTS OF THE BHAGALPUR RIOTS

(i) The vicissitudes of the movement to build the Ram temple at Ayodhya have been described at length in the chapter on Hindutva. Numerous Hindu-Muslim riots have taken place as a fallout of the movement and also in the aftermath of the destruction of the Babri mosque. The Bhagalpur riots of 1989 was one such, triggered by the Ram *shila pujan* procession, which carried the Ram *shila* (building block) destined to be taken to Ayodhya.

(ii) Like in so many cases, including the 1969 Indore riots described earlier, the 'precipitating' incident was an alleged attack on a procession, but the underlying causes are to be found in the dynamics of the relations between Hindus and Muslims prevailing at the time in Bhagalpur. The riots were waiting to happen and the attack on the procession was merely the spark that lit the fuse.

(iii) This is yet another instance where the taking out of a procession led to the outbreak of communal violence. There was every indication that such an outcome was likely and it was clearly an error of judgement on the part of the district authorities to have allowed the procession to be taken out.

OF PROCESSIONS AND AN INCIDENT AT CHANDERI IN DISTRICT, GUNA, MP

The riots at Bhagalpur are among the many instances of communal clashes that have occurred when processions, parading religious symbols, have been allowed to be taken out through the streets in different cities and towns of India. In this context, I would like to narrate an incident from my own experience, wherein we were able to prevent a communal clash by denying permission for taking out a *tajia* procession during Muharram in the year 1965. I was then posted as DM at Guna in Madhya Pradesh.

In Chanderi, a small town in the Guna district, known for its looms which produce the Chanderi saris, Shia Muslims used to take out *tajias* on each of the nine days of Muharrram in a procession through the town. On the last day, the *tajia* procession followed a route on which a temple was located, and went up to the tank (*talaab*) where the *tajias* were immersed.

During Muharram in 1965, the Hindus objected to the route as it was to pass by a temple; there was a stand-off on this issue between the Hindus and the Muslims. The SP and I tried to make the two communities arrive at a compromise. We suggested to the Muslims to slightly alter the route so as to avoid passing by the temple. The Muslims, however, refused to oblige. In our view, the procession would have surely resulted in communal violence, so we decided not to permit the procession to pass through the sensitive area. Consequently, the Muslims decided that the procession would not be taken out at all. While this diffused the situation, there was undoubtedly some resentment amongst the Shia community due to the procession not being allowed to pass through the traditional route.

Although we could not amicably resolve the matter, I do feel that the greater good was served in the light of the experience of so many processions resulting in outbreak of communal violence. There are numerous recorded instances of clashes either occurring or having been prevented – depending on the sagacity of the district officers concerned – relating to *tajia* processions during Muharram. In this connection the following account is of interest.

The height of objects carried in a procession may appear trivial but there have been cases where *tazias* (symbolic tombs) carried in a Muslim procession sparked violence when some processionists demanded that branches be taken off a Hindu-owned tree or that some other obstacle be removed to allow the procession to pass without lowering the *tazia*. This happened, for instance, at Hazaribagh in Bihar in April 1935, when Muslim processionists claimed that Hindu banners along their route would contaminate the *tazias*. Police officers in such cases sometimes tried to avoid conflict by digging the road deeper so that the tazia would not have to be shortened and would still not hit the tree. A former senior police officer, M.K. Sinha, has a good description in his memoirs of a riot averted in this way at Siwan, Bihar, in the 1930s.[9]

NOTES

1 Asghar Ali Engineer, *Lifting the Veil* (Hyderabad: Sangam, 1995), pp. 174-175.
2 Ibid, p. 176.
3 Ibid, p. 176.
4 Ibid, p. 178.
5 Ibid, pp. 179-181.
6 Ibid, p. 182.
7 '14 Convicted of Killing 116 people in Bhagalpur Riots', *The Hindustan Times*, 18 June 2007; 'Life term for 14 Bhagalpur Riot Accused', *The Hindustan Times*, 7 July 2007.
8 Engineer, *Lifting the Veil*, pp. 182-183.
9 Wilkinson, *Votes and Violence*, p. 39, footnote 72.

Bombay, December 1992 to January 1993

In December and January 1992-93, there occurred in the city of Bombay, one of the worst communal riots of independent India. The Srikrishna Commission[1] that enquired into the riots starts its report with the following vivid description. 'For five days in December 1992 (6 to 10 December) and fifteen days in January 1993 (6 to 20 January), Bombay, prima urbs of this country, was rocked by riots and violence unprecedented in magnitude and ferocity, as though the forces of Satan were let loose, destroying all human values and civilized behaviour. Neighbour killed neighbour; houses were ransacked, looted and burned, all in the name of religion ...'

The enquiry commission appointed by the government of Maharashtra in 1993, to enquire into the riots with specified terms of reference, was headed by Justice B.N. Srikrishna. Justice Bellur Narayanswamy Srikrishna, then a fifty-two-year-old, relatively junior judge of the Bombay High Court, had become an additional judge in 1990 and a permanent judge in 1991. He is a polymath of distinction who knows twelve languages and holds a Master's degree in Sanskrit and a diploma in Urdu. Justice Srikrishna was a godfearing and socially sensitive person who meticulously examined the victims, witnesses and alleged culprits and recorded the evidence for five years. There was a break of a few months when the Shiv Sena-led government disbanded the Commission in January 1996, but it was reconstituted again in March 1996. To this date the recommendations of this Commission have not been accepted or acted upon by the government of Maharashtra. It has to be understood that though an enquiry commission conducts its proceedings like a court of law, the report or its recommendations are not binding on the executive body.

The following narration draws freely from the Srikrishna Commission's brilliant and comprehensive report on the Bombay riots.

BACKGROUND

Ever since Partition an atmosphere of distrust has festered between the Muslim and Hindu communities in Bombay. The feeling of insecurity among Muslims was exacerbated in the wake of the call of Hindu communalists ('Hindutvawadis' as Justice Srikrishna calls them) for building a temple of Lord Ram in the place where the Babri Masjid stood in Ayodhya. The Rath Yatra led by L.K. Advani refocused attention[2] on the Ram Janmabhoomi – the land on which Babri Masjid stood is disputed to be the birthplace of Lord Ram and is a bone of contention between the two communities. The clashes and incidents of rioting along the route of the Rath Yatra, and in its aftermath, created tensions between the two communities all over the country, and Bombay was no exception.

From July 1992 the BJP had been organizing different campaigns and raising the pitch for building a Ram temple at Ayodhya. It held religious processions, *chowk sabhas* and meetings in order to rouse Hindus on the issue and urged them to make common cause with the party. The speeches and slogans aired on these occasions were utterly discriminatory, such as '*Mandir wahin banayenge*' (We will build the temple only on the site of the Masjid) and '*Is desh mein rahna hoga to Bande Mataram kehna hoga*' (If you want to stay in this country, you will have to sing *Bande Mataram*).

From October 1992 onwards, hectic preparations were made by BJP and its allied organizations like VHP, Bajrang Dal and RSS for the *kar seva* (religious service) on 6 December 1992. The movement was built into a crescendo through processions, speeches at public meetings, distribution of pamphlets, etc., by the Hindutvawadis. The central government's intervention to hold talks and diffuse the situation was apparently half-hearted and proved abortive. The then PM, Narasimha Rao had given assurance to the Parliament regarding the safety of the Babri Masjid. The CM of UP gave a categorical undertaking to the Supreme Court that no harm would be allowed to befall Babri Masjid during *kar seva*. What happened thereafter is well-known: despite all the assurances, hordes of *kar sevaks*, unimpeded by the police and paramilitary forces present, entered the Babri Masjid premises and demolished the mosque.

From the very day of demolition, trouble started brewing in the city of Bombay and on 6 December itself, there were series of minor incidents – recounted in detail in the Srikrishna Commission report – which indicate the build-up to the riots that followed.

THE RIOTS

In this surcharged atmosphere, the Hindutva parties celebrating and gloating over the demolition of the Babri structure raised the ire of Muslims in Bombay, who came out to protest angrily on the streets. There were certain other incidents that aggravated the situation, such as a Ganesh idol in one of the localities in Bombay being found decapitated and moved out from its place of installation. It was widely suspected that Muslim fanatics were responsible for this desecration. In the jurisdiction of Deonar, Muslims stoned the house of a local BJP leader and there were some attacks on the Hindu temples in the area. The police had to resort to firing to quell the rioting.

From 7 December the situation escalated and large-scale rioting started in different areas of Bombay. Muslim mobs came out protesting the demolition of the Babri Masjid and there were clashes between such mobs and the police. Muslim mobs damaged a number of temples and Hindus retaliated by attacking mosques and madrasas. BEST buses were also targeted. Two constables in Deonar jurisdiction were killed with choppers and swords by Muslim mobs. Police had to resort to firing on two occasions, killing twenty Hindus and seventy-two Muslims. Measures to control the situation by the police, though, had little effect.

On the following days, rioting continued and spread to the different localities in Bombay. Police had to resort to firing on numerous occasions, which mostly killed Muslims. Clashes between groups of Hindus and Muslims were at their peak on 8 and 9 December. There was improvement in the situation from 10 December onwards with only stray incidents taking place. After the 12th, the rioting petered out.

Regarding the role of the police, the Commission has found that during this period there was clear evidence of police bias against Muslims, which manifested itself in matters such as failure to register even cognizable offences on Muslim complaints.

Between 12 December to 5 January, there were a few stray incidents involving stabbing of members of both communities. However, tension continued to be built up as a result of the spurt in attendance of *namaaz* at the mosques by Muslims and *maha aartis* (big religious ceremonies) being performed by Hindus, accompanied by communally inciting speeches.

On 1 Jan 1993 an article appeared in *Saamna* (a Marathi newspaper run by the Shiv Sena), under the heading '*Hindunni*

Akramak Vhayala Have' (Hindus must also become aggressive now), openly inciting Hindus to violence. Consequent to the murders of some Mathadi workers on the night of 5 January by unidentified persons, a furore was kicked up by Shiv Sena workers alleging that the murderers were Muslims. They gave a call for Hindus to unite and retaliate. This led to large-scale rioting in various localities of Bombay city in the following days. The Hindu backlash continued for days on end. On 8 January alone there were forty-eight cases of mob violence. On 9 January, the riots had spread to the jurisdiction of forty-three police stations. Shiv Sainiks were organized to launch attacks on Muslims with military precision, carrying voters' lists and lists of Muslim establishments with them.

On 10 January the army was called in and deployed to control the riots. By this time the areas around fifty-one police stations were affected. There were numerous cases of death by stabbing and damage to property through arson, when arms and ammunition were used by both Hindus and Muslims to attack each other. Police had to resort to firing on many occasions.

There was a gruesome incident on 12 January involving an attack on two Muslim women. Although the older woman managed to escape, the young girl of nineteen was beaten and burnt alive by the violent mob. The situation showed some improvement on the 13th, though even on this day there were thirty-six cases of stabbing, sixty-seven incidents of mob violence and fifty-one incidents of arson. The police resorted to firing on twenty-one occasions.

From the 14 January there was considerable improvement in the situation, though stray incidents of violence from different localities were reported till the 19th. In the meanwhile, the deployment of the army had been increased. After 20 January the city limped back to normalcy.

The final tally of the casualty figures of December '92 and January '93 riots in Bombay given by the Srikrishna Commission are as follows.

Community	Dead (900)	Injured (2,036)
Muslims	575	1,105
Hindus	275	893
Unknown	45	–
Others	5	38

Causes	No.
Police firing	356
Stabbing	347
Arson	91
Mob action	80
Private firing	22
Others	4

Besides the human toll of the riots, the adverse economic impact on the businesses and industries in Bombay was huge. It has been estimated that losses relating to production, sales, tax revenue and property amounted to Rs 9,000 crore. Industries that largely employed Muslims, like synthetic textiles, leather, jewellery, bakeries, and government manufacturing units, were badly hit. A large number of these Muslim workers were compelled to migrate back to their homes, mostly in UP and Bihar. This extensive migration had wider ramifications for the country's economy. It caused impoverishment of the migrants' hometowns in the respective states due to the drying up of regular remittances from Bombay.[3]

CAUSES OF THE RIOTS

The Srikrishna Commission appointed a 'Committee of Experts' from the Tata Institute of Social Sciences (TISS) to undertake an analysis of the December '92–January '93 riots in Bombay from the political, socio-economic and demographic perspectives. Briefly, it may be stated that the report of the Committee ruled out class conflict or economic competition between Hindus and Muslims as causes for the riots. It, however, noted that decline in employment in the organized sector in Bombay and the growth of the informal sector was a contributory factor, since there is rank exploitation of workers in the informal sector. These workers, who are victims of riots in the first instance, become potential aggressors in future communal riots.

Other factors identified by the Committee were increase in the number of footpath-dwellers and slum-dwellers, their sense of deprivation, the concentration of minorities in distinct pockets leading to exclusivist tendencies amongst them, all conducive to the creation of a cauldron for riots to erupt.

More importantly, the Committee identified the changing political discourse in the country as an underlying cause. The propagation of the Hindutva ideology and militant Hinduism had gradually come to the fore. The Muslims too were driven more and more to assert their identity and become increasingly exclusivist due to the rise of Hindutva forces.

The conclusion was that certain socio-economic and demographic factors contributed to the development of a situation conducive to ethnic violence. The political factors aggravated the cleavage between the two groups, functioning as a proximate contributory cause for the riots and violence in Bombay.

The immediate cause, of course, was the demolition of the Babri Masjid followed by aggravation of Muslim sentiments over Hindus celebrating the event.

The Srikrishna Commission also noted the role of professional criminals in whipping up communal frenzy for their advantage and the inciting writings in print, particularly in *Saamna* and *Navkar*, which fuelled rumours about an imminent attack by Muslims using sophisticated arms. An interview given to *Time* magazine by Bal Thackeray, the head of the Shiv Sena, who expounded the doctrine of 'retaliation', and also those by other leaders such as Shah Poddar and Manohar Joshi, were responsible for the misplaced vigilantism of the Shiv Sainiks.

The police were criticized, inter alia, for the failure of their intelligence machinery to anticipate the fallout of the damage to the Babri Masjid; for treating the *maha aartis* as purely religious activities, ignoring the communal overtones; for failing to enforce curfew and a ban against assembly of five or more persons effectively.

The police too, allegedly, did not maintain a list of communal *goondas* and failed to take action against such persons who indulged in arson and rioting.

Although the army was alerted on 6 December itself, its deployment and utilization was delayed and they were not given an operational role to swiftly and decisively put an end to the riots.

It has been noted that the response of police to appeals for help from desperate victims, particularly Muslims, was cynical and utterly indifferent. The Commission even commented on the inbuilt bias of police officers and of men, particularly at the junior levels, against Muslims. The police also failed to take action against certain newspapers that published false and inflammatory news. While certain cases were registered under section 153A of the IPC, these were not properly followed up.

While every riot has distinctive characteristics, there are common elements or themes across the board in such riots that were again evident in the Bombay riots. It is, therefore, with a feeling of déjà vu that we revisit these aspects listed below:

(i) A failure of intelligence and the utter lack of preparedness to meet the outbreak of violence on the part of the state authorities and the police.

(ii) The vernacular press played a devious role in spreading rumours and stoking communal fires through provocative writings.

(iii) The police failed to effectively enforce prohibitory orders under Section 144 CrPC.

(iv) The police showed bias against the minority community.

(v) The police failed to control antisocial elements from taking advantage of the situation. It is known that such elements have a vested interest in whipping up communal frenzy, as demonstrated in the chapter on causal factors and dynamics of riots.

(vi) There was ineffective deployment and use of army columns in controlling the riots.

(vii) Organizations such as the BJP, RSS, VHP and Bajrang Dal played their part in inciting violence through propagation of Hindu militant ideals.

NOTES

1 Justice B.N. Srikrishna, 'A Report of the Commission of Enquiry on Communal Riots in Bombay in December 1992–January 1993' (1997).

2 Refer to the chapter, 'Religious Nationalism and Hindutva' for a history of the conflict.

3 Wilkinson, *Votes and Violence*, pp. 14-15.

Gujarat, 2002

It is generally agreed that subsequent to the post-Partition riots, the carnage in Gujarat in 2002 was the worst to have occurred in independent India.

Although the events pertaining to this riot have been extensively covered in the media, as yet we have no authentic account of the incidents which occurred on the day the Sabarmati Express was torched at Godhra on 27 February 2002 and of the riots in the state on subsequent days.

As far as the Godhra incident is concerned, two judicial enquiry commissions have gone into it and submitted their reports. Soon after the rioting, on 6 March 2002, the Gujarat government appointed a commission headed by Justice G.T. Nanavati, a retired judge of the Supreme Court, to enquire and report on all the events that had occurred. This commission has come out with its first interim report pertaining only to the Godhra incident. Before the Nanavati report, however, the UC Banerjee Commission, appointed by the Ministry of Railways in the central government on 2 September 2004, came out with its report. Justice U.C. Banerjee, also a retired judge of the Supreme Court, carried out this enquiry.[1]

It is difficult to treat either of these two reports as wholly credible because they have arrived at divergent conclusions. Perhaps for this reason, the two reports have attracted the stigma of political bias, a charge levelled against them by the two sides of the current political divide in India – the UPA headed by the Congress and the NDA headed by the BJP. National Human Rights Commission (NHRC) chairperson, Justice S. Rajendra Babu has been quoted to say that 'One thing is normally not done is partial report [*sic*]. Both Nanavati and Banerjee gave partial reports'.[2]

For a description of the events, therefore, one has to rely on the media investigations and reports, as also on the observations made by the courts and the NHRC. To describe the happenings and draw conclusions based on such material alone is hazardous because their veracity can be questioned and deemed to be coloured by the predisposition of the narrator and by the leanings of the organization. Thus, I will not attempt to cover, in any detail, the various episodes and incidents of the riots. The description will be restricted to certain major incidents of defining nature, the facts of which are incontestable, having been drawn from various reliable sources.

THE FIRE IN THE TRAIN AT GODHRA

The incident that triggered off the violence in the state of Gujarat occurred when the Sabarmati Express from Faizabad to Ahmedabad caught fire a few minutes after it left Godhra railway station on 27 February 2002. Fifty-nine persons were killed in this fire, many of them being *kar sevaks* returning from a pilgrimage to Ayodhya, though amongst the dead were also women and children travelling in the ill-fated train. Godhra is a town with Muslim majority, mainly belonging to the Ghanchi community. It was widely suspected that miscreants from this community were responsible for the attack on the train and the burning of the coach.

One version about what transpired is that there was an altercation between a few *kar sevaks* and a Muslim tea-vendor at the station. The *kar sevaks* attacked the vendor, abducted a Muslim girl and took her to the railway carriage forcibly. This resulted in a retaliatory attack on the carriage. The Forensic Science Laboratory (FSL) at Ahmedabad concluded controversially that since the doors of the coach were latched from inside, there was slim possibility that liquid fuel was thrown from outside, prior to setting the coach on fire.

The UC Banerjee Commission report too concluded that the fire was accidental and not deliberate. U.C. Banerjee dismissed theories regarding conspiracy and surmised that the fire could have resulted from food being cooked in the railway carriage designated S-6.

The Nanavati Commission, however, has come to the conclusion that the burning of the carriages of Sabarmati Express was a pre-planned conspiracy hatched by local Muslims. On the basis of the evidence before it, the Commission has held that burning rags and other things that were thrown inside the coach had caused the fire. Some persons had, thereafter, forcibly opened the interconnecting door between the coaches S-6 and S-7 and sixty litres of highly inflammable liquid material was thrown into the coach. This resulted in a big fire in which fifty-nine persons died and many were injured.

According to the Commission, one Maulvi Umarji planned the conspiracy that was hatched at Aman Guest House. Several persons and conspirators, allegedly involved in buying petrol and attacking the coach, have been named. Sometime before the Sabarmati Express was to start from Godhra railway station, a false rumour was spread in the Signal Falia locality – apparently by the conspirators – that a Ghanchi Muslim girl had been forcibly taken away into the train. This was done to induce the people of the locality to come to the station and attack the train.[3]

The Nanavati Commission also avers that it found no evidence to show that either the chief minister, or any of the ministers in his council, or police officers, had played any role in the Godhra incident.[4]

The Gujarat government initiated proceedings under POTA against 134 persons, accused in connection with the attack on the train at Godhra, in March 2002. However, for the subsequent post-Godhra riots, a description of which follows, cases were registered only under normal laws and POTA was not applied. A twist has been given to this controversy by a judgement of the Gujarat High Court[5] delivered on 12 February 2009, holding that the Godhra train incident was not an act of terror and hence POTA was not applicable to those arrested in connection with this incident. The division bench of the High Court upheld the recommendations of the Central POTA Review Committee (CPRC) that had held in May 2005 that there was no conspiracy alleged to have been hatched in Godhra and hence POTA could not be invoked against the accused. This judicial pronouncement exposed the discriminatory approach adopted by the state government in Gujarat.

POST-GODHRA VIOLENCE IN GUJARAT

In the light of the contradictory findings of the two eminent jurists who conducted the enquiries, the real truth of what actually happened will perhaps never be known. Whatever be the truth about the burning coach, it can never be trotted out as a reason to justify the unprecedented violence which was unleashed in the state on the minority community.

The Sangh Parivar and even the state government tried to defend it as a spontaneous reaction to the burning of the Sabarmati Express. A senior politician, holding a responsible position, reportedly justified the violence which followed the Godhra incident as 'action and reaction'. Through this cynical invocation of a law of physics, the desecration of countless Muslim shrines, killing of Muslim men, women and children, and destruction of their businesses and property were sought to be justified.

Attacks by large mobs commenced on 28 February at various places in the districts of Ahmedabad, Vadodara and Saberkantha. On the next day it spread to the rural districts of Panchmahal, Mehsana, Kheda, Junagadh, Banaskantha, Patan, Anand and Narmada. In the subsequent days, Bharuch, Rajkot and Surat were also affected.[6] The capital of Gujarat, Gandhinagar, situated at a short distance from Ahmedabad, was affected by communal violence for the first time. The offices of the Wakf Board and Minority Development Board were burnt down. Other institutions of the state and judiciary were attacked too. A number of trucks with the drivers were set on fire in front of the main gate of the High Court. While all this vandalism on properties of the state occurred, the police allegedly looked the other way.

The scale and magnitude of the riots were tremendous. As many as 151 towns and 993 villages in fifteen to sixteen of the state's twenty-five districts were affected by post-Godhra violence, which was particularly severe in about five or six districts. The violence raged largely between 28 February and 3 March. After a good deal of hesitation, curfew was imposed in twenty-seven towns on the evening of 28 February. Though minority leaders and concerned citizens had been repeatedly urging the state government to call in the army to bring the riots under control, this was done only on the afternoon of 1 March.[7] Rioting resumed on 15 March and continued till mid-June. Northern and central Gujarat, as well as the north-eastern tribal belt, where Hindutva mobilization efforts were strong, were the worst affected while Saurashtra and Kutch remained largely peaceful.

It needs to be stated at the outset that the riots in Gujarat were not one-sided with only the Muslims being victimized. There were attacks on Hindus by Muslim mobs in Danilimda, Modasa, Himmatnagar, Bharuch, Sindhi Market, Bhanderi Pole, and other localities in the city of Ahmedabad in Gujarat.[8] There was significant loss of life and property in these attacks and a large number of Hindus including Dalits fled their homes to stay in makeshift shelters. However, it is indisputable that Muslims suffered considerably more in these riots, which have been frequently described as a 'pogrom' against them.[9]

According to an official estimate, 1,044 people were killed in the violence: 790 Muslims and 254 Hindus, including those killed in the

Godhra train fire. Another 223 people were reported missing; 2,540 were injured; 919 women were widowed and 606 children orphaned. Unofficial estimates put the death toll closer to 2,000, with Muslims forming a high proportion of those killed.[10]

I will focus on some incidents that were archetypal of the kind of violence that followed in the wake of the Godhra incident.

Attack on Gulbarg Housing Society and killing of Ehsan Jafri

Among the Muslims residing in the Gulbarg housing society, former Congress MP, Ehsan Jafri was one. On 28 February, when a mob attacked this colony, Jafri asked for help from the police commissioner, the chief minister's office, and people at the centre, but no help came his way despite reassurances. The Muslim families in the colony waited to be rescued in vain, for over five hours.[11]

When no help arrived and even Jafri's house was attacked, he opened fire and injured a few people. He pleaded with the attacking mob to spare his life and that of other Muslims. But he was attacked, killed and his body was hacked and mutilated. Many hours later, the police came and rescued some of the Muslims who had survived the mob's fury.

The relevant portion of the NHRC team report, citing the incident, is worth reproducing because it graphically underscores the fact that the topmost functionaries of the state government and the police were totally indifferent to the fate of the Muslims facing dangerous onslaughts from the Hindu mobs:

> Shri Amar Sinh Chaudhary, former Chief Minister, Gujarat, narrated to the team his futile efforts in seeking police help for Shri Ahsan Jaffrey [*sic*], former MP. He claimed to have personally contacted the Police Commissioner, P.C. Pande, at 10.30 AM on 28 February and apprised him of he imminent danger to the life of Shri Jaffrey. The Police Commissioner assured him that police assistance will be dispatched rapidly. He reminded him again after receiving another frantic call from Ahsan Jaffrey that no police reinforcement had reached his place and that the few policemen present were ineffective and unwilling to control the violent mob. Shri Chaudhary said that he also spoke to the CM Narendra Modi in the afternoon and found him well informed about the presence of a violent crowd outside Shri Jaffrey's house. He also spoke to the Chief Secretary and

Home Secretary between 12.30 and 2 PM. Shri Jaffrey was burnt alive along with his family and 39 others (total killed – 50).[12]

Violence in Naroda Patiya

In the immediate aftermath of the Godhra incident, Ahmedabad was the most affected in the riots. It is alleged that Bajrang Dal activists attacked the Muslim neighbourhoods in Naroda Patiya and Naroda Gaon. The estimates of the number of persons killed in the area vary. If the official figure is right, eighty-three Muslims were killed. Unofficial estimates point to a much higher figure of casualties.

The media has reported many horrific incidents related to the attack on Muslims at Naroda Patiya: 'Kauser Bano was nine months pregnant; her belly was torn open and her foetus wrenched out, held aloft on the tip of a sword, then dashed to the ground and flung into a fire. ... Another victim, twenty-two-year-old Sufiya Bano, was raped and burnt in front of her father.'[13]

Serious allegations were levelled against the police for covering up the crimes in these areas. Most of the survivors fled and are yet to be rehabilitated. It was alleged in the media that investigations by the police were tardy, much of the evidence was lost and cases involving rape were ignored. The trials in the cases put up in the courts have been stalled since the NHRC sought intervention of the Supreme Court to transfer the cases outside the state.

There have been important developments in this case since then. A special investigation team (SIT), appointed by the Supreme Court for investigating the case, approached the Gujarat High Court for cancellation of anticipatory bail to State Women and Child Welfare Minister Maya Kodnani, an accused in this case.[14] She was thus arrested. This is one instance of a highly placed person in the Gujarat government being allegedly involved in the riots.

Best Bakery Case

Best Bakery, a small outlet in the Hanuman Tekri area of Vadodara, was attacked on 1 March 2002 by a mob. They burnt the bakery along with fourteen people, twelve of them Muslims. Zaheera Sheikh, a nineteen-year-old girl who lodged the First Information Report (FIR), was an important witness in the case. She stated that she saw her family members being burnt to death by the mob shouting communal slogans.[15]

The trial of the case went through several ups and downs. A number of witnesses, including Zaheera Sheikh, turned hostile, denying they had seen anything on the night of the attack. The fast track court acquitted twenty-one accused Hindus on 27 June 2003. In the judgement it was held that though it was proved beyond doubt that a violent mob had attacked the bakery and killed around twelve people, there was no legally acceptable evidence to prove that any of the accused presented before the court had committed the crime. The judgement was critical of the police for its delay in filing the FIR, poor investigation, etc.

A retrial was ordered. Zaheera Sheikh was separately prosecuted for perjury. The Supreme Court sentenced her to one-year imprisonment for perjury in a murder case and she was fined Rs 50,000. In February 2006, after retrial, nine of the twenty-one accused of the bakery murders were convicted and sentenced to life imprisonment. The court acquitted eight others while issuing warrants for the arrest of four missing persons. The case was unique in that after the accused had been acquitted, a retrial on the same charges took place under the orders of the Supreme Court, outside the state of Gujarat, which ended in conviction.

Bilkis Bano Case

The case of Bilkis Bano too is unusual in that after a tortuous process in which the tragedy was first hushed up, then brought to light, justice finally prevailed.

Bilkis is a simple uneducated village girl. Journalist Sheela Bhatt, who met her, wrote, 'She found it difficult to understand the event that had devastated her. To her, the most incomprehensible and unbearable aspect of what had happened was the fact that people whom she knew since childhood, who were like her brothers, had raped her.'[16]

The incident dates back to 3 March 2002. The six-month-pregnant girl was gang-raped and beaten up in Dahod district. She witnessed the massacre of fourteen of her family members. Her three-year-old daughter's head was smashed on a stone that resulted in her death.

With the intervention of the Supreme Court, Bilkis's was the second case to be transferred out of Gujarat. The trial was held at Bombay instead of at Ahmedabad. After six long years, twelve persons were convicted of the crime, of whom eleven were awarded life sentences. One of the accused, a policeman, was awarded a sentence of three years in prison for recording a distorted complaint.

It must be said that for one Bilkis Bano who got justice, there were many who were denied it.

DISPLACEMENT AND OSTRACIZATION

Soon after rioting commenced in the various towns and cities, many Muslims, fearing for their lives, left their homes and flocked to the relief camps set up for them by NGOs and the state government. By 27 March nearly 1,00,000 had moved to 101 relief camps. This number increased to 1,50,000 in 104 camps within the next two weeks.[17]

Media reports have shown, on different occasions, how the state government officials compelled the inmates to leave the camps, which the former were trying to close down. Most of the Muslims felt insecure about returning to their erstwhile homes and they felt safe about going back only to the Muslim-dominated areas. This resulted in the 'ghettoization' of Muslims in Gujarat.

Initially, the state government sanctioned Rs 2,00,000 as compensation to the families whose members had died in the Godhra train fire and Rs 1,00,000 to those who died in the subsequent riots. This was later increased to Rs 1,50,000. Muslims considered this discriminatory. Much later, on 23 May 2008, the central government announced a compensation package of Rs 3,50,000 for families of those who died in the Gujarat riots and each of the 2,540 wounded were to receive Rs 1,50,000.[18]

The NHRC team made some observations – on the basis of the evidence gathered – of the social and economic boycott of the minority community during the riots. The relevant observations in its report are excerpted below:

> Organised attempts for effecting a social and economic boycott of the minority community was another distressing feature of the current riots stressed by many. Pamphlets and handbills were widely circulated exhorting Hindus to boycott Muslims in matters of employment and business activities. Shri R.K. Sayed, a retired Secretary to the Govt. of India and former adviser to the Governor of J&K said in anguish that the husband of his maid servant, Rayeesa Banu, has been told not to report for work at a motor garage whose Hindu owner has been threatened not to employ any Muslim workers. He further said that the authorities of Don Bosco school have also received threats not to allow students from the Muslim community to attend.[19]

....

Media reports suggest that many shops and commercial establishments owned by Muslims have not been re-opened and their businesses have suffered.

CRIMINAL PROSECUTIONS

A very large number of cases were registered in connection with the Gujarat riots. There has been much finger-pointing about the handling of the investigation by the Gujarat police. The Supreme Court strongly criticized the state government's investigation and prosecution of those accused of violence in the riots and directed the police to review 2,000 of the 4,000 riots cases that had been closed due to lack of evidence. The police then identified about 1,600 cases for reinvestigation, arrested 640 accused persons and launched investigations against forty officers for their lapses.[20]

A reflection of the way our system of criminal justice operates is that even among cases for which charge sheets were filed in the courts, very few have been decided some seven years after the riots. The trials in these cases are still ongoing. The exceptions are the Best Bakery and Bilkis Bano cases, whose outcome was different, perhaps only due to the intervention of the Supreme Court.

ROLE OF THE STATE GOVERNMENT AND THE PRESS

The role of the state government in dealing with the riots came under severe criticism in the media. Both national TV channels and mainstream English newspapers highlighted the failures of the state government in dealing with the situation. The state administration was also accused of its complicity in the victimization of Muslims by Hindu activists and for its failure to prevent the rampaging mobs from attacking the Muslims, their shops, establishments, homes and places of worship at many locations in the state.

Three eminent journalists, Dileep Padgaonkar (former executive managing editor, the *Times of India*), Aakar Patel (former editor, *Mid-Day*) and B.G. Verghese (former editor, the *Hindustan Times*), were deputed on a fact-finding mission by the Editors Guild of India and their report is called 'Rights and Wrongs – Ordeal by Fire in the Killing Fields of Gujarat'.[21] In the report, this mission has made very pertinent observations concerning the role played by the media and the state government in aggravating the situation in Gujarat.

Numerous provocative press notes issued by the state government have been cited; for instance, the press note issued immediately after the chief minister's visit at the Godhra site on 27 February described the torching of Sabarmati Express as a 'pre-planned, inhuman, collective violent act of terrorism'. The press notes of the state government most often used phraseology like 'inhuman genocide', 'inhuman carnage', and 'massacre' to describe the Godhra incident, while the subsequent riots were invariably termed as 'disturbances' and occasionally as 'violent disturbances or incidents'. On 4 March, the press release on the occasion of L.K. Advani's visit to Gujarat stated that 'Home Minister L.K. Advani today said that Godhra genocide had given setback to the four years of peaceful Bharatiya Janata Party rule in Gujarat'.[22]

The two leading Gujarati newspapers, *Sandesh* and *Gujarat Samachar*, which compete with each other for circulation in the state, took a pro-Hindutva approach and sensationalized their reports, contributing to the generation of antipathy against Muslims and to the consequential perpetration of violence against the community. As a result, both newspapers profited through increased circulation. The fact-finding mission has reported that *Sandesh's* circulation increased by about 1,50,000 copies since the riots began.

The English media and the national TV news channels, which mostly took an independent line and sometimes highlighted the atrocities committed on Muslims, were criticized as being biased against Hindus. A group of VHP storm troopers, whose ire the Editors Guild of India's mission had to face,[23] demanded that the 'licence' of Aaj Tak be revoked. This channel was perhaps the first to show live footage of the rioting in Gujarat. The *Times of India* and the *Indian Express* also had to face the wrath of VHP activists.

Since the Nanavati Commission has so far only given the report regarding the Godhra train burning incident and has not covered the subsequent events of the Gujarat riots, the lone authentic account available is a summary of the NHRC report that was placed in the Lok Sabha, in answer to a starred question, on 16 July 2002.[24]

The NHRC has been highly critical of the role of the state government and, inter alia, castigated it for the assault on the dignity and worth of the human person, particularly of women and children, through acts of rape and other humiliating crimes of violence and cruelty. The Commission reached the definite conclusion that 'the principle of *res ipsa loquitur* applies in this case and that there was a comprehensive failure on the part of the State to protect Constitutional rights of the people of Gujarat, starting with the tragedy in Godhra on 27 February 2002 and continuing with the violence that ensued in the weeks that followed'.[25]

The NHRC has faulted the state government on several counts, including the failure of intelligence. Given the volatile situation that was developing in Ayodhya at that time and considering the reports in the press warning of the danger of inter-communal violence, the Gujarat Intelligence Bureau should have kept a close and continuing touch with their counterparts in UP and with the Central Intelligence Bureau. Their inability to establish a two-way flow of intelligence was in part responsible for the tragic consequences.

Besides the failure of intelligence, there was a 'failure to take appropriate anticipatory and subsequent action to prevent the spread and continuation of violence'. In view of the gravity of the Godhra incident, there should have been a higher degree of responsiveness from the state government to control the likely fallout, especially in the wake of the call for the Gujarat Bandh. Instead, the state government publicly announced its support of that call.

With regard to other aspects of handling the riots, the Commission found that the state government failed to identify the local factors and players, did not handle the major cases equally, recorded distorted FIRs, etc. Although the chief minister of the state made claims that the situation was brought under control within seventy-two hours, in reality, communal violence continued till the middle of June 2002.

A high-level team of the NHRC, headed by its chairperson, visited Gujarat during 19–22 March 2002. In its report the NHRC team observed:

> While in the previous riots also political elements did play a major part and the police and administration failed to control violence, they were not accused of direct involvement in the carnage. The failure of police and administration in the current riots is attributed not to their professional incompetence but to their attitude of apathy and callousness in general and the accusation of connivance and complicity was made in some cases.[26]

The case of former congress MP, Ehsan Jafri has been mentioned earlier in this chapter, with respect to the apathy and/or complicity of the state administration and police. The NHRC team has also mentioned numerous other cases where it found evidence of connivance of the police in the incidents of arson and looting by the marauding crowds. Such happenings invoked the feeling of insecurity not only among the poorer sections of Muslims but even among the highly placed ones. The following extract from the report brings this out clearly:

> Describing the prevailing sense of insecurity and fear in the minds of the members of the minority community, a number of representatives of the NGOs/activists including A.P. Ravani, former Chief Justice, Rajasthan, referred to the cases of Justice A. Divecha, retd. Judge of Gujarat High Court who was forced to leave his house which was later burnt and Justice Qadri, a sitting High Court Judge who had to leave his bungalow in Law Garden area and move to the Judges' Colony as no one assured safety and security to him and his family.
>
> Even the police officials belonging to the minority community were targets of threats from the marauding mobs. A number of gazetted police officers belonging to the minority community were advised by their superiors to remain confined in their homes during the period of violence. The incident involving IGP Saiyed who was in uniform with name tag and was menacingly accosted by a mob in the presence of some policemen was mentioned by a number of speakers.[27]

These instances seem to bear out the allegation that the administration and the police were often complicit in the victimization of Muslims in the post-Godhra riots. However, a caveat needs to be added here that even though such a conclusion appears to emerge from the findings of responsible entities such as the NHRC, there can be no definitive conclusion in this regard as yet.

COMMENT BY THE PRESIDENT OF INDIA

Consequent to an interview given to the press by the then president of India, K.R. Narayanan, it came to notice that he had exchanged correspondence with the then prime minister, Atal Bihari Vajpayee, in which the president had expressed his concern about the handling of the Gujarat riots by the central and the state governments. The correspondence was asked to be put in the public domain through the Central Information Commission (CIC) under the RTI Act 2005. However, the government did not agree to make the correspondence public, stating, 'the disclosure of which would prejudicially affect the sovereignty and integrity of India and security, strategic, scientific or economic interests of the state, etc. In these circumstances copies cannot be provided'.[28] The CIC did not accept the contention but the matter has not been resolved and the correspondence is yet to be made public. Nevertheless, Narayanan himself disclosed the nature of the correspondence in a press interview in March 2005, which is excerpted below:

> There was governmental and administrative support for the communal riots in Gujarat. I gave several letters to Prime Minister Vajpayee in this regard on this issue. I met him personally and talked to him directly. But Vajpayee did not do anything effective. ... Had the military been given powers to shoot, the carnage in Gujarat could have been avoided to a great extent. I feel there was a conspiracy involving the state and central governments behind the Gujarat riots.[29]

It is evident that the president felt concerned about the way in which the government dithered in acting effectively to control the riots in Gujarat and he went to the extent of hinting at a conspiracy between the state and central governments. This is indeed a very damaging indictment.

LONG-TERM EFFECTS

The riots got over in June 2002 but the impact on the lives and psyche of the people has been a long-lasting one. Many Muslim families, who were displaced from their homes in the riots, have not been fully rehabilitated even now. During their sojourn in the relief camps they have had to face both deprivation and discrimination that has resulted in their isolation from the system and the majority community within the state.

The riots yielded political dividends for the BJP inasmuch as the party was returned to power by large majorities in two successive state elections since 2002, perhaps as a direct consequence of the polarization of the electorate in Gujarat. The people of Gujarat, however, have been left with a legacy of strained relations and persisting mutual hostility between the Hindu and Muslims.

As in the other instances, the role played by the vernacular media was found to be objectionable. This underscores the need for regulation of what is published at such times, for which hardly any strong mechanism exists as of today. The powers of the Press

Council of India are severely circumscribed. It is time legislation is brought out to arm this body with effective powers enabling it to rein in errant sections of the media, wont to act in a manner that creates disaffection among communities. While freedom of the press is sacrosanct, it should be amenable to imposition of certain curbs in the larger national interest.

✪

NOTES

1 The UC Banerjee Commission was set up two years after the Gujarat riots, when the opposition coalition, the UPA, came to power at the centre, replacing the BJP-led coalition of NDA.

2 'Godhra probe findings are "partial": NHRC', Press Trust of India, 12 October 2008, http://newsx.com/story/31184.

3 G.T. Nanavati and A.H. Mehta, 'Report by the Commission of Enquiry into the facts, circumstances and all the course of events of the incidents that led to setting on fire some coaches of the Sabarmati Express Train on 27-2-2002 near Godhra Railway Station and the subsequent incidents of violence in the State in the aftermath of the Godhra incident' (18 September 2008), Ahmedabad.

4 'Both Godhra probe reports are partial, says rights panel', *The Financial Express*, 13 October 2008.

5 'POTA not applicable in Godhra riots case: Guj HC', *The Times of India*, 13 February 2009.

6 '2002 Gujarat Violence', http://en.wikipedia.org/ wiki/2002_Gujarat_violence.

7 Achyut Yagnik and Suchitra Sheth, 'Whither Gujarat? Violence and After', *Economic and Political Weekly*, 16 March 2002 as in *The Gujarat Carnage*, ed., Asghar Ali Engineer (New Delhi: Orient Longman, 2003), pp. 85-86.

8 Ibid.

9 Brass, *Production of Hindu-Muslim Violence*, pp. 386-392.

10 Ibid.

11 'Safehouse of Horrors', *Tehelka* 4 (43), 3 November 2007, pp. 74-76.
12 'Report of NHRC Team', http://nhrc.nic.in/guj_annex_1.htm.
13 'Naroda Patiya Massacre: Muslims. They don't deserve to live', *Tehelka* 4 (43), 3 November 2007, pp. 66-73.
14 IBNLive, http://ibnlive.in.com/news/guj-minister-maya-kodnanis-bail-to-be-cancelled /86156-3.html
15 'Best Bakery Case', http://en.wikipedia.org/wiki/Best-Bakery_case.
16 Sheela Bhatt, 'The tragedy of Bilkis Banu' (7 August 2004), http://in.rediff.com/news/2004/aug/07spec1.htm.
17 Brass, *Production of Hindu-Muslim Violence*, p. 388.
18 BBC News, http://news.bbc.co.uk/2/hi/south_asia/7416073.stm.
19 'Report of NHRC Team', http://nhrc.nic.in/guj_annex_1.htm.
20 'Gujarat Violence', http://en.wikipedia.org/wiki/2002_Gujarat_violence.
21 Aakar Patel, Dileep Padgaonkar and B. G. Verghese, 'Rights and Wrongs – Ordeal by Fire in the Killing Fields of Gujarat' (3 May 2002), eds., Guild Fact Finding Mission Report, New Delhi, p. 2.
22 Ibid, p. 16.
23 Ibid, p. 20.
24 Lok Sabha Starred Question No. 23 by Vilas Muttemwar and Jyotiraditya Scindia on NHRC Report on Gujarat and Answer given by Ch. Vidyasagar Rao, Minister of State in the Ministry of Home Affairs, GOI.
25 Ibid.
26 'Report of NHRC Team', http://nhrc.nic.in/guj_annex_1.htm.
27 Ibid.
28 A.G. Noorani, 'Matters Of Policy: A President's Letters on the Gujarat Pogrom to a PM are the Nation's Property – Dear Atalji', *The Hindustan Times*, 23 May 2002.
29 Ibid., First appeared in the Malayalam monthly, *Manava Samskriti*, the interview was given to a Congress legislator from Kerala, P.T. Thomas, http://in.rediff.com/cms/print.jsp?docpath=//news/2005/mar/07inter1.htm

A Non-astrological Peep into the Future

In the global perspective, the view that future conflicts would be between civilizations, across certain fault lines, is indeed questionable. It is more likely that political and economic factors and the imperatives of achieving global or regional dominance will be the drivers for such conflicts. Whether or not, and when and where such conflicts occur will also depend on the effectiveness or otherwise of international institutions, such as the United Nations, in fulfilling their role as forums for conflict resolution.

At the regional, sub-regional and national levels, however, such conflicts will not easily abate in the near or medium-term: such as the ones between Israel and Hezbollah in Lebanon, Israel and Hamas in Gaza, Shias and Sunnis in Iraq, the Tamils and the Sinhalese-dominated government in Sri Lanka, and Hindus and Muslims in India.

We have seen that Hindu-Muslim riots have been an enduring phenomenon for more than a century. In the earlier part of British rule, in the nineteenth century, communal riots were few and far between. Coinciding with the consolidation of nationalist forces against imperial rule and resulting from the tactics resorted to by the British to prevent such consolidation by the adoption of a divide-and-rule policy, the schism between Hindus and Muslims widened. This led to sporadic eruptions of Hindu-Muslim violence in the earlier part of the twentieth century; the Kanpur riots of 1930 being one such example of conflagration in this period.

Then came the trauma of the partition of the country with the bloodbath on both sides of the borders, preceding the event and following in its wake as well. The administration at the time was in shambles and did not have the capacity to deal with violence on the scale it happened. While governance was at a standstill, the herculean efforts of one individual, Mahatma Gandhi, injected some sanity into the people and gradually brought back life on an even keel. The magnitude of the violence perhaps proved to be self-limiting inasmuch as well after the Mahatma had fallen to an assassin's bullets, the decade of the fifties remained nearly free from communal discord and violence.

Since the 1960s to the present day, Hindus and Muslims have clashed from time to time; the frequency and intensity of the clashes have varied, but the problem has stayed with us.

It would be invidious to ascribe these clashes to religious or cultural dissonance for no religion sanctifies violence nor do our inherent cultural traditions. We have seen how political and economic factors, primarily the former, have been responsible for most of the conflicts. There are scholars – Paul Brass for instance – who argue that it is futile to try and identify a cause or even a multiplicity of causes for communal riots because the dynamics of 'riot production' are such that they defy causal analysis. It is indubitable, however, that differences between the two major communities have been exacerbated, at different times, through political mobilizations around certain emotive issues and the fallout has been the eruption of communal violence.

By far the most significant political mobilization that gained considerable political traction for the protagonists of Hindutva was around the issue of building a Ram temple at Ayodhya. Some of independent India's worst communal conflagrations have been the offshoots of this political mobilization, three of which have been covered in this book, namely, Bhagalpur (1989), Bombay (1992-93) and Gujarat (2002).

The fact that there has been no major outbreak of Hindu-Muslim violence since the Gujarat riots gives us the space to consider and reflect on the possibility of cessation of such tragic happenings in the future. Although the Ayodhya temple issue has not been resolved, it does appear that the prospects of gaining further political and electoral advantage by milking it any more have greatly diminished.

The general elections of 2004 and the state elections in UP in 2007 are indicative of that. This has been further reinforced by the outcome of the 2009 general elections, which show that ideological issues of the revivalist brand seem to no longer sway the voters one way or the other. That is not to say that sentiments cannot be whipped up around similar emotive issues in the future. Unless a consensus develops not to exploit such issues to gain or consolidate their following among political parties and religious leaders – the *mahants*, the *shankaracharyas*, the imams and the ulamas – the cycle of episodic violence will continue.

....

In recent times, when the elections were coming up in several states to be followed by the general elections in mid-2009, it appeared that the forces that could benefit from outbreaks of sectarian violence were at work.

About 150 persons died within a few months since April 2008 in communal clashes across a number of states in different locations such as Burhanpur in Madhya Pradesh, Dhule in Maharashtra, Central Assam districts (where nearly fifty were killed in clashes between Bodo tribals and Muslims) and Adilabad in Andhra Pradesh. Lives were lost in numerous clashes between the Bajrang Dal activists and Christians in the states of Orissa and Karnataka. These developments do not bode well for the future.

The issue really is one of steering away from the politics of identity, for it quickly tends to degenerate into the politics of hatred. Currently, most political parties are guilty of practising it. The identities that are played up are religious, caste-based, regional or linguistic and passions are sought to be aroused to polarize electorates around these identities. There seems little possibility that the nature of political discourse will rise above these identity issues.

In recent years, incidents of terrorism have added a new dimension to this age-old problem. In the chapter on this topic, we have drawn a clear distinction between acts of terrorism and outbreaks of communal violence; but these two do get linked in public perception. Many victims of terrorist violence are Muslims, yet Muslims are adversely profiled whenever an act of terror occurs.

It is posited by experts that these terrorist strikes are aimed at destabilizing our society by creating discord among communities. The police, to ward off blame, and the media to gain viewership or readership, highlight the identities of the suspects leading to the adverse profiling of Indian Muslims. More often than not these are false leads and the suspects turn out to be innocent. But the damage is done. Unless some regulation can be enforced against premature publicity being given to such so-called 'breakthroughs', the situation can only get worse. As we have discussed, the problem can be resolved only by developing the capability in our agencies to prevent these terror-related incidents from taking place.

The outlook for communal riots ending in the proximate future is bleak. Nonetheless, since 'hope springs eternal in the human breast', some fuzzy light is visible at the end of the tunnel. In developed countries, such conflicts are rare. Even in an ethnically diverse and multicultural society like the United States, the

Caucasians and African-Americans (as well as the Hispanics and Asians) have learned to live together without overt display of animus degenerating into what we describe as 'riots'. Economic development, therefore, may be the key. As people are lifted out of poverty, and more people, including those from among the minorities, are gainfully employed, it would be increasingly difficult for manipulative agents to find foot soldiers to carry out their nefarious designs.

Our economy could soon enter into a phase of double-digit growth and this could divert the attention of our politicians to genuinely focus on 'issues of development' in their electoral strategies rather than divisive communitarian issues – away from the politics of identity.

That is how we hope the future will unveil itself as, in this Asian century, India ascends to become the third-largest economy in the world.

Annexure

STATEMENT OF P.K. LAHIRI, DISTRICT MAGISTRATE, INDORE, SUBMITTED TO JUSTICE T.C. SRIVASTAVA JUDICIAL ENQUIRY COMMISSION

ORIGIN

1. On 2nd June, 1969 Master Chandgi Ram 'Hind Kesari' came to Indore. Certain programmes had been arranged to fete him at Indore, including a Civic Reception on 3rd June. After being received at the Railway Station at about 7:30 p.m., he was taken out from there in a procession organized by the Dugdh Vikreta Sangh, Indore.
2. On the same day, a freestyle wrestling show was also arranged by certain other sponsors at the Nehru Stadium in the evening. On account of the past disturbances on such occasions, a large force under gazetted police officers and magistrates was deputed for the arrangements. In the absence of SP, Indore, I had discussed the arrangements made by the police at the Stadium and with Chandgi Ram's procession with CSP-I Shri Bhatnagar. He explained to me the details of the police arrangements at the Stadium and also informed me that CSP-II Shri Shukla had been detailed to look after Chandgi Ram's procession with a sizeable contingent of police force. Though no trouble was apprehended, as a precautionary measure a license to take out the procession in honour of Chandgi Ram was granted u/s 30 of Police Act by the CSP-I describing the route and with a specific condition that no *'akhadas'* would be associated with the procession. The procession was to terminate at Ahilya Chowk and a police force consisting of one inspector, 5 SIs, 15 HCs and 50 constables was under the charge of Shri S.L. Shukla, city superintendent of police accompanied it to ensure its smooth passage. Master Chandgi Ram was enthusiastically greeted by the populace, both Hindus

and Muslims as he wended his way towards Ahilya Chowk in the procession. There were originally about 300 persons in the procession and it proceeded through different localities without any incident till it reached Bombay Bazaar area of Jawahar Marg at about 9:00 p.m. From the start, a few volunteers with *lathis* accompanied the procession clearing the way for it to progress towards its destination.

3. A crowd of about 300 spectators, mostly belonging to the minority community, stood at the Bombay Bazaar crossing. It appeared at first that they were bystanders who had gathered to cheer Chandgi Ram on his way. But their presence caused some obstruction to even the progress of the procession. The police officers tried to clear the way for the procession to proceed ahead. A few members of the procession brandished their *lathis* to force a passage for the processionists. Perhaps this infuriated the crowd and stones were pelted on the procession. There was some retaliation. Acting with presence of mind the police officers sent the jeep with Chandgi Ram speeding away from the scene to safety. The procession also automatically broke up and dispersed. In the meanwhile mobs of both the communities gathered on both the sides of Jawahar Marg near the Bombay Bazaar crossing and soda water bottles, iron bars, stones, etc., were used in the ensuing fracas. The CSP Shukla and the TI received injuries in their efforts to bring the situation under control. But as the situation deteriorated the CSP requisitioned arms and ammunition from the nearest police station i.e., PS Sarafa. On receipt of arms the CSP and his party had to open fire at about 2120 hrs. to disperse the rioting crowds. 11 rounds were fired at this juncture.
4. I received a telephone call from CSP Shri Shukla at about 9:30 p.m. at my residence asking for reinforcement of police force as the situation was going out of hand. I immediately rushed to the stadium where, as stated earlier, strong police arrangements had been made in connection with the freestyle wrestling being staged there. The wrestling was over and a police truck, with a contingent of 2 PCs, 6 HCs, and 65 constables with Town Inspector Shri Sugan Singh, was dispatched by me to the Bombay Bazaar area at about 9:35 p.m. Soon after CSP-I Shri Bhatnagar and City Magistrate Shri Singh were located in the stadium and sent to Bombay Bazaar area at about 9:50 p.m. I also instructed Shri Kailash Saxena, DSP, to proceed immediately to the Control Room to mobilize all available police force. The remaining force

....

in the stadium was directed to proceed to the Control Room. I and the Addl SP, Indore, in the absence of Shri C.S. Kadam on leave, thereafter proceeded to the Control Room to take charge of the situation reaching there at about 10:00 p.m.

FURTHER DEVELOPMENTS

5. The trouble at first spread quickly in the Bombay Bazaar area and the neighbouring localities. Several shops were looted on the main Jawahar Marg and the crowd set fire to some shops and the plundered goods collected in heaps on the road. In the lanes forking out from the main road there was indiscriminate stone throwing particularly coming from the rooftops, windows and other openings of residential houses.
   CSP-I P.S. Bhatnagar and his party and the town inspector had to open fire on a few occasions in defence of person and property and to disperse the menacing crowds. In all thirty-six rounds were fired in this area.
6. On reaching the Control Room I contacted the ADM Shri Thakur and asked him to come to the Control Room immediately. Shri Mathur, deputy collector and magistrate, was also contacted by me on phone and asked to rush to the Control Room along with the other dy. collector/magistrates. Shri Bhatnagar CSP-I informed me on phone about the situation in the Bombay Bazaar area, from PS Sarafa, shortly after 11:00 p.m. He suggested imposition of curfew in view of the serious situation and I thereupon decided to impose curfew in the city limits of Indore and conveyed to him that announcement of curfew be made through loud-speakers. Personnel was also dispatched from the Control Room to make similar announcements. The announcement of curfew was made effective from midnight till 8:00 a.m. on 3.6.1969.
7. After Shri Thakur, ADM, arrived I sent him with a police officer and force to the Bombay Bazaar area at about 10:45 p.m. Meanwhile, I was informed that the electricity in the Bombay Bazaar area had failed and I requested the commissioner on phone to take up the matter immediately with the MPEB authorities and after some time the power failure was rectified. I also requested the commissioner to immediately call for more police force from Bhopal and other places. The commissioner informed me afterwards that one company of SAF was being immediately rushed from Ujjain and one or two companies would also start from Bhopal.
8. I learnt meanwhile that though the situation had improved a little

in the Bombay Bazaar area, mischief mongers were still throwing stones, setting fire and committing other acts of hooliganism in the area, particularly in the lanes and by-lanes. I therefore decided to proceed to Bombay Bazaar with a contingent of police force at about 11:40 p.m. On reaching the scene I found that the main street had been cleared but at several places plundered goods were lying in heaps on the road which had been set on fire by hooligans. The fire brigade was active in extinguishing the fire and in none of the arson cases the fire had been allowed to spread over a large area. I found the roads and the lanes littered with stones and, at some places, with wreckage of glass. On both sides of the Jawahar Marg mischief mongers could be seen in the by-lanes. I also saw a few stones being pelted by them. Under my orders the police force was rushed to the lanes on both sides from the Bombay Bazaar crossing to clear the crowds. After I had made sure that the area was cleared, I returned back to the Control Room.

9. All the available police force had been speedily brought to the Central Kotwali. But as the trouble escalated and spread to other localities the police force available appeared to be wholly inadequate to meet the situation and ensure enforcement of the curfew. I received a telephonic call from the DIG Administration Shri Nagu from Bhopal and I stressed the necessity of rushing as much force as possible to Indore. He informed me that some police force was already on the way and some more would be shortly dispatched. I contacted the commissioner also several times on phone to request for more force and he informed me that he was making every effort to secure forces from Bhopal and other places. He also informed me that he had contacted the IG of police at Gwalior and the latter had asked him to direct Shri S.P. Mishra, commandant 1st BN SAF, Indore, to take charge of the situation as the SP, Indore, in view of the fact that Shri C.S. Kadam was on leave and Shri Sorang was absolutely new to Indore. Shri S.P. Mishra had already been called to the Control Room and as soon as he arrived I informed him of these orders. Shortly after midnight Shri S.P. Mishra accordingly assumed charge of the situation.

10. As the situation was being brought under control in the Bombay Bazaar area, reports were received of arson, stone throwing, etc., from Juni Indore area. Some of the available force was immediately dispatched by me with Magistrate Shri Mathur and a gazetted

police officer to proceed to the affected area in Juni Indore at about 11:40 p.m. As stated earlier, I left for Bombay Bazaar at the same time and returned shortly after midnight.

There was some trouble in the area of PS Malharganj and sometime after midnight the police party had to fire four rounds to disperse a riotous mob also intent on committing arson.

11. Shri Suresh Seth, mayor, and some other local leaders came to the Control Room and informed me that the situation in the Juni Indore area was not being brought under control. CSP-I Shri Bhatnagar had returned to the Control Room from the Bombay Bazaar area and I proceeded to Juni Indore with him and a contingent of police force at about 12:50 a.m. I found that although several engines of the fire brigade were operating the fire was enveloping a large number of houses and its further spread was not being contained. I found that the mud-houses surrounding the mosque at the crossing were all on fire and it was immediately necessary to concentrate on extinguishing the fire in these houses to save the mosque. I accordingly asked Shri Rishi, superintendent of fire brigade to concentrate efforts to save these houses. After some time the fire in the area was brought under control though considerable damage was caused mostly to the shacks and mud-houses in the area. The mosque, however, remained practically unaffected and could be saved. Meanwhile, CSP-I Bhatnagar rushed with the force and chased away the crowd collected in the alleys and the by-lanes ahead, towards right and left of the road, committing arson and mischief. He had to order firing in defence of person and property and to drive away the mischief mongers.

12. After the situation had improved in this area and the fire was on the way of being brought under control, I returned with CSP Bhatnagar to the Control Room and subsequently remained there through the early hours of the morning directing measures to bring the situation under control. The police reinforcements began to come in during this period. The forces as they arrived were deployed in various parts of the city to bring the situation under control.

13. A meeting of the senior police officers, station officers of the town and magistrates available in the Control Room was held at about 3:00 a.m. on 3.6.1969. I and Shri S.P. Mishra addressed the officers. It was decided to put into operation the 'Internal Security Scheme' for Indore City. The station officers were accordingly

directed to commence arrests of the listed bad characters other anti-social elements and *goondas* likely to indulge in communal rioting. Shri S.P. Mishra divided the city into 5 sectors, placing a gazetted police officer in charge of each sector. The posting of piquets was also finalized at important points listed in the Internal Security Scheme and also at some other strategic places. The piquets were further strengthened and supplemented as reinforcements of police force came in front of the different parts of the state. However, throughout the 2nd and the 3rd of June we continued to be handicapped by the lack of adequate police force. Along with the posting of piquets and division of the city into sectors, several mobile parties were constituted for intensive patrolling in the town. The DIG of police, Indore, also returned from Bhopal in the early hours of the morning on 3rd June.

14. On 3rd June 1969, the period of curfew was extended since trouble spread to some other localities, particularly the Jinsi and the neighbouring areas of PS Malharganj. During the day there were sporadic cases of arson and other mischief. The tension spread in the city and the Swadeshi and Malwa Mills did not function in the first shift.

    There were a number of cases of arson and assaults during the afternoon in the area of PS Malharganj. There was also a report of firing from a house belonging to a member of the minority community. In order to disperse an unruly mob and prevent arson the police had to resort to firing in the area. One youth of the majority community died of a bullet injury in the Jinsi area on 3.6.1969.

15. In the course of the afternoon a few public leaders including Shri Khadiwala and Shri Jhanisriya came to the Control Room and complained that the situation in the Jinsi area was out of control. The CSP, magistrate and police force had already been sent to the area. However, in view of the gravity of the situation I and Shri S.P. Mishra decided to proceed to the scene ourselves. On reaching PS Malharganj we learnt that crowd at the Jinsi crossing had been dispersed by the force with Shri Batnagar, CSP-I, but a big mob had collected near the Hammalon Ki Masjid in the Malharganj area and was setting fire to the mosque. The fire brigade was dispatched to the scene as soon as it arrived. At this stage I heard some persons, who had come running to the PS, crying out about a boy having been shot in the vicinity. The ambulance van which was available at the PS was immediately

sent to attend to this casualty. We later came to know that this was the boy of the majority community who had succumbed to bullet injury.

16. I and Shri S.P. Mishra proceeded with a few constables to Hammalon Ki Masjid. The front portion of the mosque had already been set on fire by the crowd which had now collected at the rear of the mosque and appeared to be intent on mischief. This crowd was chased away by the small police force available with us. Some members of the crowd shouted that a large crowd of the minority community, armed with lethal weapons, had gathered inside the mosque and were preparing for an attack. The crowd was speedily dispersed and chased away by show of force and we succeeded in persuading the persons inside the mosque to open the door and come out. We found some 12 persons including a few women and children huddled inside the mosque. When they came out they were in a state of abject fear and panic. They were escorted to the PS for safety. The mosque was full of smoke and as far as we could see there was no collection of lethal weapons inside. Had the persons within the mosque not been rescued at our instance they would perhaps have met with a tragic fate; and it would truly have been the worst calamity in the course of the communal disturbances at Indore.

17. We had heard of the rumour of a boy of majority community having been shot dead by one Haidar Pahelwan. Therefore, I and Shri Mishra proceeded to the Kadabin area where Haider Pahelwan's house was searched and a few *lathis*, spears, etc., which had been thrown out of the house were seized. Haidar Pahelwan was taken into custody. Haider Pahelwan and his brother Pyaremiyan are known to run a notorious gambling den in Kadabin. Shri Mishra also left instructions with the sector commander Shri Naidu to arrest Gangacharan and Devicharan, two notorious *goondas* who also thrive by encouraging the vice of gambling. The arrest of Haider Pahelwan and Gangacharan on the 3rd itself had a very salutary effect in preventing further escalation of trouble in the Malharganj area.

18. After ensuring that the situation in the Malharganj area was well on the way to being brought under control, I and Shri Mishra returned to the Control Room where a meeting had been called of prominent citizens and local leaders to solicit their help in dealing with the situation. We listened to the suggestions made by the various persons attending the meeting and also impressed

upon them the need to stand together to work for restoration of communal harmony.

ARMY CALLED OUT

19. During the afternoon I had alerted the station headquarters at Mhow to keep the Internal Security Column of the army standing by in case we required their help. I had also requested for the posting of a liaison officer at the Control Room at Indore and accordingly Capt. Raghuvir Singh of the 20th Punjab had come to station himself at the Central Kotwali. At 5:15 p.m. I asked Capt. Raghuvir Singh to call in the military contingent from Mhow. I also rang up the administrative commandant, station hqs., Mhow, and he asked me to confirm the requisition by sending a telegram. This was done. The Internal Security Column arrived from Mhow late in the evening and they were asked to stand by at the Control Room.

The SP, Indore, Shri Kadam returned sometime after 9:00 p.m. with the IG of police who arrived from Gwalior to supervise the measures.

20. On the 3rd itself two dead bodies of members of the minority community were found – one near the aerodrome and the other in the Malharganj area. The dead body of another Muslim, having succumbed to stab wounds, was found in Banganga. His wife was also reported to have been raped. In the Toda area of PS Juni, Indore, some miscreants opened fire on a police party later in the evening on 3.6.1969 and one constable of the 7th BN SAF was killed and another of the DEF was injured. The police returned the fire in self-defence. One member of the minority community was also killed as a result of the firing by the miscreants. In the Daulatganj area also the police had to fire 7 rounds in defence of persons and property on mobs indulging in violence and to prevent arson and looting.

21. The strengthening of the police piquets as a result of reinforcements coming in and intensive patrolling by officers as well as the patrolling parties had a salutary effect. The curfew was very effectively enforced during the intervening night between 3rd and 4th June. The task of rounding up of bad characters had been taken up in earnest and large number of arrests of *goondas* and anti-social elements, were made on the 3rd (and subsequently), under Section 151 CrPC and of others for specific offences which were registered from time to time in connection with incidents arising out of the disturbances.

....

22. From 4th June 1969 the situation improved gradually. In the morning a Flag March was carried out by the army contingent through the streets of the city of Indore. This appeared to have a wholesome psychological impact on the citizens. TI Sugan Singh had to open one round of fire in the air in self-defence to bring a difficult situation under control in Lal-ka-bagicha in the Goma-ki-fel area of PS Tukoganj. Some more cases of arson and looting were reported. Shri Gangaram Tiwari, Minister for Labour, also arrived in Indore to take stock of the situation.

    As a result of the precautionary and preventive measures taken by the administration and the police and with the cooperation of the citizens and local leaders, acts of organized violence were prevented from the 4th onwards though stray incidents continued to occur for some more days. At the instance of the IG of police, strong police reinforcements also arrived by this time from different parts of the state and strengthened the hands of the local administration in dealing with the situation. As I have stressed earlier, paucity of adequate police force was keenly felt on the 2nd and 3rd of June.

23. On the 5th of June, 1969, there were 19 incidents of arson, mostly involving properties belonging to the minority community. The most serious case of arson took place in Chhoti Gwal Toli where some miscreants set on fire a few auto-garages. This case has been detected and some of the accused persons have been arrested. The fire brigade did commendable work in bringing under control the arson cases and in most of them, only minor damage was caused to property. Two dead bodies, one of a Muslim named Suleman, which was identified later, and another of an unknown Hindu, who was later identified as a beggar, were found in Nehru Nagar and Nayapura areas respectively. A case of murder has been registered. The death of the beggar did not appear to be connected with the communal disturbances. Late in the evening on 5th June, one round was fired at a police party in Daulatganj area causing no mishap. Earlier at about 4:30 p.m. the same day, a head constable had to fire 2 rounds in Shakkar Bazaar area to prevent a belligerent crowd from spitting away two persons arrested by the police for looting. No one was injured.

24. On the 6th of June, there had been some improvement in the situation. This trend continued on 6th of June as well, though one of the injured in the hospital succumbed to his injuries. The same day at about 4:15 p.m. some members of the majority

community were reported to have proceeded towards a mosque in the Mukeripura area of PS Malharganj, armed with *lathis*, iron bars, etc., and pelting stones. The police piquets had to fire 2 rounds to disperse the crowd. Late in the evening at about 11:15 p.m. on 6th June some miscreants broke into the house of a Muslim in the Patnipura area and made away with some household goods. The police party had to fire one round in the air to scare away the crowd.

As stated earlier, from the 4th of June onwards the situation remained largely under control with only stray incidents of arson, looting, etc., taking place. The curfew continued to be enforced strictly with brief periods of relaxation. The curfew hours were progressively reduced and the curfew was entirely lifted for the first time on 16th June 1969. The prohibitory order u/s 144 CrPC continued to be extended from time to time and has been currently extended upto 24th July 1969.

THE AFTERMATH

25. The Internal Security Column of the army after staying in reserve in Indore for a few days, returned to Mhow on 7th. A total of 135 rounds were fired by the police. The death toll in the disturbances has been 12 though one of them may not have died in circumstances connected with the communal incidents. The total number of persons injured has been 258; 22 of them received gunshot wounds, 10 from sharp instruments and remaining from hard and blunt objects. The total cases of arson are 112. The total number of arrests todate is 1,727. Out of them 76 have been arrested for specific offences, 625 *goondas* and anti-social elements were arrested u/s 151 Cr PC and 944 were arrested for breach of curfew.

At the instance of the IG of police who continued to stay and supervise the police arrangements till 12th June 1969, several experienced police officers arrived at Indore to assist the local administration in restoring normalcy. Some of these police officers including CID inspectors commenced the investigation of the important offences.

TEXTILE MILLS

26. During the initial stages of the disturbances the workers of the minority community in the textile mills had taken leave from work. The position with regard to the number of such workers in the textile mills of Indore is indicated below:

....

Name of Mill	Hindu Workers	Muslim Workers	Total
Hukumchand Mills	4,255	145	4,400
Rajkumar Mills	1,773	144	1,917
Kalyanmal Mills	3,038	53	3,039
Malwa Mills	4,479	131	4,610
Swadeshi Mills	2,652	2	2,654
Bhandari Mills	5,597	1	5,598
Grand Total	21,794	476	22,270

The total number of Muslim workers is thus 476 which is an insignificant minority in relation to the total strength of the textile mill workers in Indore. The Muslim workers refrained from going to work voluntarily from the 3rd June till 13th June 1969. However, when some of them went to the mills on 14th June, the workers of the majority community resented their entry and demanded that the Muslim workers should not be allowed to work. Every effort was made by the local administration, the police and the labour department to ensure the return to work of the workers of minority community. The cooperation of labour leaders of different unions was also enlisted in this behalf. For some time, however, the problem persisted and workers of the majority community refused to work whenever the Muslims entered the mills. Vigilance exercised by the authorities and the mill managements prevented any untoward incident. Ultimately the problem was solved on the 2nd of July and from then onwards the Muslim and Hindu workers have been working together in the mills in an atmosphere of amity and communal concord. This problem was solved by the administration with the help of responsible labour leaders and the mill management in a very tactful and restrained manner.

With the normalization of the work in the textile mills, much of the bitterness engendered in the city of Indore during the disturbances also gradually disappeared.

DAMAGE TO PROPERTY

27. On 5th June itself an assessment party comprising the addl. tehsildar Nazul, Indore, an assistant engineer of the PWD, together with a police officer to assist the two was formed under my orders to carry out on-the-spot assessments of the property damaged during the disturbances. This party went round all the

....

affected areas in the town and carried out detailed assessments of the damage to property sustained during these disturbances. As per the report of this party the brief abstract of the assessment of damage to property is given below:

Categories Affected	Persons	Extent of Damage
Small traders	220	Rs 4,41,720
Buildings	99	Rs 1,74,455
Automobiles (Scooter, etc.)	6	Rs 23,500
Garages	12	Rs 80,100
Grand Total	337	Rs 7,19,775

Note: Losses of personal effects sustained during the disturbances has not been including in the above statement, but it is very roughly estimated at Rs 93,440/-. The expeditious manner in which the assessment party had carried out its work enabled us to organize the relief measures and this had the desired effect in boosting the morale of the citizens in the affected areas.

RELIEF MEASURES

28. The state government initially sanctioned Rs 20,000/- for relief. Thereafter, further sanctions were received from time to time and total amount of Rs 3,25,000/- has been placed at our disposal in accordance with certain proposals submitted to the state government. The manner in which relief operations were organized and succour provided to the distressed persons is recounted briefly below.

29. Shri V.K. Mandloi, chairman, Town Improvement Trust, Indore, was placed in charge of relief operations with the staff of the improvement trust and several experienced revenue officers to assist him.

The first step was to provide immediate relief to the affected families, particularly of the poorer classes, rendered homeless or destitute. Each family thus affected was contacted and sums up to Rs 50/- granted by way of immediate relief to them to meet their daily needs. Some of the persons seriously injured during the riots were given amounts upto Rs 200/- by way of relief. Thus a total amount of Rs. 11,380/- has been distributed by way of immediate relief to 249 affected persons and families.

30. The chief minister had announced that the nearest of kin of persons killed during the disturbances would be given ex-gratia grants of Rs 3,000/-. Accordingly, Rs 27,000/- has been disbursed to the members of the families of 9 deceased persons.

....

31. Two school buildings were thrown open by the local administration for housing the distressed persons but most of them preferred to stay with their relatives. The corporation authorities had similarly opened two camps and some families remained in these camps for a number of days.
32. The state government also undertook the repairs of the religious places damaged during the disturbances. Four mosques, 1 temple and 1 graveyard were damaged and the repairs to the same have been undertaken.
33. To help set up the petty traders, affected by the disturbances, in their business again, ex-gratia grants up to a maximum of Rs 500/- have been disbursed among traders of this class and the total amount thus expended is Rs 81,874/-.
34. With the approval of the state government it was decided to provide relief to the persons whose houses and structures have been damaged. The basis on which such relief is being given is that the owners would be disbursed a maximum amount of Rs 3,000/-; in case the damage to their properties is assessed at a figure in excess of Rs 3,000/-, the amount payable as ex-gratia relief would be equivalent to the amount of loss sustained as assessed by the party constituted for the purpose. By way of relief to persons whose houses and structures have been damaged, Rs 45,565/- have already been distributed amongst 56 house owners. This work of disbursement of the amounts is continuing and the amounts are being disbursed after proper verification regarding title, etc.
35. It would be thus seen that the administration has been quick in providing relief to persons affected during the riots. The repairs to the religious places of the different communities has also acted as a balm to aggrieved sentiments.

    The precise assessment made of the damages has given lie to the rumours and widely exaggerated accounts of extensive damages to property caused during the disturbances. The relief given to the distressed persons has projected the image of the welfare state in its true perspective and restored the confidence of the citizens.

RELATIONS WITH THE PRESS

36. The relation with the press generally speaking remained cordial throughout. I, in the presence of senior police officials, personally briefed the pressmen from time to time, sometimes twice during

the same day, about the incidents. They were always taken into confidence. In addition, authorized press releases were also regularly issued.

37. The Hindi daily *Swadesh*, published from Indore, from the initial stages, continued to publish material with a view to incite hatred between the communities. When they could not be otherwise persuaded the matter was first reported by me to the state government for action u/s 12 of the Public Security Act vide my letter No. Q/St./69 dated 8.6.1969. The publications considered objectionable were also brought to the notice of the state government. In accordance with the orders of the state government a warning was issued to the editor and the publisher of *Swadesh* on 17th June 1969 vide my letter No. Q/St./69 dated 17.6.1969. While reporting the communication of the warning to the state government, I again made a request for action u/s 12 of the Public Security Act vide my letter No. 490/St./69 dated 28.6.69. Finally, the state government vide Notification No. 1707-3424/I-X/69 dated 9th July 1969 issued in the extraordinary gazette, dated 9th July 1969, stopped publication of this newspaper for the period of one month.

    Action to prosecute this newspaper for publication of specific items with a view to incite hatred between the communities has also been taken by the police u/s 153-A of the IPC and two challans in this connection were put up on 30th June 1969 and 1st July 1969 respectively.

38. The police took action against the publication of one *Saptahik Matribhoomi* from the *Swadesh* press for breaches of certain provisions of the Press and Books Registration Act and u/s 153-A of the IPC on 18.7.69. SDM Dhar also cancelled the declaration, on certain legal grounds, of one *Dainik Kiran* on 17.7.69 which was being published from the *Swadesh* press.

    The publications in *Swadesh* press definitely, in our opinion, were responsible for the persisting tension in the city and mill areas; and in this context I feel that the district authorities should be vested with wider powers to control such publications. Material which inflame communal passions should not be allowed to be published with impunity in the name of freedom of the press.

    An objectionable press telegram, which could have had adverse repercussions on public order, was also stopped by me u/s 5 of the Indian Telegraph Act, on a reference made by the telegraph authorities on 12.6.1969.

....

COOPERATION OF LOCAL LEADERS AND CITIZENS

40. During the course of the disturbances, efforts were made at every stage to seek participation of the local leaders and citizens in the restoration of normalcy. As mentioned earlier, on the 3rd of June 1969 a meeting of the local leaders of various political parties was convened in the Central Kotwali and their views regarding methods to be adopted to restore peace and communal harmony were obtained and acted upon as far as practicable. The local leaders also resolved to work for restoration of normal life in the city. On the 6th of June leaders of different political parties and others again got together in the Central Kotwali and assured to work for maintenance of peace and tranquillity in the city. A joint appeal was also published on their behalf in the local daily newspapers. Peace committees, with the active encouragement of the police and local administration, were formed in various affected localities. A peace committee comprising both communities did commendable work in the Kagdipura, Silavatpura, Tatpattibakhal and Chatribag areas. Peace committees were formed also in Labriyabheru, Juna Risala, Tajikuwar on Jawahar Marg as well as in Jinsi, Shankerganj and Malharpaltan areas. The various peace committees worked sincerely in the localities to maintain peace and order.
41. On 12.6.69 a Central Peace Committee for the city was formed with Shri Kanhaiyalal Khadiwala as the president and Johrilal Jhanjariya as the secretary. On 16.6.69, under the presidentship of Shri Suresh Seth, mayor of Indore, an all-party peace committee was formed. Both these committees played their part in healing wounds and reducing the tension between the communities.
42. Besides the peace committees certain other institutions also made their contribution in providing people with the bare necessities of life. The Bharat Yuvak Samaj worked zealously in the Juni, Indore, and Jinsi areas, which were two of the most affected localities. The Jan Sangh formed a relief committee and the Muslims also formed a similar relief committee with Khurshid Hassan Khan, a corporator, as its convenor. The Mayor of Indore Shri Suresh Seth worked indefatigably to restore communal harmony in the town. He was always a source of strength to the district administration and the police. Shri Gangaram Tiwari, Minister for Labour, remained at Indore throughout the most troubled period and his presence was of invaluable help.

....

CONCLUSIONS

43. Although the communal disturbances were of an unprecedented nature for Indore, as a result of the measures adopted by the police and the local administration, and with the cooperation received from the press, the local leaders and the public, the trouble was contained within limits. The situation was quickly brought under control and it did not spread beyond certain localities. I must mention that the police fire brigade at Indore, with the assistance received from the fire engines coming in from Ujjain, did a great job in controlling the numerous cases of arson. The total damage caused by arson would have been greater but for the speed and efficiency shown by the fire brigade.

44. The trouble appears to have blown over for the present. To prevent its recrudescence in future a strict watch must be kept on anti-social elements interested in fanning communal trouble. The district authorities and police must also be armed with wider powers to take immediate and deterrent action against agencies spreading communal poison through the medium of the press.

The strength of the local police has to be augmented and our experience was that the local administration was greatly handicapped in dealing with the situation, particularly in the initial stages, due to lack of adequate force. Some more police stations will have to be opened in strategic areas in the town. Details of such reorganization must be quickly worked out by the police department and the sanction of the government obtained.

NOTES

1. Justice T.C. Srivastava, 'A Report of the Commission of Judicial Enquiry on Communal Disturbances in Indore, MP in June, 1969' (1969).

Bibliography

Akbar, M.J. *Nehru: The Making of India*. New Delhi: Roli, 2003.

Aiyar, Mani Shankar. *Confessions of a Secular Fundamentalist*. New Delhi: Penguin, 2004.

Alexander, Yonah. *Combating Terrorism: Strategies of Ten Countries*. New Delhi: Manas.

Aziz, K.K. *Muslims Under Congress Rule 1937–1939: A Documentary Record*. Islamabad: National Commission on Historical and Cultural Research, 1979

Burke, S.M. and Salim Al-Din Quraishi, *The British Raj in India: An Historical Review*. Karachi: Oxford, 2004.

Brass, Paul R., *The Production of Hindu-Muslim Violence in Contemporary India*. New Delhi: Oxford, 2003.

Brass, Paul R., ed. *Riots and Pogroms*. London: Macmillan, 1996.

Basu, Amrita and Atul Kohli, ed. *Community Conflicts and the State in India*. New Delhi: Oxford, 2000.

Chandhoke, Neera. *Beyond Secularism: The Rights of Religious Minorities*. New Delhi: Oxford, 2002.

Chandra, Bipan. *Communalism in Modern India*. New Delhi: Vikas, 1984.

Collins, Larry, and Dominique Lapierre. *Freedom at Midnight*. New Delhi: Vikas, 1976.

Dalrymple, William. *The Last Mughal: The Fall of a Dynasty, Delhi, 1857*. New Delhi: Penguin, 2007.

Das, Veena, ed. *Mirrors of Violence: Communities, Riots and Survivors in South Asia*. New Delhi: Oxford, 1990.

Engineer, Asghar Ali. *The Gujarat Carnage*. New Delhi: Orient Longman, 2004.

Engineer, Asghar Ali. *Communal Riots in Post-Independence India* Mumbai: Sangam, 1997.

Engineer, Asghar Ali. *Communal Riots After Independence: A Comprehensive Account*. Delhi: Shipra, 2004.

Engineer, Asghar Ali. *Lifting the Veil: Communal Violence and Communal Harmony in Contemporary India*. Hyderabad: Sangam, 1995.

Engineer, Asghar Ali. *Essays in Contemporary Politics of Identity, Religion, and Secularism*. Delhi: Ajanta, 1999.

Engineer, Asghar Ali and Uday Mehta. *State Secularism and Religion – Western and Indian Experience*. Delhi: Ajanta, 1998.

Engineer, Asghar Ali and Pradeep Nayak. *Communalisation of Politics and 10th Lok Sabha Elections*. Delhi: Ajanta, 1993.

Engineer, Asghar Ali. *Communal Challenge and Secular Response*. Delhi: Shipra, 2003.

Engineer, Asghar Ali, ed. *Babri-Masjid Ramjanambhoomi Controversy*. Delhi: Ajanta, 1990.

Gandhi, Rajmohan. *Understanding the Muslim Mind*. New Delhi: Penguin, 2000.

Gandhi, M.K. *Hindu Dharma*. Ahmedabad: Navajivan Publishing House, 1950.

Gauba, K.L. *Assassination of Mahatma Gandhi*. Ahmedabad: Navajivan Publishing House, 1969.
Gray, R. M. and Manilal C. Parekh. Builders of *Modern India: Mahatma Gandhi, An Essay in Appreciation*. Calcutta: Association Press, 1931.
Gopal, Sarvepalli. *Jawaharlal Nehru: A Biography, Vol. One, 1889–1947*. Oxford, UK: Oxford, 1984.
Guha, Ramachandra. *India After Gandhi: The History of the World's Largest Democracy*. London: Picador, 2007.
Hasan, Mushirul. *Islam in the Subcontinent: Muslims in a Plural Society*. New Delhi: Manohar, 2002.
Hasan, Mushirul. *Moderate or Militant: Images of India's Muslims*. New Delhi: Oxford, 2008.
Hasan, Mushirul, ed. *India's Partition: Process, Strategy and Mobilization*. New Delhi: Oxford, 2005.
Hansen, Thomas Blom. *The Saffron Wave: Democracy and Hindu Nationalism in Modern India*. Princeton (NJ): Princeton, 1999.
Huntington, Samuel P. *The Clash of Civilizations and the Remaking of World Order*. New Delhi: Penguin, 1997.
Huntington, Samuel P. *Who are We: The Challenges to America's National Identity*. New York: Simon & Schuster, 2005.
Jalan, Bimal. *The Future of India: Politics, Economics and Governance*. New Delhi: Penguin, 2005.
Jaffrelot, Christophe. *The Hindu Nationalist Movement and Indian Politics: 1925 to the 1990s*. New Delhi: Penguin, 1999.
Kaur, Ravinder, ed. *Religion, Violence and Political Mobilization in South Asia*. New Delhi: Sage, 2005.
Kher, V.B., ed. *In Search of the Supreme, Vol. III*. Ahmedabad: Navajivan Publishing House, 1962.
Kriplani, Krishna. *Tagore: A Life*. New Delhi: Orient Longman, 1971.
Kriplani, Krishna. *All Men Are Brothers: Life and Thoughts of Mahatma Gandhi as Told in His Own Words*. Ahmedabad: Navajivan Publishing House, 1960.
Lacey, Jim, ed. *A Terrorist's Call to Global Jihad: Deciphering Abu Musab Al-Suri's Islamic Jihad Manifesto*. Annapolis, Maryland: Naval Institute Press, 2006.
Mamdani, Mahmood. *Good Muslim, Bad Muslim: Islam, the USA and the Global War Against Terror*. Delhi: Permanent Black, 2006.
Madan, T.N. *Modern Myths, Locked Minds: Secularism and Fundamentalism in India*. New Delhi: Oxford, 2005.
Mehta, J.K. *Gandhian Thought: An Analytical Study*. New Delhi: Ashish, 1985.
Musharraf, Parvez. *In The Line of Fire: A Memoir*. New York: Free Press, 2006.
Mukherjee, Hiren. *The Gentle Colossus: A Study of Jawaharlal Nehru*. Calcutta: Manish, 1964.
Mukherjee, Hiren. *Gandhi: A Study*. New Delhi: People's Publishing House, 1960.
Nanavati, Justice G.T. and Justice Akshay H. Mehta. Report by the Commission of Enquiry on Gujarat Riots 2002. September 2008.
Narayan, Shriman, ed. *The Selected Works of Mahatma Gandhi, Vol. 4, The Basic Works*. Ahmedabad: Navajivan Publishing House, 1968.
Narayan, Shriman, ed. *The Selected Works of Mahatma Gandhi, Vol. 1, An Autobiography*. Ahmedabad: Navajivan Publishing House, 1968.
Nair, P.M. *Combating Organised Crime*. New Delhi: Konark, 2002.
Nehru, Jawaharlal. *Jawaharlal Nehru: An Autobiography with Musings on Recent*

Events in India. London: John Lane the Bodley Head, 1947.

Nikhilananda, Swami, *Vivekananda: A Biography*. Calcutta: Advaita Ashrama, 1982.

Noorani, A.G. *The RSS and the BJP: A Division of Labour*. New Delhi: LeftWord, 2000.

Noorani, A.G. *The Muslims of India: A Documentary Record*. New Delhi: Oxford, 2004.

Noorani, A.G. *Citizens' Rights, Judges and State Accountability*. New Delhi: Oxford, 2002.

Panikkar, K.N. *Communal Threat, Secular Challenge*. Madras: EarthWorm, 1997.

Page, David [et. al]. *The Partition Omnibus*. New Delhi: Oxford, 2004.

Prakash, Virendra. *Hindutva Demystified*. New Delhi: Virgo, 2002.

Puniyani, Ram, ed. *Religion, Power and Violence: Expression of Politics in Contemporary Times*. New Delhi: Sage, 2005.

Pyarelal. *Mahatma Gandhi, the Last Phase, Vol. I*. Ahmedabad: Navajivan Publishing House, 1958.

Rajeshwari, B. *Communal Riots in India: A Chronology (1947–2003)*. IPCS Research Papers, March 2004.

Rai, V.N. *Combating Communal Conflict: Perception of Police Neutrality During Hindu-Muslim Riots in India*. New Delhi: Manas, 2008.

Ray, Annada Sankar. *Yes, I Saw Gandhi*. Bombay: Bharatiya Vidya Bhavan, 1976.

Rozen, Henry S. *Prospects for Peace in South Asia*. Stanford (CA): Stanford, 2005.

Reuter, Christoph. *My Life is a Weapon: A Modern History of Suicide Bombing*. New Delhi: Manas, 2004.

Sharma, Jyotirmaya. *Hindutva: Exploring the Idea of Hindu Nationalism*. New Delhi: Penguin, 2003.

Sharma, Rajeev. *Global Jihad: Current Patterns and Future Trends*. New Delhi: Kaveri, 2006.

Sen, Amartya. *The Argumentative Indian: Writings on Indian History, Culture and Identity*. London: Penguin, 2005.

Sen, Amartya. *Identity and Violence: The Illusion of Destiny*. London: Penguin, 2006.

Safi, Omid, ed. *Progressive Muslims: On Justice, Gender and Pluralism*. Oxford: One World, 2006.

Smith, Donald Eugene. *Nehru and Democracy: The Political Thought of an Asian Democrat*. Calcutta: Orient Longman, 1958.

Tharoor, Shashi. *The Elephant, the Tiger and the Cellphone: Reflections on India in the Twenty-first Century*. New Delhi: Penguin Viking, 2007.

Varshney, Ashutosh. *Ethnic Conflict and Civic Life – Hindus and Muslims in India*. New Delhi: Oxford, 2005.

Wilkinson, Steven I. *Votes and Violence: Electoral Competition and Communal Riots in India*. Cambridge (UK): Cambridge, 2005.

Weber, Karl and Muhammad Yunus. *Creating a World Without Poverty: Social Business and the Future of Capitalism*. New York: Public Affairs, 2007.

Zakaria, Rafiq. *The Man Who Divided India*. Mumbai: Popular Prakashan, 2004.

Zakaria, Rafiq. *Communal Rage in Secular India*. Mumbai: Popular Prakashan, 2003.

Index

Note: *g* has been used for graph and *t* has been used for tables